TABLE OF CONTENTS

PART TWO: THE LINGUISTIC DOCTRINES

HUMBOLDT'S LINGUISTIC DOCTRINES

AMSTERDAM STUDIES IN THE THEORY AND HISTORY OF LINGUISTIC SCIENCE

Series III - STUDIES IN THE HISTORY OF THE LANGUAGE SCIENCES

Volume 32

Martin L. Manchester

The Philosophical Foundations of Humboldt's Linguistic Doctrines

THE PHILOSOPHICAL FOUNDATIONS OF HUMBOLDT'S LINGUISTIC DOCTRINES

MARTIN L. MANCHESTER

JOHN BENJAMINS PUBLISHING COMPANY
AMSTERDAM/PHILADELPHIA
1985

Library of Congress Cataloging in Publication Data

Manchester, Martin L.

The philosophical foundations of Humboldt's linguistic doctrines.

(Amsterdam studies in the theory and history of linguistic science. Series III, Studies in the history of the language sciences, ISSN 0304-0720; v. 32)
Bibliography: p.
Includes indexes.
1. Humboldt, Wilhelm, Freiherr von, 1767-1835 -- Contributions in linguistics. 2. Linguistics -- History -- 19th century. I. Title. II. Series.
P85.H8M36 1985 410'.92'4 85-9209
ISBN 90-272-4514-2 (alk. paper)

PREFACE

This study was initially completed in the Spring of 1980 as a doctoral dissertation at the University of Toronto. The version here published varies from that version by a number of revisions. The several additions to the Humboldt literature in the intervening period (most notably Borsche 1981) have not led me to alter the basic claims made in this study, but several tangential sections have been deleted, Chapters two and seven have been rewritten, a brief conclusion added, and the whole text somewhat streamlined. A shortened version of Chapter seven was published in the interim as an article (Manchester 1982).

My hope is that the book may succeed both in being of interest to specialists on Humboldt, and serving as an introductory survey of Humboldt's ideas on language, accessible to the general student. If it only manages to accomplish one of those purposes, however, I would prefer the latter. The Humboldt literature contains many treatments of special themes in Humboldt's work, but very few attempts to establish a general framework within which the mutual relationship of those special themes is clearly determined. Regardless of whether or not such a framework can indeed be justly attributed to Humboldt (itself an issue of considerable disagreement), it seems clear that Humboldt interpretation will remain fragmented until it at least attempts to move in this direction.

I am indebted to a number of people who assisted me at various points in this project. In particular I am grateful to Graeme Nicholson, Kenneth Schmitz, Harry Roe, Brendon Gillon, and Vahan Benglian. The comments of the publisher's reader were very helpful in revision of the dissertation, especially in pointing out sources which I had overlooked earlier. I am thankful for the graciously given technical assistance of Joel Taunton in the final preparation of the manuscript. I am grateful to the publisher for their acceptance of this study for the SiHoL series, and for their patience over the long period between their acceptance and the appearance of the book at this time. Finally, and most of all, I appreciate the direction and attention provided by the editor of the series, Konrad Koerner, whose insistence upon clarity and consistency, as well as attention to details of format, have improved this study both in terms of presentation and substance. His prompt and pointed attention to my revisions has been in marked contrast to the slow pace with which I have completed those revisions, and I greatly appreciate his patience and the perspicuity of his advice.

Concord, Massachusetts
September, 1984 M.L. Manchester

KEY TO ABBREVIATIONS

The following list is composed primarily of Humboldt's writings on language from the period 1820-1835, although several earlier works are included. For convenience of citation I use, both in the text and in the endnotes, the abbreviations given in the left hand column. All of these writings are to be found in the basic edition of Humboldt's works, Wilhelm von Humboldts Gesammelte Schriften, Berlin, 1903ff, edited by the Prussian Academy of Sciences. The date indicated is that of publication, in those cases where the essay was published during Humboldt's lifetime. In other cases the date is the approximate date of composition, as determined by Albert Leitzmann, principal editor of the Gesammelte Schriften. I cite that edition throughout. All translations, unless otherwise indicated, are my own.

Engels Vortr.	Aus Engels philosophischen Vorträgen. 1785-86.
Kleins Vortr.	Aus Kleins Vorträgen über Naturrecht. 1785-86.
Tagebücher I and II	Tagebücher, vol. I. 1788-98; vol. II. 1799-1835. (The journals end in 1801. Other materials are included here.)
DuS	Ueber Denken und Sprechen. 1795-96
ges. Sprachst.	Einleitung in das gesamte Sprachstudium. 1810-1811.
Sprachverwandtschaft	Ueber Sprachverwandtschaft. 1812-14
vergl. Sprachstudium	Ueber das vergleichende Sprachstudium in Beziehung auf die verschiedenen Epochen der Sprachentwicklung. 1820
Entstehen	Ueber das Entstehen der grammatischen Formen und ihren Einfluss auf die Ideenentwicklung. 1821
Einfluss	Ueber den Einfluss des Verschiedenen Charakters der Sprachen auf

	Literatur und Geistesbildung. 1821
<u>griech. Akzent</u>	Ueber die allgemeinsten Grundsätze der Wortbetonung mit besonderer Rücksicht auf die griechische Akzentlehre. 1821
<u>Nationalcharakter</u>	Ueber den Nationalcharakter der Sprachen. 1822
<u>Zusammenhang</u>	Ueber den Zusammenhang der Schrift mit der Sprache. 1823-24
<u>Buchstabenschrift</u>	Ueber die Buchstabenschrift und ihren Zusammenhang mit dem Sprachbau. 1824
<u>Lettre A-R</u>	Lettre à Monsieur Abel-Rémusat sur la nature des formes grammaticales en général et sur le génie de la langue chinoise en particulier. 1825-26
<u>Grundzüge</u>	Grundzüge des allgemeinen Sprachtypus. 1824-26
<u>Bau der chines.</u>	Ueber den grammatischen Bau der chinesischen Sprache. 1826
<u>Dualis</u>	Ueber den Dualis. 1827
<u>Essay</u>	An essay on the best means of ascertaining the affinities of oriental languages. 1828
<u>Vom gram. Baue</u>	Von dem grammatischen Baue der Sprachen. 1827-29
<u>Verschiedenheiten</u>	Ueber die Verschiedenheiten des menschlichen Sprachbaues. 1827-29
<u>Einleitung</u>	Einleitung zum Kawi-Werk: Ueber die Verschiedenheit des menschlichen Sprachbaues und ihren Einfluss auf die geistige Entwicklung des Menschengeschlechts. 1836

GS — <u>Wilhelm von Humboldts Gesammelte Schriften</u>. 17 vol. Edited by A. Leitzmann et al. for the Königlich Preussische Akademie der Wissenschaften. Berlin: B. Behr, 1903ff. (Repr., Berlin: W. de Gruyter, 1967-68.)

INTRODUCTION

0.1 Introduction

Wilhelm von Humboldt (1767-1835) was a Prussian aristocrat who served the state as minister of education, diplomat, and envoy to the Vienna congress in 1815. He traveled extensively throughout Europe and maintained close personal contact with the German academic and literary community, contributing publications to various fields. In 1819 he retired from public service and devoted the remaining fifteen years of his life to the study of language and languages.

Humboldt's writings on language are a mixture of philosophical theorizing about mind and language on the one hand and, on the other hand, specialized studies of the most detailed sort of both the classical languages and languages which only in Humboldt's day were becoming known to European scholars, such as Sanskrit, Chinese, and native north and south American languages. In the long series of essays which he wrote between 1820 and 1835 these two complementary emphases are constantly interwoven, as Humboldt moves from very general theoretical statements about language as such to discussion of specific problems of word-formation, accent, grammar, etc. in particular languages. In the present study I am predominantly interested in the philosophical theory. Most of these essays are fairly short, around twenty to thirty pages in length, although several are much longer. Some of them are unfinished and many were not published during Humboldt's lifetime. His rather unsystematic style is one reason that his thought is also often branded as unsystematic.[1]

Humboldt himself saw his philosophical orientation towards language as a very broad one. It was his intention to approach language not just as a medium of interpersonal communication but also as a deeply rooted psychological force. This, for him, meant that language must be studied in its interaction with thought, perception, imagination, and other psychological 'faculties':

> The intellectual process of language is taken in its broadest extension, not merely in the relationship of it to discourse and to its supply of word elements, but also with respect to its influence on the thinking and perceiving capacities. I take under consideration the whole way in which, proceeding out of the intellect, it reacts back upon the intellect again.[2]

> Language is, however, not a mere means of communication, but rather the impression (Abdruck) of the intellect and of the world view of the speakers; ...[3]

Humboldt is convinced that language plays a constitutive role in the formation of concepts; that language is necessarily involved in 'thinking' itself, apart from all questions of expression and communication; that each natural language represents a particular way of understanding the world. Claims like these obviously implicate a philosophical framework which goes beyond the study of language itself. It is my intention in the following chapters to explore the penetration of this broader philosophical framework into Humboldt's views about language.

Two themes guide the examination as a whole. (1) Systematic: I want to show that Humboldt's work on language is a coherent system of thought. Towards this end I avoid focusing on any specific theme as 'central'. Rather I endeavor to recapture and expose the systematic structure of assumption, hypothesis, argument and conclusion, and to assign many of the specific themes in Humboldt's writings to a place within this structure. (2) Historical: In many respects Humboldt's thoughts on language are by no means original. He borrows and uses ideas and idioms from sources as diverse as Enlightenment philosophy, romantic literature and early comparative linguistics. I try to show in the book what the appropriate background source is for Humboldt's ideas, and in some specific cases to discuss that background itself in order to illuminate those ideas.

The main writings by Humboldt which I will examine here are the essays which he wrote between 1820 and 1835. On the one hand this may seem too broad a focus. Many writers on Humboldt have limited their consideration only to his final work, the introduction to his projected study of the Kawi language of Java, assuming that this represents the complete and final statement of his views. In many cases I have found that earlier essays give clearer statements or more illuminating examples, and thus I have freely drawn on all the essays of this period to represent Humboldt's views.

On the other hand it might be felt that this focus is too narrow. Humboldt wrote about language at least as early as 1795, and there are several essays in the intervening years which are of obvious relevance to his philosophy of language, for example, the introduction to his translation of Agamemnon (1816). Several studies have concentrated on the development of Humboldt's views in his earlier writings.[4] Although I have occasionally drawn on these earlier writings, in general it seems to me to be unnecessary. All of Humboldt's philosophical views about language are present, often in repeated treatments of the same persevering issues, in the essays following 1820, and for the purpose of a systematic exposition and examination of those views it is not really necessary to go beyond those texts.

It is perhaps evident from the preceding remarks that I will not be much concerned to discriminate between various phases of Humboldt's development, as if there were an 'early' and a 'late' Humboldt, etc.. In most respects there is remarkably little change in Humboldt's positions over time. There are of course certain shifts of terminology and minor changes of doctrine, and these will be duly noted. For the most part, however, with the exception of Chapter six, I will consider Humboldt's writings as presenting an essentially unchanging set of positions, without regard to date of composition. With a few exceptions[5] the literature on Humboldt acknowledges the basically static character of his views. It is of course difficult to justify in advance the assumption of a lack of significant change in an author's work over time; this can be demonstrated only by the exposition itself. Nevertheless in Humboldt's case there is prima facie evidence for such an assumption. He has the tendency to borrow passages from earlier works, often whole paragraphs or even several pages, and use them verbatim in later essays. Certain key formulations occur again and again, unchanged in successive essays. Long passages in Einleitung (1836) for example, were first written as early as Grundzüge (1824-26), and used in several intervening essays as well.[6] This stylistic tendency to borrow from earlier writings can be taken as evidence that Humboldt himself did not perceive much significant alteration in his views.

The main themes and arguments which I pursue in the

book are developed primarily through exposition and interpretation of Humboldt's writings. I have introduced consideration of the secondary literature on Humboldt only where it is particularly helpful in clarifying specific issues. For this reason it may be appropriate to begin here with a brief overview of the scholarly discussion of Humboldt's philosophy of language. My intention is not to critique the literature but rather only to point out several of the different trends which have characterized it. After this review of the literature I will give a preliminary summary of the chapters which follow.

0.2 A brief review of the secondary literature.

Very few large scale attempts at a systematic exposition of Humboldt's work on language exist. Three long studies have appeared in recent years in German. Volume II of Bruno Liebrucks' vast undertaking, Sprache und Bewusstsein (1965), is a lengthy discussion of Humboldt's philosophy of language, subtitled 'zur dialektischen Sprachbewegung bei Wilhelm von Humboldt'. Liebrucks' work has the advantage of surveying a wide selection of Humboldt's writings where earlier authors had often limited their study to Humboldt's magnum opus, the introduction to his three volume work on the Kawi language of Java. Nevertheless his discussion is often rambling with many short sections whose over-all plan or relationship is never explained. Missing from Liebrucks' study are any treatments of the concept of 'national character' or the inflectional superiority thesis, which I have treated in the present study as central aspects of Humboldt's thought. The reception of Liebrucks' work in the Humboldt literature has been decidedly cool, perhaps because many of those who work on Humboldt are not philosophers and Liebrucks' work is so obviously part of a larger philosophical enterprise. Volker Heeschen's assessment (1975: 5) is typical:

> As stimulating and many-sided as Liebrucks' reading may be, we believe that we are nevertheless justified, not only on account of the extent of his contribution but just as much because of its peculiarity (Eigenart), in being able to waive throughout argumentation and mention of it.[7]

The same can not be said of the recent book

by Tilman Borsche, Sprachansichten: Der Begriff der menschlichen Rede in der Sprachphilosophie Wilhelm von Humboldts (1981). More compact and organized than Liebrucks' work, it is nevertheless as ambitious in scope. Borsche emphasizes the Kantian elements in Humboldt's early writings on anthropology and aesthetics, and attempts to clarify Humboldt's linguistic ideas by reference to those earlier writings. While his arguments in this respect remain unconvincing, like the similar arguments in Ross (1970), the later chapters of the book, focusing on Humboldt's linguistic writings proper, contain some of the most detailed and best documented explorations in the Humboldt literature. The chapters on 'Articulation' and 'Sprache und Kunst' are seminal, and I will have more to say about them in the chapters below.

The other full length study to appear in recent years is Die Sprachphilosophie Wilhelm von Humboldts, a dissertation by Volker Heeschen at Ruhr-Universität, Bochum, 1972. This study is much shorter and less ambitious than Liebrucks', but more clearly organized. The main topics which Heeschen discusses are the same as those which dominate most of the Humboldt literature; namely, Humboldt's version of the linguistic relativity thesis, and his concept of the 'inner form' of language.

Although there are no other studies beyond these three which even claim to attempt a systematic overview, the following full-length studies of Humboldt should be mentioned here. Kurt Müller-Vollmer has focused upon Humboldt's poetics and theory of art, especially in Humboldt's writings in the 1790s. His book Poesie und Einbildungskraft: zur Dichtungstheorie Wilhelm von Humboldts (1967), and a later article (1976), have concentrated on exposition of Humboldt's writings on poetry and language, as well as on comparison of Humboldt to his contemporaries. Roger L. Brown's book, Wilhelm von Humboldt's Conception of Linguistic Relativity (1967), is the closest thing in English to a systematic survey of Humboldt's philosophy of language. Although Brown's discussion ranges broadly over many of the main concerns which I have examined in the present study, his treatment of those themes is oriented primarily towards the theme of linguistic relativity, as if that were the focal point towards which all of Humboldt's considerations point. This orientation conceals the fact that many of Humboldt's philosophical assumptions and arguments were held by him quite independently of their relation to the linguistic relativity thesis, and indeed also provide a philosophical basis for other claims which Humboldt makes, such as the inflectional superiority thesis. Aside from unjustly narrowing the focus of Humboldt's philosophy of language, Brown's book is marred by various mistakes in detail, such as mistranslation and the neglect of texts, and I shall have more to say on this below. One other full-length study which should be mentioned here is a dissertation by Roberta Graber Ross, _Wilhelm von Humboldt's philosophy of language: The genesis of its basic concepts_, completed at Stanford in 1970. This study is not primarily concerned to examine Humboldt's later writings on language, but rather to trace the emergence and development of his ideas about language _prior_ to 1820. Although I do not believe that her occasional arguments that Humboldt's ideas underwent significant change and development are convincing, her extensive survey of Humboldt's correspondence and non-linguistic writings is often very helpful, and I draw on it frequently in the present study.

In recent years a number of journal articles have appeared whose intention seems to be to provide a general overview of Humboldt's philosophy of language. Representative of this genre are: Helmut Gipper (1965), Hugo Mueller (1966), and Herbert Seidler (1967). The general approach of these articles is to find some two or three 'central concepts' in Humboldt's philosophy of language, and focus the discussion around these. For example:

> If we now inquire into what are the most important central concepts of Humboldt's conception of language, the answer can not be difficult. They are: (1) the concept of linguistic world view, (2) the concept of _energia_, (3) the concept of the inner form of language. (Gipper 1965: 10)

> As is well known two concepts in particular characterize Humboldt's understanding of language, which are also important for our considerations. They are indeed, corresponding to Humboldt's peculiar way of thinking, not completely easy to understand and have therefore called forth varying meanings and discussions. They are the concepts of language as _energeia_ and of the inner form of languge. (Seidler 1967: 436)

In the discussion of these themes some deeper consensus is readily apparent as well. It is emphasized, for example, that Humboldt's use of 'form' should be understood primarily in the sense of a 'forming process' rather than as some static 'forming thing'. This sense of _forma formans_, as contrasted to a _forma formata_, is usually explained as typical of the intellectual environment within which Humboldt worked. 'Form', so meant, is then intimately joined with the characterization of language as _activity_, or _energeia_.[8]

Such attempts to elucidate Humboldt's philosophy of language by focusing on 'central themes' seem to me to essentially fail to represent the systematic structure of his claims and arguments. In giving the impression that Humboldt was a thinker of several fascinating ideas whose mutual relationship and philosophical motivation is unclear, they only serve to perpetuate the image of Humboldt as a somewhat eccentric essayist, an unsystematic thinker. This reading can only be countered by a convincing exposition of the structure of Humboldt's philosophy of language, not by the elucidation of this or that 'central theme'. These articles seem to try to walk the middle line set forth by Cassirer (1923: 156) in this regard:

> Fundamentally, Humboldt was a thoroughly systematic thinker; but he was hostile to any purely external technique of systematization. In his endeavor to set the _whole_ of his view of language before us at every point of his inquiry, he resists any clear and sharp analysis of this whole.

Apart from these general treatments, the literature on Humboldt has tended to concentrate on the following questions. (1) What intellectual forces decisively influenced Humboldt's philosophy of language? (2) What does Humboldt mean by the term 'innere Sprachform'?

0.2.1 _Humboldt's philosophical background_

Probably the most divided and acrimonious aspect of the literature on Humboldt has to do with evaluating the philosophical influences on Humboldt's philosophy of language. This problem is exacerbated by the lamentable fact that Humboldt himself rarely gives references to philosophical literature.

The traditional attitude, dating back to Rudolf Haym's biography, _Wilhelm von Humboldt: Lebensbild und Charakteristik_ (1856), is that Humboldt is a 'Kantian', although it is not always clear exactly what this term is meant to imply. In 1908 Eduard Spranger published an article, "Wilhelm von Humboldt und Kant", in which he analyzed the influence of Kant insofar as it is evident in Humboldt's published works and correspondence. He claims (1908: 62) that "Humboldt was formed by two intellectual powers: by the Greeks and by Kant". He qualifies this statement by admitting (1908: 61) that the 'Identitätsphilosophische-speculative Standpunkt' appears with greater clarity in the writings of the 1790s than in the 'sprachphilosophischen' works. Further, he notes (1908: 63) that Humboldt would have been influenced by the 'Berlin Enlightenment philosophy':

> We have taken Humboldt's most Kantian period to be the years 1789-1798, although in the beginning, naturally, many strong reminiscences of the Berlin Enlightenment philosophy remain.

This view of Humboldt as a Kantian was continued by Cassirer, in the first volume of _The Philosophy of Symbolic Forms_ (1923). More recently Nathan Rotenstreich (1974) has emphasized Kantian elements in Humboldt's early fragment _Ueber Denken und Sprechen_ (1795-96), although he also notes the significance of the use of some terms, for example, 'reflection', by Locke and Herder.

Arguments that Humboldt's philosophy of language may be viewed as not essentially influenced by Kant were advanced in 1965 by Karl-Heinz Weimann in his article "Vorstufen der Sprachphilosophie Humboldts bei Bacon und Locke". Hans Aarsleff (1975: 449, and cf. 432-33) has argued that, although Humboldt was a 'good Kantian', he was decisively influenced in his views about language by the French empiricist Condillac. Aarsleff also discounts any influence by Herder on Humboldt:

> As I have suggested earlier, it is very hard indeed to escape the impression that Humboldt's philosophy of language was strongly influenced, in fact initially it seems determined by, what he met in Paris. Humboldt of course postulated a sort of language power or speaking power, ... This conception is fully in agreement with Condillac. Though it has often been asserted in the secondary literature that Humboldt was influenced by Herder, I have never seen this claim substantiated.

Aarsleff's claims have recently been emphatically

rejected in an article by Wulf Oesterreicher (1981). He points out (1981: 125) that all of Humboldt's notes on his reading of Condillac are clearly critical, and that Aarsleff's rejection of Herder's influence on Humboldt is supported only by quotation out of context. Oesterreicher (1981: 123) cites approvingly Coseriu's maxim that one can assume a significant influence of Herder on Humboldt despite the lack of direct reference to him. I have argued in Chapter one that, although Humboldt may have been interested in Condillac, as his notes indicate, his views could not have been essentially and initially formed by that reading. Müller-Vollmer (1976: 228) is convinced that Fichte (and especially Fichte's concept of imagination) was a central determining influence both on Humboldt's poetics and his philosophy of language.

My own primary goal is to set forth and demonstrate the presence of a systematic philosophy of language in Humboldt's works. This in itself does not require taking a position on these matters of historical influence, but it does seem to me that an examination of Humboldt's philosophy of language shows very little influence by Fichte or the romantic movement in literature, although it is indisputable that other parts of his writings, particularly those on aesthetics, are deeply influenced by those sources.

0.2.1 Humboldt's concept of 'innere Form'

The theme which has dominated much of the secondary literature on Humboldt is the meaning of his term 'Form of language', and the related terms 'inner form of language' and 'outer form of language'. The term 'inner form of language' has exercised a special fascination, although in fact it appears only very rarely in Humboldt's writings. In 1934 Reinhold Schwinger concentrated particularly on the aesthetic connotations of 'inner form' in his dissertation: Innere Form: Ein Beitrag zur Definition des Begriffes auf Grund seiner Geschichte von Shaftesbury bis W. von Humboldt. In 1969 Karl-Wilhelm Eigenbrodt wrote a dissertation which concentrated on exposition of many other terms in Humboldt's writings which help explain his usage of 'innere Form'. A very helpful part of Eigenbrodt's study is his summary of how the concept of 'innere Form' has been interpreted by a number of commentators.

Perhaps the most lively debate over interpretation of 'inner form of language' was initiated by Noam Chomsky's effort to appropriate Humboldt as part of the history of 'Cartesian linguistics'. In his book Cartesian Linguistics Chomsky (1966: 19) argued that by the 'form of language' Humboldt meant essentially the system of rules, grammatical and phonetic, which are employed in creating sentences. These rules would correspond to what Chomsky called 'generative rules', or sometimes 'transformational rules':

> There is a constant and uniform factor underlying this 'Arbeit des Geistes'; it is this which Humboldt calls the 'Form' of language. It is only the underlying laws of generation that are fixed, in language. ... The concept of Form includes the 'Regeln der Redefugung' as well as the rules of 'Wortbildung' and the rules of formation of concepts that determine the class of 'Grundwörter'.

In 1970 Eugenio Coseriu published an article, "Semantik, innere Sprachform und Tiefenstruktur", which is primarily a rebuttal of Chomsky's interpretation of Humboldt. Coseriu argues (1970: 53) that Chomsky's assertion of a parallel between Humboldt's 'Sprachform' and Chomsky's 'generative rules' fails to appreciate that Humboldt's concepts are rooted in different 'Denkweisen'. He examines (1970: 58) three meanings of the concept of 'form' in Humboldt, as applied to language, and concludes that "The deep structure of transformational grammar has absolutely nothing to with Humboldtian inner form". Similar criticisms of Chomsky's interpretation of Humboldt were made by Hans-Heinrich Baumann (1971), apparently written before Coseriu's article appeared. The general appropriateness of Chomsky's interpretation of Humboldt has been the subject, more recently, of a dissertation by Scharf (1977). This debate about the proper meaning of 'form of language' is, I think, too complicated a matter to be dealt with in a brief review of the literature, and I have discussed the positions of Chomsky and Coseriu at more length in Chapter four.

0.3 The structure of Humboldt's philosophy of language

My primary goal is to present Humboldt's philosophy of language as a system of thought. As previously mentioned, Humboldt has often been regarded as both an unsystematic thinker as well as unorganized and obscure in his presentation. I believe that this assessment is incorrect, and that, despite the obviously unsystematic and rambling style which often characterizes his writing, the underlying ideas reveal a remarkably consistent and enduring set of interlocking views about language.

A system of thought is defined by its logical structure. That is to say, a mere conglomeration of unrelated ideas is not a system. A system of thought builds from a foundation of axioms, assumptions and hypotheses to a set of conclusions. The conclusions will be related to the foundations by a set of arguments. In this book I will try to divide Humboldt's various concerns with language into the systematic categories of axioms, hypotheses, arguments and conclusions. This will provide, hopefully, a framework for future, more detailed, investigation of the various parts of his system. I will here try to give an anticipatory schematic overview of the themes treated in the following chapters.

The basic strategy of this study begins by dividing Humboldt's various concerns with language into two general groups. The first group includes those areas where language is taken up in connection with traditional philosophical issues, such as the nature of thinking, self-consciousness, designation, and perception. The second group includes those areas more closely limited to the analysis of language, such as investigation of grammatical structure, accent, writing, theory of poetry and metaphor. To this second group I add the so-called 'linguistic relativity' thesis, although this is one theme which must be viewed as more complex and overlapping both groups. I call the first group of concerns the philosophical foundations, and the second group the linguistic doctrines. To some extent this sweeping distinction is too artificial. Nevertheless I shall argue that it does help capture a certain flow of argument in Humboldt's work which remains concealed if one merely concentrates separately on each of these various themes. I have tried to show that several of Humboldt's linguistic doctrines are based not upon his voluminous empirical research on many languages or upon his cultural prejudices (as has sometimes been claimed), but rather upon several philosophical assumptions, hypotheses, and arguments. In Part I of the book I explore these philosophical foundations, and in Part II I show how they are operating in the linguistic doctrines.

In Chapter two I take up the crucial question of the relationship of language and thought, as Humboldt sees it. Here I argue that Humboldt adhered to several key assumptions about the nature of thinking and consciousness. These assumptions can be traced back to Enlightenment philosophy, and primarily to the works of Descartes, Locke, Leibniz, and Kant. In addition, Humboldt argues that language plays a necessary part in the formation of concepts and in the emergence of self-consciousness. Following Humboldt I call this the 'articulation doctrine'. In this chapter, more than in any other, I think it is crucial to highlight the historical background of Humboldt's assumptions and arguments, and thus I devote a considerable amount of space to discussion of the original views of the philosophers Humboldt seems to be influenced by. Humboldt, unfortunately, does not often cite philosophical sources. This fact has contributed to a rather chaotic spectrum of claims in the secondary literature as to what the philosophical influences on Humboldt were.

In Chapter three I explore Humboldt's theory of designation. The central points discussed in this chapter are the distinction between 'lexical' and 'grammatical' designation, and Humboldt's speculations about sound symbolism. In this section I concentrate on exposition of Humboldt's views without extensive discussion of the historical background of those views.

In Chapter four I introduce the topic of language variation by taking up several general aspects of that topic. I show what Humboldt meant by variation among languages, stressing the location of variation at the phonetic, syntactic, and semantic levels. This is followed by a consideration of some of Humboldt's terminology, with respect to the question of language variation, and an exploration of his views on 'universal grammar'. Although his consideration of universal grammar is not extensive it represents an important restriction on the extent of variation among languages.

In Chapters five and six I look at the question of linguistic variation, concentrating on Humboldt's own orientation towards a genetic account of variation. I have distinguished two aspects of this account. In Chapter five I consider Humboldt's attempt, half-hearted though it is, to base linguistic variation upon perceptual variation. This attempt employs a philosophical definition of perception and conceptualization which I trace to Herder and Kant. In Chapter six I explore Humboldt's long preoccupation with the concept of 'national character'. This is one area in which his views *do* undergo a considerable degree of development over time; hence I follow that chronological development in my exposition. I argue that the concept of 'national character' is developed by Humboldt essentially as an explanatory hypothesis. Although Humboldt's theory of national character is related to many of his other interests beyond philosophy of language, I restrict my discussion to his use of it as an explanation of language variation.

In Part II of the book I discuss two areas where the various philosophical assumptions and arguments exposed in Part I are operating as motivations for claims which Humboldt advocated. The two cases in which I try to delineate these connections are: (a) the inflectional superiority thesis; (b) the linguistic relativity thesis.

(a) The inflectional superiority thesis. Humboldt, like many other linguists of his period, claimed that languages which had highly inflectional grammatical systems were superior to other kinds of languages. In Chapter seven I clarify the meaning of this claim and show how it is motivated by Humboldt's view of thought and language (the articulation doctrine) and his theory of designation.

(b) The linguistic relativity thesis. This ancient philosophical thesis revolves around the claim that thought is determined by language. The way a person thinks is dependent upon the language he or she speaks. Thus people who speak different languages 'think' differently: thought is relative to language. In Chapter eight I clarify the meaning which this claim had for Humboldt, and show how it is based on the assumption of conceptual variation among languages; on the arguments of the articulation doctrine (that languge has an instrumental role in the process of thought); and on the hypothesis of national character.

One could, I believe, show the influence of Humboldt's philosophical assumptions and hypotheses in other areas of his linguistic studies. His account of accent in the 1821 essay *Ueber die allgemeinsten Grundsätze der Wortbetonung*, for example, shows employment of the 'articulation assumption' I discuss in Chapter two. The two cases I have sketched out in Chapters seven and eight are not intended to exhaust the linguistic conclusions in Humboldt's work, but rather only to suggest the general paths of thought which characterize the mind of this rich, often original, thinker, who eloquently synthesized many diverse ideas of his time.

PART ONE

THE PHILOSOPHICAL FOUNDATIONS

CHAPTER ONE
HUMBOLDT'S PHILOSOPHICAL BACKGROUND

In several of the following chapters I have attempted to illuminate and explain Humboldt's arguments and claims by discussing earlier philosophical thinkers who advanced the same or similar arguments and claims. Much of the secondary literature on Humboldt's philosophy of language is devoted to relating his viewpoints to the influence of many different thinkers upon him, and a great deal of disagreement is evident in that literature, as I have shown briefly above. One basic fact remains clear amidst this disagreement. Humboldt almost never quotes philosophical writings nor refers by name or footnote to philosophical sources he sees himself as drawing upon, arguing against, or in any way concerned with. This is true of all his works in general, and none more so than the essays on language from 1820 on.[9]

It is important to take note here, if only briefly, of the ways in which claims about historical influence are established and demonstrated. There are two basic kinds of evidence in this regard. (1) Direct citation, i.e., reference by name to another thinker. (2) Doctrinal similarity, where the position taken by one thinker seems so to resemble or be a reaction to the views of a second thinker that this resemblance is taken as evidence that the first thinker was consciously orienting his discussion towards the second thinker's views, although without making this explicit.

Most of the various attempts to relate Humboldt to Herder, Kant, Fichte, Condillac, Hegel, James Harris, Port Royal Logic, and so on, are of necessity based only on claims about doctrinal similarity, since Humboldt gives so few references. For example, Roberta Graber Ross (1970: 123) relates Humboldt's 1820 essay _vergl. Sprachstudium_ to Kant's influence as follows:

> Among these categories he included Kant's
> four categories of the understanding --

> quantity, quality, relation, and modality--and the _apriori_ forms of intuition, space and time, as well as all possible degrees of emotion. Following Kant, he considered these categories of thought to be universally valid and common to all men.

Kant is not, of course, mentioned anywhere in the essay, nor does the specific passage referred to by Ross appear, in fact, to be very Kantian in tone.

It is not my intent here to discredit the importance of noting doctrinal similarities, especially in the case of a writer, like Humboldt, where there is very little alternative. Indeed I shall often be concerned to point out such similarities myself. Nevertheless I wish to emphasize that assertions about historical influences based only on doctrinal similarities are always somewhat speculative. These similarities may merely indicate the common wisdom of the period, indirect influence, or even quite accidental similarity of views. While such speculative discussions of Humboldt-Herder, Humboldt-Fichte, etc. are interesting in their own right, it is crucial to try to substantiate, by his own explicit references, which philosophers Humboldt studied and what his views about them were. In this way doctrinal similarities can be supported by showing what writings Humboldt was familiar with, and what he had to say about them.

Although Humboldt rarely gives references in his writings, there are three sources wherein his philosophical background can be ascertained. These are: (1) his correspondence, (2) his early study notes from 1785-86, (3) his personal journals, covering the period from 1789-1801. Much of Humboldt's correspondence was published around the turn of the century, but many of the early collections are long out of print and there is as yet no comprehensive critical edition. The latter two sources, published in the _Gesammelte Schriften_, were generally neglected until Lammers' (1935) dissertation, _Wilhelm von Humboldts Weg zur Sprachforschung_, but have more recently become the subject of critical discussion, notably by Aarsleff (1975) and Oesterreicher (1981).

Before proceeding to discuss Humboldt's philosophical views, accordingly, I will begin by briefly describing his philosophical background, on the basis of these three sources. There is a certain polemical intent to this description, since it acts as a corrective to the confusion in the literature about philosophical influences on Humboldt. But there is also a more direct need for it here. I will emphasize, later on, doctrinal similarities between Humboldt and the Enlightenment philosophers, and this emphasis receives further support from the direct evidence of Humboldt's familiarity with these philosophers.

Humboldt's early education consisted of a series of private tutors drawn from the academic circles of Berlin. His first, and most comprehensive, introduction to philosophy was a year long private seminar, in 1785-86, with Johann Jakob Engel. Engel (1741-1802), at this time professor at the Joachimsthal Gymnasium in Berlin, was a rationalist and popularizer of the Leibnizian-Wolffian school, and was primarily interested in logic and aesthetics.[10] Humboldt was nineteen at the time. In 1787-88 he attended a number of seminars at the Universities of Frankfurt and Göttingen. These seminars, however, were oriented primarily around his preparation for a diplomatic career, and there is little evidence that his philosophical reading at the university seminars was of much significance.

Surviving from the seminar with Engel are Humboldt's notebooks, 264 pages with marginal notes by Engel himself. Leitzmann published these notes in the _Gesammelte Schriften_ (hereafter GS), vol. VII/2, under the title _Aus Engels philosophischen Vorträgen_. He describes the format of the notes as follows:

> What we have in Humboldt's manuscripts are not notes taken down during the seminar hours, properly called _Kollegienhefte_, but rather free reworkings done at home, philosophical essays in which the whole systematic structure of the material must be reproduced with reference to the textbooks and notes from the seminars.[11]

The basic themes of the notes are traditional issues of Enlightenment thought: Cartesian doubt, innate ideas, classification of concepts (clear and distinct, etc.), proofs of God's existence, and towards the end a bit of ethics. Engel's instruction inevitably favors the Leibnizian line in these controversies, but not uncritically. Most of Humboldt's discussion centers around Descartes, Locke, and Leibniz. A few references occur to Spinoza, Kant, Condillac, Malebranche, and Herder. There is no discussion of Kant's 'critical turn': apparently it had not yet penetrated as far as Berlin.[12]

Not surprisingly, Humboldt often adheres to Leibniz's position when evaluating, for example, the controversy between Leibniz and Locke on innate ideas. Leibniz's _New Essays on Human Understanding_ are often cited in these notes. Humboldt says, for example:

> I continue to trace out, here, Leibniz's train of ideas, and allow him to speak for himself, because this is the easiest way to set forth these difficult and obscure matters. (GS VII: 429)[13]

On the issue of innate ideas, Humboldt cites Leibniz's doctrine: 'There are no innate ideas (angebohrne Begriffe) but there are innate principles'.[14] Ten years later he will agree with Condillac on the non-existence of innate ideas (GS XIV: 449).

On the issue as to whether the mind 'always thinks', Humboldt presents Locke's position, but calls it 'very superficial' (GS VII: 370). Similarly, with respect to the continuity of forces he says:

> The second question, with respect to the powers of things, is, whether they constantly continue unbroken, or not. Leibniz says they do; Locke however seeks to refute him. In this matter however the former is clearly right. For, according to the Lockean system, every time that a previously discontinuous force begins to work again, a new production must be forthcoming. Also, experience does not conflict with Leibniz's position. (GS VII: 413)[15]

Probably the most interesting aspect of these notes, in our present context, is Humboldt's long treatment of 'concepts' (Begriffe). Following Leibniz the concept is defined in terms of a conjunction of perception and consciousness, which here, as generally at the time, means self-consciousness or apperception, as opposed to the perceptions which consciousness reflects on:

> Definition of the concept. Leibniz calls the pure representation perception, consciousness apperception; the concept then is a conjunction of perception and apperception.
>
> The mere representation in itself thus does not give a concept. For in it is lacking the consciousness necessary to a concept. (BS VII: 369)[16]

After a short discussion of attention (Beachtung)

Humboldt devotes twelve pages to a three part classification of concepts. They are classified: (1) according to their origin (sensual, immaterial, or mixed origin); (2) according to their further reworking (individual, universal); and (3) according to their content (simple, complex, positive, negative, mixed). This classification follows Leibniz in many respects,[17] but also owes a surprising amount to Locke. The discovery of 'concepts of mixed origin', 'idées mixtes', is attributed to Locke (GS VII: 373), and, like Locke, Humboldt divides simple concepts (einfache Begriffe) into two areas, those of sense and those of understanding (GS VII: 377-78).

In general these notes show us a classical rationalist education in philosophy, oriented primarily towards Descartes and Leibniz but well aware of recent developments in empiricist and even French 'sensualist' trends. Language is only mentioned a few times (e.g., GS VII: 371-72).

Humboldt's further reading in philosophy can be traced in his journals, written during the 1790s. These unfortunately end by about 1801. The Tagebücher were edited by Leitzmann and published in 1916 and 1918 as volumes XIV and XV of the Gesammelte Schriften.

These journals reveal basically only two significant facts about Humboldt's philosophical interests: his developing familiarity (and sympathy) with Kant's 'critical' works, and his familiarity (and lack of sympathy) with Condillac's work. Leibniz and Descartes are almost never mentioned in these journals: the former three times, the latter once. Locke is mentioned more often but always in the context of comments on Condillac (e.g. GS XIV: 445,558). Humboldt clearly links the two together.

With respect to Kant these journals are, unfortunately, not very helpful. Although there are many references to Kant, they are mostly just passing references with no substantial content. The only point which Humboldt mentions repeatedly is Kant's emphasis on 'self-consciousness' as a necessary condition of experience as we know it. He regards this as a crucial difference between Kant and the empiricists, especially the French school. Most noteworthy in this regard perhaps is Humboldt's report of a 'metaphysische Zusammenkunft' between himself and several others during his stay in Paris in 1798.[18] After discussing the directions the conversation took, he concludes:

> At the basis of all philosophy lies the pure intuition of the I, outside of all experience; either explicitly, so that one can

> proceed explicitly on its basis, as Fichte did, or only in an implicit fashion, so that one shows how the clarification of the phenomena leads to it, as in Kant. The French absolutely do not recognize this, having neither the sense of it nor the concepts for it, and so we were in two different worlds. (GS XIV: 486)[19]

Given this opposition which Humboldt felt it is all the more remarkable that in this period of May and June 1798 he read closely all of Condillac's major works, and recorded notes on them in the journal.[20] These notes show a fascination with Condillac's radical 'sensualization' of Locke's empiricism, hedged by a constant criticism, namely that Condillac has no treatment of, and cannot account for, self-consciousness. Of Condillac's Essai sur l'origine des connaissances humaines (1746) he says:

> Here however is the basic error, that everything is explained as an appearance; that actual self-consciousness, which can no longer be explained, in general he fails to recognize, ... (GS XIV: 446)[21]

Although there is very little mention of language in these notes, Aarsleff (1975: 449, and cf. 433) has suggested that Humboldt was decisively affected, in his philosophy of language, by this reading of Condillac, despite their 'metaphysical differences', stating:

> As I have suggested earlier, it is very hard indeed to escape the impression that Humboldt's philosophy of language was strongly influenced, in fact initially it seems determined by, what he met in Paris.

There may indeed be something to this suggestion; Humboldt may have found some of his own thoughts on language confirmed in Condillac. But this is speculation, since he does not say so. And, although this is not the place to engage in polemic, there are two reasons why Humboldt's philosophy of language could not have been 'initially determined' by Condillac. First, as I have pointed out, he is unceasingly critical of Condillac's treatment of consciousness, which is quite important with respect to the later essays on language. Müller-Vollmer (1976:236ff) considers this strong reason to deny the importance of French influence on Humboldt, and Oesterreicher (1981) has recently argued persuasively against Aarsleff's views on this matter. Second, and more telling, is the fact that Humboldt's first reflections on language, Ueber Denken und Sprechen,[22] are dated by Leitzmann as written in 1795-96, two years before the reading of Condillac. These reflections contain many anticipations of Humboldt's writings on language twenty years and more later. It would seem more likely to suggest that these reflections may have been influenced by Locke, since it is clear that Humboldt was more familiar with Locke than with Condillac prior to Ueber Denken und Sprechen. Weimann (1965) has pointed out the doctrinal similarities between Humboldt's and Locke's treatment of language.

Humboldt's correspondence is especially rich in the period of the 1790s. Here we can find confirmation that Humboldt was studying Kant occasionally during this period, and also further evidence that he was familiar with Fichte's writings. There is, however, very little systematic discussion of the views of those philosophers, so one must extrapolate Humboldt's reactions to them on the basis of the brief remarks which he does make.

Humboldt apparently began studying Kant's critical writings in 1788, at the university of Göttingen. In September of that year he was introduced to the philosopher Friedrich Heinrich Jacobi, and spent five days visiting Jacobi in Düsseldorf. Humboldt's letters to Jacobi over the next several years often allude to his on-going study of Kant. They also indicate a dissatisfaction with a purely abstract or conceptual approach to philosophy, which is typical of Humboldt throughout his life. In a letter to Jacobi of 17 November 1788 he criticizes the 'dry' (trocken) Wolfian metaphysics, where, Humboldt says: "I demonstrate and demonstrate and yet the results never produce conviction."[23] He opposes to this approach the need 'to view the objects themselves in their full life and truth'[24] and suggests to Jacobi the following position:

> How is truth to be distinguished from illusion (Täuschung)? I believe through no other means than by continuously turning the object about and regarding it again from new sides. For the analysis of concepts, I feel, can not even be of critical use here, since it never brings us even the smallest step over from the formal into the material aspect of knowledge. ...sensibility is, I believe, the single condition under which we can receive new concepts from outside;

> every intuition which is related either indirectly or immediately to sensibility I would regard as sensation, not as perception.[25]

In a letter to Jacobi on 20 June 1790 Humboldt gives a lengthy comparison of Jacobi's and Kant's philosophical standpoints. It is clear from this sketch that he was familiar with at least the Critique of Pure Reason and Kant's ethical writings. Although Humboldt's sympathies are clearly with Jacobi, the comparison seems objective and informed:

> It seems to me that between you and Kant there isn't even the smallest point of contact; in general you move in completely different directions. ... With you all knowing is immediate, revelation of the object, perception of the subject; with Kant it is assumed on the basis of a kind of necessity. Thus he assumes things outside of us in general because in our representations, when we develop them, there is still something material which must be related to something real outside of us, ...[26]

By the Fall of 1791 Humboldt indicates to Jacobi that he is studying the Kantian system 'anew':

> I am especially concerned now with metaphysics again. I have taken it upon myself to make a serious new revision of my own convictions, and am studying the Kantian system anew.[27]

Humboldt's letters to Schiller in the 1790s also often mention Kant, but with even less systematic discussion then in the Jacobi letters. In a letter to Schiller on 30 October 1795 Humboldt notes that he has been reading Kant's essay on perpetual peace:

> Altogether I can not call the work very important. I have not encountered a single idea in it which was not already given in earlier writings, including the a priori principle of politics.[28]

Humboldt remarks at one point that traces of Kant's later doctrines can be found in his earlier, precritical writings.[29] Here again there is no further discussion of Kant's views; the comment arises in the context of, in fact, Humboldt's characterization of Schiller's philosophical development.

Many references to Herder can also be found in the Schiller letters, but none refer to Herder's philosophical writings. It is clear, of course, from the Berlin lecture notes, as discussed earlier, that Humboldt had read Herder's 1770 essay on the origin of language. References to Herder in the Schiller letters arise always in discussion of Herder's contributions to Schiller's journal Die Horen, to which both Herder and Humboldt contributed. Herder's contributions were either verse or commentary on ancient literature. A typical comment by Humboldt is the following, in a letter to Schiller on 25 August 1795:

> Herder's Parthenope is completely Herderian, full of his excellence but, as it appears to me, at least, also of his bad habits (Unarten). The piece has on the whole a beautiful touching course and in many infinitely beautiful passages, but also much that is mystical, and such a permeating twilight obscurity that many can easily get confused by it.[30]

Although it is evident from these and similer references to Kant, Herder, and occasionally Fichte that Humboldt was familiar with the works of these authors, I think it would be somewhat premature to conclude that his philosophy of language was centrally influenced by those thinkers any more than by the Enlightenment philosophers he had studied earlier. Indeed his attitude towards idealism is ambivalent from the beginning, as was evident in the 1788 letter to Jacobi cited above. In a letter to Johann G. Schweighauser in 1801 Humboldt describes himself as 'neutral' in this regard:

> But it is awful that he (Degerando), even according to Villars, still does not see that the Kantian philosophy is different than the Lockean. It becomes more and more clear to me that only infinitely few men actually feel what metaphysics is, and that actually the struggle about philosophy is only between those few and the masses-- a struggle in which the former call the latter blind and the latter call the former crazy, and which may easily be interminable. For myself, always very neutral, I am actually undecided as to whose side is correct.[31]

By 1803, when Humboldt had entered the Prussian foreign service, and was serving as minister in Rome, his antipathy to Fichte, in particular, is quite evident in a letter to Karl G. von Brinkmann:

> I am quite finished with German metaphysics, with which you have been so much concerned, at least with respect to books. But I believe that I have arrived at metaphysical ideas in another way. ... Fichte's absolute ego (I speak merely from memory) was to me always contrary and obscure (widrig und dunkel), because to me it appeared to sublate the actual egos and to hypostatize a thoroughly chimerical one. Of Schelling's pantheism I have scarcely the faintest idea. But if you tell me that in each metaphysics there is a more solid and clear point, from which one proceeds, and a more obscure (though not less secure) one to which one proceeds, then I think that Fichte takes as first that which actually is last, the absolute actual ego.[32]

In the present study I will concentrate upon Humboldt's writings on language from the 1820s, and it would be particularly helpful to find evidence of what philosophy, if any, he was reading during this period. There is, however, very little such evidence. The correspondences which dominate this period are with A. W. Schlegel and Franz Bopp,[33] the latter being professor of Sanskrit at the University of Berlin since 1821. In the letters with Bopp and Schlegel, throughout the twenties, there is no mention whatsoever of Kant, Fichte, Herder, Leibniz, Locke, or indeed any other philosophers of note. These letters, especially those with Bopp, are almost completely concerned with detailed technical discussion of specific languages which Humboldt was studying. In the letters with Schlegel there is a fair amount of more general discussion of language, for example of the proper definition of inflection, and I shall make some use of this correspondence in chapter seven.

On the basis of the absence of references to philosophers in these letters, as well as in his published works of this period, I would tentatively conclude that Humboldt's extremely ambitious schedule of language study and his writing left little time for reading philosophical literature. In a letter to Friedrich Gottlieb Welcker on 3 December 1828 he laments the fact that his language studies have left him little time to pursue traditional philology:

> In language I believe, indeed, that I have established myself and even to have come to a new insight to which philology in the traditional sense does not lead. ... But the reading of authors and the aesthetic and antiquarian part of the study necessarily suffers, since I have taken a different direction in my principal investigations.[34]

A further curious fact which might be mentioned in this regard is the complete absence of any reference to Hegel in Humboldt's writings of this period. Given that both lived in Berlin throughout the 1820s, and that Hegel's lectures at the University were popular, Hegel is conspicuous by his absence from Humboldt's work. Borsche (1981: 92) suggests that Humboldt and Hegel were on friendly terms but admits that there is no evidence of direct influence by Hegel over Humboldt's views despite occasional striking similarities.

I have tried here to give an overview of the philosophy and philosophers that Humboldt studied, and what his reactions to them were, insofar as this can be explicitly documented from study notes, journals, and correspondence. This sort of documentation is of course only biographical information and proves no philosophical assertion whatsoever. I conclude by noting that Humboldt had a broad familiarity with Enlightenment philosophy which was complemented in the 1790s with a study of Kant and Fichte. There is evidence, however, that Humboldt's enthusiasm for idealism was tempered by a persistent antipathy to its abstractness. Humboldt's own inclinations were always towards detailed empirical study mixed with philosophical speculation, as is nowhere more evident than in his writings on language. I suggest then that we might at least reserve judgment when, for example, Müller-Vollmer ((1976: 228) asserts that:

> The model of human intellectual activity that lies at the basis of Humboldt's philosophy of art and language is derived from Fichte's Wissenschaftslehre.[35]

Such an assertion, at least with respect to Humboldt's philosophy of language, can only be based on doctrinal similarity. And there are several crucial assumptions and arguments underlying Humboldt's central claims about language which, I believe, can be more clearly and correctly understood as an appropriation of Enlightenment philosophy rather than of Kant and

Fichte. As professor Clemens Menze says, Humboldt is no 'Transcendentalphilosoph'.[36] In the following chapters I discuss several of these central assumptions and arguments which I believe are at work in Humboldt's philosophy of language.

CHAPTER TWO
THE PSYCHOLOGICAL FUNCTION OF LANGUAGE

2.1. Introduction

One enduring theme that runs through all of Humboldt's writings on language is the conviction that language should not only, or even primarily, be regarded as a medium of interpersonel communication. In addition it is intricately involved in the psychological processes of concept formation and perception. We may speak in this respect of a psychological function of language.

The key to understanding why Humboldt was convinced that language had a psychological function, and what he meant by this, lies in elucidation of his assumptions about the nature of thought itself. This I will attempt to do in this chapter, both by exposition of his own texts on the subject and by some exploration of the philosophical background which shaped his beliefs in this area. Humboldt's philosophical perspective on the nature of thinking, conceptualization, perception, and other psychological activities seems to parallel closely ideas developed among several Enlightenment philosophers whom he was familiar with, both in the 'rationalist' and 'empiricist' traditions.

The central belief which characterizes Humboldt's description of the psychological function of language is that language is, as Esper puts it, "the vehicle both of autistic sequences, 'thinking', and of social interactions" (Esper 1968:4). Typical formulations of this belief in Humboldt are the following passages:

> Language is, however, not a mere means of communication, but rather the impression of the intellect and of the world-view of the speaker. The social aspect is the indispensable aid to its unfolding, but not, by far, the only purpose with which it is concerned, ... (GS VI: 23)[37]

> Therefore, without regard to communication between men, speaking is a necessary condition of the thinking of an isolated individual. (GS V: 377)[38]

This latter sentence, as well as the ones which follow it there, in the Grundzüge des allgemeinen Sprachtypus (1824-26), is taken over literally into the long essay of 1827-29, Ueber die Verschiedenheiten des menschlichen Sprachbaues (GS VI: 155). Both of these essays were unpublished in Humboldt's lifetime. It first appears in print, still unchanged (GS VII: 56), in Humboldt's last published work, Ueber die Verschiedenheit des Menschlichen Sprachbaues und ihren Einfluss auf die geistige Entwicklung des Menschengeschlechts (1836), the famous introduction to his projected three volume work on the Javanese language. In general, this final work often draws, unaltered, whole sentences and even paragraphs from unpublished essays over the previous decade. The point is that this distinction, whatever it amounts to, is not a passing fancy.

But just what does it amount to, to claim that language is the 'impression of the intellect', or that speaking is a 'necessary condition of the thinking'? Humboldt occasionally glosses this claim by stating, for example, that "... it is impossible to think without language." (GS V: 323), or that language plays a necessary role in the 'formation of thought':

> ... language is not simply the designation of thoughts formed independently of it, but rather is itself the formative organ of thinking.(GS V: 374)[39]

The claim, in brief, is that 'thinking' requires language, that language is a necessary condition for the occurrence of thinking. It is clear that such a claim is not based upon empirical investigation of languages. It is not an inductive claim which makes appeal to many particular instances wherein thinking requires language. Rather it is a deductive claim, based upon a theory about what thinking and language are in general, such that language is a necessary condition for thinking.

I will proceed by first describing in a preliminary fashion what I take to be the most significant aspects of the theory of thinking and language which Humboldt accepts. Then I explore, in section 3, the appearance of the claim that thinking requires language, as it appears in many passages throughout Humboldt's works, emphasizing the reliance of this claim upon the broader philosophical definitions of thinking and language. Finally, having clarified the meaning of and motivations for this claim in Humboldt, I end with a more extensive discussion of the appearance of this theme in Enlightenment philosophy. This glance backwards is not meant as a mere appendix to the examination of Humboldt's views, but rather is of significant help in clarifying those views further. Humboldt's claim that thinking requires language is not essentially original to him, but involves an appropriation of a set of assumptions and arguments drawn from these earlier thinkers.

2.2 The term 'articulation' and the articulation argument.

In the years following 1820 the term 'articulation' becomes progressively more important in Humboldt's writings, and it is particularly relevant to explaining his view of the relationship of language to thinking. Although its meaning will be explored more fully in the exposition below, some preliminary clarification may be helpful here. The term must be understood, in Humboldt, primarily by emphasizing its original Latin sense of a severing or cutting activity, a division of something into parts. In this sense thinking, as (in Humboldt's view) a continuous linear flow of states of consciousness, may be 'articulated', that is, cut up or divided into individual elements by a self-conscious activity usually called <u>reflection</u> by Enlightenment philosophers (and by Humboldt). 'Articulation' in this sense is a necessary prerequisite for the subsequent formation of concepts, both simple and complex. Similarly a continuous stream of sound may be 'articulated' into a number of separate sound units, capable of repetition and of use as a symbolic medium. It is Humboldt's thesis (although not original to him) that just such an articulation at the symbolic (sound) level is a necessary condition for articulation to occur in thought, and thus for conceptual thought proper to develop.

Among modern commentators Borsche (1981) has best understood the pivotal role of articulation for Humboldt. He quite correctly resists reducing it to its psychological meaning, insisting that Humboldt's argument for the psychological function of language is only consistent if one retains both the mental and phonological levels of articulation:

> Articulation as such cannot be conceived as a natural phenomenon, and indeed neither

> acoustic nor physiological. However it is not, as Humboldt emphasizes, to be separated from natural sounds. Rather human thinking is 'connected to the necessity of entering into a connection with sound', it 'cannot otherwise attain to clarity'. (Borsche 1981: 274)

Articulation thus may be viewed as a process of self-analysis by a subject of its own stream of consciousness. That stream of consciousness itself, prior to such analysis / articulation, is generally viewed by Enlightenment philosophers from Hobbes and Locke through to Kant as a linear one-dimensional concatenation of states of consciousness which may include such disparate elements as sensual intuitions, feelings, and instincts. This type of thinking is commonly described by philosophers of the period as the 'flux' or 'train' of thoughts, although Kant's favored term is the 'sensory manifold'. Humboldt accepts not only this viewpoint but also the terminology. We may speak, therefore, of two types of thinking, according to this view; a prelinguistic 'pre-articulated' thinking, and a linguistic, articulated, and thus 'conceptual' thinking. Borsche makes the point fairly succinctly:

> The 'thinking' from which Humboldt proceeds in the first sentence of the fragment, is a prelinguistic thinking, that, as is shown, requires language for its realization. ... Later he occasionally contrasts the prelinguistic indeterminate thought as 'intellectual activity' with the linguistically determined 'thinking' proper. (Borsche 1981: 305)

The presence and significance of this treatment of 'thinking' has not been generally appreciated in the Humboldt literature until Borsche, although it was pointed out as early as Oertel (1901: 62). He argued that Humboldt's discussion of 'innere Sprachform':

> ... involved a distinction between 'prelinguistic' and 'formless' psychical processes and similarly 'formless' (i.e., inarticulate) physical speech on the one hand, and integrated or analyzed psychical processes and articulated speech on the other. (Esper 1968: 55)

With this brief indication of the meaning and role

of articulation for Humboldt as background, I shall first summarize what I take to be the essential structure of his claim that language is necessary for thinking. This claim may be broken down into: (a) the articulation assumption, and (b) the articulation argument.

2.2.1 The articulation assumption

A distinction is made between two modes of thinking. The first mode is non-conceptual and non self-conscious. This may be regarded as simply a basic state of sensory awareness, a type of awareness which we might, for example, attribute to animals and to very young human infants. The second mode is conceptual self-conscious thinking. It is perhaps tempting to label this distinction as that between thinking and consciousness. Indeed to some extent the presence of the distinction can sometimes be monitered by watching how those terms are used (as I shall do below in sect. 4). Nevertheless, shifts in the usage of such terms make it dangerous to depend upon them to label a persevering theme. Hence I shall use the simpler, if less revealing, terms 'primitive thinking' and 'articulated thinking'. ('Primitive' is not intended here to carry pejorative implications.) 'Articulation' refers to the process of concept formation. It does not refer to actual speaking, to precise diction, etc., but rather to a psychological process. Humboldt uses the term 'articulation' in this sense, particularly in his later writings. Articulation is to be associated with the activities of reflection, attention, and abstraction which play an important role in the transition from primitive to articulated thinking. The value of noticing this distinction is that when Humboldt (and others) make the claim that language is a necessary condition for thinking, it means necessary for articulated thinking.

The distinction between primitive and articulated thinking operates essentially as an assumption in Humboldt's philosophy. There are reasons why this distinction seemed an appropriate, even natural, one to many philosophers of the period, but I can not explore here what those reasons were. In sketching out this theme in several philosophers prior to Humboldt I will be concerned merely to show the presence of this distinction as Humboldt would have seen it, and not examine further the motivations for the distinction itself.

2.2.2 The articulation argument

Connected with the assumption of the distinction between primitive and articulated thinking is an argument, which I shall call the articulation argument. This argument essentially claims that language is necessary for the move from primitive thinking to articulated thinking. Put more briefly, language is necessary for concept formation. The most developed version of this argument before Humboldt seems to be in Locke's _Essay on Human Understanding_ (1691), which Humboldt knew well. Locke argues that language is necessary for the formation of _complex ideas_. Since complex ideas are collections of simple ideas, they would have no autonomous existence, no status as an idea in their own right, unless the collection as such, over and above any specific constituent simple idea, is signified. Locke argues that the _attachment_ of a _name_ to the complex idea is an essential part of its formation. Without a name signifying the whole idea, so to speak, that idea would remain nothing more than a concatenation of simple ideas. In the case of forming a complex idea, for Locke, the whole must be more than the sum of the parts, and the name is that which makes it so. Humboldt makes the same claim. Language, viewed generally as signification of a thought-unit by a sensual symbol, is necessary for the very formation and preservation of any thought-units (concepts), even before any interpersonal expression or communication. To 'articulate' our (primitive) thinking, (that is, to separate _this_ element from _that_ element, and so on, to initiate divisions within the 'train of thoughts'), we turn our attention upon some particular element. This attention-turning is the key Enlightenment concept of _reflection_. Yet as soon as we turn our attention away the thought-unit singled out by that initial attention vanishes; unless, that is, we have attached a persevering signifying symbol to it.

2.3 Signification and conceptualization

In investigating Humboldt's claim that language is a 'necessary condition of thinking' I will look first briefly at his earliest writing on language, the aphoristic _Ueber Denken und Sprechen_ (1795-96), and then see how the same theme appears in his later essays.

Ueber Denken und Sprechen is constituted by sixteen

brief theses. The first six, which are the most relevant here, I quote in full:

> (1) The essence of thinking consists in reflecting, i.e., in distinguishing the thinking from that which is thought about.
>
> (2) In order to reflect, the spirit must in its progressive activity stand still for a blink, to gather what was just represented into a unity, and in this manner to posit it as an object against itself.
>
> (3) These units, of which it can form several in this manner, it in turn compares with each other, and separates and combines them according to its need.
>
> (4) The essence of thinking consists, therefore, in making sub-divisions in its own course; thereby to form totalities out of certain portions of its own activity; and these formations singly among themselves, but all together as objects, to posit against the thinking subject.
>
> (5) No thinking, not even the purest, can take place but with the aid of the universal forms of our sensuality; only in them can we comprehend it and, as it were, hold fast.
>
> (6) Now, the sensuous signification of units, into which certain portions of thinking are united, in order, as parts to be posited against other parts of a bigger totality, as objects to the subject, is called in the broadest understanding of the word, language. (GS VII: 581-83)[40]

I will now try to briefly relate these theses to the two themes sketched out above, i.e., to the distinction between primitive and articulated thinking and to the argument following from that distinction that language is necessary for articulated thinking, i.e. consciousness.

Humboldt does not, in this text, use the word 'consciousness' (Bewusstsein), although he does say, in thesis seven, that man encounters language as soon as he 'awakens to self-consciousness'. 'Thinking' (Denken) here has the meaning of articulated thinking, then, which is already indicated by the first phrase 'the essence of thinking consists in reflecting'.

Nevertheless the distinction I have drawn above, between 'thinking' in the primitive sense ('presentations' of any sort) and 'articulated thinking', is present here. Although Denken means, for Humboldt, 'articulated thinking', the other level of awareness, of raw on-going presentations, as it were, is indicated by the catch-phrases 'its progressive activity' (in 2), and thinking's 'own course' and 'its own activity' (in 4). 'Reflection' occurs when the subject of thinking, instead of just indiscriminately following this progressive activity, 'stops' for a second, and 'posits' that mental activity as an 'object' which it is observing (thesis 2). Thus consciousness is distinguished from the mere 'thinking activity'.

Reflection consists then not in a blind acceptance of the 'flux of thoughts' (a locution Humboldt will often use later), but in an organization of it, breaking it up into different 'units'. These 'thought units' Humboldt will call concepts (GS VII: 582, thesis 13). Articulated thinking, then, comes into being by the creation of partitions or sub-divisions in the activity of thought. The 'units' thus created can be compared, separated, and combined, etc. (thesis 3). Concepts admit of "... free handling, recurring separation, and new conjunction" (thesis 13). Thus consciousness can manipulate its content, rather than being at its mercy.

The key point, however, is now that in this chore of creating concepts, or 'thought-units', consciousness must employ 'signs' for the concepts. Otherwise the created unit will lose its unity, and collapse back into the unformulated presentations from which it was constructed. To comprehend (i.e. conceptualize) our thinking a sensual sign must be attached to 'hold it fast' (thesis 5). Thus conscious thought employs 'signs' to cement and retain the created thought units. Ultimately it is only by the attachment of signs that one can present in thought the constructed concept as such, in its unity, rather than just as a representation of the various constituent parts of that concept. Thus the 'sensuous signification of units' is necessary for conceptualization to occur and necessary, therefore, for articulated thinking:

> (Thesis 8) The language-seeking man seeks signs, from among which, by virtue of the partitions he makes in his thinking, he can gather totalities into a unit. (GS VII: 582)[41]

It is this employment of signs in maintaining and presenting the constructed concept in its unity, rather than as a mere aggregate of elements, which Weimann (1965: 502) sees as a significant similarity between Humboldt and Locke:

> The general ideas which so arise, as new unities and abbreviations, would each time fall apart again after they have been thought, ... here language intervenes in a decisive way. The word, arbitrarily attached as a representative sign, allows to the fleeing idea permanence ...[42]

Although Humboldt did not turn his attention primarily towards linguistic studies until about 1820, there are some brief discussions of language to be found in other works in the period 1800-1820. One of the most interesting of these is the introduction to his translation of Agamemnon, worked on from 1797 until its first publication in 1816. Here we find discussion of problems of translation, synonymy, linguistic variation, and also this notion of language as involved in forming thought into concepts. He says, for example:

> A word is so little a sign of a concept that indeed the concept, without the word, could not arise, let alone be retained. The indeterminate working of the power of thought gathers itself together in a word, ... Now it is an individual thing, of determinate character and determinate form, ...[43]

The possession of concepts is seen by Humboldt to allow man to comprehend the 'objects of reality' which are, as it were, contained 'dissolved' in ideas (gleichsam aufgelöst in Ideen enthalten) and to alter, define, separate, and combine them (verändern, bestimmen, trennen, und verbinden) (GS VIII: 131).

Humboldt's essays on language dating from the 1820s exhibit well his tendency to be torn between presenting his empirical research on specific languages and engaging in more abstract theorizing about language. Although the theme of the inner or 'psychological' role of language appears in almost all of these essays, it rarely does so in any systematic or lengthy fashion.

In these essays Humboldt begins to use the term 'articulation' to refer both to the reflective process which changes primitive to conceptual thinking, and to the role of language in this process. This word is not to be taken in the sense of speaking to another person, as, for example, eloquence in expressing oneself, precise diction, etc. Rather, it has the more etymologically primitive meaning of 'dividing' or 'cutting up', as in the German 'Gliederung'. Humboldt uses the term to indicate the 'reflective' activity of dividing or partitioning a linear flux of thoughts into 'thought units' or concepts, and thereby to make possible the subsequent conscious manipulation of our thoughts by the activities of combination, separation, comparison, etc. Humboldt had seen these activities as essential to 'reason' already in 1789 in Ueber Religion[44], and by his last published work he will say that 'thinking' consists in such activities; "Since all thinking consists in separation and connection, ..."(GS VII: 121). Man always strives after the construction of new combinations of thought and higher unities:

> He strives however after comparison, separation and connection, and, in his higher purposes, after the formation of ever more encompassing unities. (GS VII: 54)[45]

As we have already seen, Humboldt claims that language, a system of signification, is necessary for this very activity of concept formation to be possible; necessary both for the construction and the retention of concepts, and thus for conscious thought itself. 'Articulation' comes in Humboldt to stand for both the activity of dividing and manipulation of thought and (as a noun) for the system of thought-units so produced. Occasionally in these essays the term 'Articulationsinn' will replace the more customary 'Sprachsinn' or 'Sprachvermögen'.[46]

It would be tiresome and redundant to follow this theme through all of the essays on language which Humboldt produced from 1820 to 1835, although it does appear in most of them. I will be content, here, to indicate its formulation in several. The general theme, that language is necessary to thought, appears relatively unchanged throughout this period. Phrases like "man thinks only by means of language, ..." (1820); "Thinking, which occurs by means of language, ..." (1821); and "For since the requirement of thinking awakens language in man, ..." (1836)[47] are fairly common. The background of assumptions and arguments for this doctrine is also fairly evident.

Perhaps the earliest of several attempts by Humboldt to give a general introduction to comparative linguistics is the 1820 lecture Ueber das vergleichende Sprachstudium in Beziehung auf die verschiedenen Epochen der Sprachentwicklung. Most of the dominant concerns of Humboldt's work can be found in it, including the theme of articulation and the inner function of language. 'Articulation' is the activity of molding the 'material of the phenomenal world' into the form of thoughts. It is necessary to 'form' thought so that it will be composed of parts which admit arrangement in various ways (e.g., combination, separation, etc.):

> The principle dominating through the whole language is articulation; the most important quality of each (language) is consistent and facile arrangement, but this presupposes simple and in themselves inseparable elements. The essence of language consists in molding the material of the phenomenal world into the form of thoughts. (GS IV: 17)[48]

The 'forms of thought' which language helps to mold out of inner perceptions and sensations are later called 'concepts' (GS IV: 22), and words are seen as necessary to make concepts into the individual parts of thought, the cognitive building-blocks, as it were: "The word, which first makes the concept into an individual element of the sphere of thought ...".[49] In the 1821 essay on the Mexican language Humboldt attributes a similar psychological function to the word; it assists in the transition from 'formless' thought to 'individualized' thought:

> Out of the mass of indeterminate, as it were formless, thought, a word pulls out a certain number of features, connects them, gives to them structure and color and thereby individualizes them. (GS IV: 248)[50]

A somewhat longer discussion of concept formation and the articulation of thought occurs in the lengthy essay Grundzüge des Allgemeinen Sprachtypus (1824-26), a fragment which consists primarily of an introduction of about one hundred pages on the 'Natur der Sprache überhaupt'. The essay was first published in 1906 in the Gesammelte Schriften.

Here Humboldt claims that language does not merely designate thoughts, for the purposes of communication, expression, etc., but also has an essential role in the 'formation' of thought. Language is regarded as a way to form and preserve the inner activity of thought, which, without language, passes 'without a trace'. Thus the development of thinking and language are inseparably connected. Without language "the representation cannot become a concept":

> ... language is not simply the designation of thoughts formed independently of it, but rather is itself the formative organ (<u>das bildende Organ</u>) of thinking. The intellectual activity, throughout spiritual and internal, and to a certain extent passing without a trace, becomes, by the tone in discourse, externalized and perceptible for the senses, and receives through writing a persevering body. ... The intellectual activity and language are therefore one and inseparable from one another; one can not merely regard the former as that which produces and the latter as that which is produced. ... Intellectual activity is connected to the necessity of entering into a connection with a tone; thinking cannot otherwise attain to clarity, the representation cannot become a concept. (GS V: 374-75)[51]

The word gives to the concept a certain form (Gestaltung, GS V: 419), so that it can be dealt with as a unit. The concept 'first attains its completion' through the word, and the two cannot be separated from one another. Indeed Humboldt goes so far here as to say that overlooking this active inner role of words in the formation of concepts, and regarding words as 'mere signs' is a basic error which destroys a correct evaluation of language:

> ... but the concept only first attains its completion through the word, and the two cannot be separated from one another. To confuse this, and to regard words as mere signs, is the basic error which destroys all linguistics and all correct evaluation of language. (GS V: 428)[52]

Numerous similar formulations may be found in Humboldt's essays of this period. In the famous lecture <u>Ueber den Dualis</u> he characterizes the formation of a concept as follows:

> It (i.e., the concept) is produced when it is separated out of the moving mass of (our) representing and formed into an object

contrasted to the subject. (GS VI: 26)[53]

Many such passages could be cited from Humboldt's final long essays on grammatical structure and the variation of languages.[54] These would, however, add little new to the passages already mentioned. Some, indeed, are direct re-usages of parts of earlier essays, especially the Grundzüge.[55]

The claim that thinking is 'discursive', is 'performed' by language, is a general kind of claim that has occasionally been raised in the history of philosophy, often in a rather obscure, unclarified fashion. Humboldt is part of this tradition, and I have tried here to clarify some of the underlying assumptions and arguments about thought and conceptualization involved in the claims which he makes. These claims are not empirically based, nor did he see them as such. They depend, rather, upon a view of thinking and language which was already present in a number of earlier philosophers whom Humboldt had studied. In order to further clarify the background of assumption and argument which Humboldt is drawing on I now will turn to a direct examination of those philosophers, still concentrating on the themes of the distinction of primitive and articulated thinking and the resulting argument for the necessity of language within the process of articulation.

2.4 Earlier versions of the articulation argument.

2.4.1 The distinction of primitive and articulated thinking.

The terms I have used here, 'primitive thinking' and 'articulated thinking' are, as indicated above, my own labels for a general distinction which is present in Enlightenment philosophy and still operative in Humboldt's claim that language is a necessary condition for (articulated) thinking. We can not expect the distinction to appear neatly labeled by these terms, of course, in philosophers of the period. In earlier philosophers, such as Descartes, it may be seen as the distinction between 'thinking' and 'consciousness'. As late as Hegel's Phenomenology of Spirit (1807) essentially the same distinction emerges, I think, labelled as that between 'consciousness' and 'self-consciousness'. In the following I try to elicit the distinction primarily by looking at the usage of 'thinking' (sometimes 'thought') and 'consciousness'.

The first thing which must be indicated is that the

terms 'thinking' and 'consciousness' carry significantly different connotations in the seventeenth century than they do in current (especially English) idiom. 'Thinking' now would generally be used only to indicate self-deliberative reasoning activity, ('I think that ...'), whereas 'consciousness' indicates a more inclusive awareness, including sensation, emotion, willing, etc.. For example, many modern dictionaries attribute 'consciousness' to sentient creatures as such, including higher animals, while reserving 'thinking' for human mental activities, and indeed only for certain kinds of these activities. (Note, for example, Rodin's sculpture 'le Penseur', dating from about 1880).

'Consciousness' however has not always had this broader base of meaning. McRae (1976: 13) notes this shift in his recent book on Leibniz:

> The notion of consciousness as it occurs within the context of modern epistemological theories has lost this relation to action-- and passion-- and therefore necessarily to the ego which it had in the seventeenth century. It now stands for any kind of awareness and no doubt does useful work because it is as loose as that. But it had not yet had time to spread itself so thinly when Leibniz, and _a fortiori_ Descartes, used it.

Just as consciousness had a narrower, more 'self-conscious' meaning at that time, 'thinking' (at least in philosophical usage) carried a broader meaning than it has today. Descartes' definitions of thinking often include sensing, perception, emotional feelings, etc., a usage which strikes the modern ear very strangely. In his _Principles of Philosophy_ (1644) he says (1973. I, 222):

> By the word thought (_cogitationis_) I understand all that of which we are conscious as operating in us. And that is why not alone understanding, willing, imagining, but also feeling, are here the same thing as thought.

Similarly, in the _Arguments_ (1641) Descartes says:

> _Thought_ is a word that covers everything that exists in us in such a way that we are immediately conscious of it. Thus all the

> operations of will, intellect, imagination, and of the senses are thoughts. (1973. II, 52).

By these definitions 'thought' is 'that in us' _of which_ we are conscious or 'immediately' conscious. Thinking and consciousness would have an equivalent range, so to speak, existing as different yet parallel psychological levels. Nevertheless 'thought' and 'consciousness' are often treated as synonymous terms for Descartes. Anscombe and Geach attempt to impose the modern English senses of 'consciousness' and 'thought', as noted above, ('consciousness' broader, 'thought' narrower), on Descartes' text in their recent volume of translations. In their comments on the problems of translating Descartes' _cogitare_ and _penser_ they note the wider sense of 'thought' in Descartes' time, but suggest that a modern translation should generally use 'consciousness' (which they do) for both terms, thus avoiding the 'intellectualistic' modern meaning of 'thought'.[56] While this policy may seem to do the modern reader a service by using our all inclusive term (consciousness) for Descartes' all-inclusive term (_cogitare_, or _penser_), in fact it does Descartes a disservice by making it seem as if _consciousness_ and _thought_ are synonymous for _him_, which they are not.

Robert McRae (1972, 1976) has gone to some lengths to clarify the distinction between 'thought' and 'consciousness' in Descartes. Since I am here primarily concerned only to establish an historical context for understanding Humboldt, I can not go into the problem in more detail, but instead will use McRae's (1972: 57) formulation of the distinction:

> Taking our departure from Descartes' definition of thought we can say that the difference between thought and consciousness can be expressed in these two kinds of sentences:
>
> a) I think.
> b) I am conscious that I think.
>
> For the variable 'think', in both of these sentences can be substituted the values 'doubt', 'understand', 'affirm' 'deny' 'desire' 'refuse', 'imagine', 'see', 'hear', 'feel'. No term other than a synonym can be substituted for 'am conscious'. (McRae 1972: 57)

The essential point here is that 'thinking' covers a broad spectrum of mental activity, whereas 'consciousness' indicates an attentive self-awareness of that activity:

> Thus we see that consciousness is for Descartes the kind of knowledge which we attribute to agents. To be conscious is preeminently to know what we are doing or to know what is happening to us. (McRae 1972:57)

We are not here simply reversing the roles of thought and consciousness, however, making the former a more inclusive term. Rather, they are co-extensive, for Descartes says that we are always conscious of all of our thoughts. This is already evident from the definition of thought as 'everything that exists in us in such a way that we are conscious of it'. Descartes reiterates this point in the reply to Arnauld. (1973. II, 31) The distinction seems to be one between two different aspects of human mental activity; the thinking activity, and the consciousness of the thinking. That these always coincide in man is a contingent fact, the result of the fact that he is a self-conscious creature. We can imagine the two _not_ coinciding. Animals, for example, may 'think' in this sense (e.g., sense red, feel fear) but not be conscious of those thoughts. Similarly we might say that human infants only 'think' without being 'conscious'. As they grow older and develop consciousness the thinking is not _lost_, but rather the new psychological level of consciousness is superimposed upon it. Kant, in a similar vein, distinguishes the 'sensory manifold' of mental activity from its conscious 'categorized' product, experience. But the distinction is only abstract for Kant. The two always coincide in fact. We begin with experience and only by subsequent analysis make the distinction.

Locke adopts Descartes' broad sense of 'thinking'[57] although he disputes Descartes' dictum that the mind 'always thinks'. But he disputes this not because he misinterprets Descartes' use of 'thought' as indicating only a narrower 'intellectualistic' activity, as Anscombe & Geach suggest.[58] Rather, his caution is based on the much more mundane observation that sometimes man sleeps and does not dream (Locke _An Essay concerning Human Understanding_, Book II, chap. I, 9-14). But whenever man _does_ think, he is 'conscious' of it:

> If they say that man thinks always, but is not always conscious of it, they may as well

> say his body is extended without having parts. ... as thinking consists in being conscious that one thinks. (*Essay*, II,I,19).

We might say, to treat Locke very cursorily, that 'thinking' is the occurrence of 'ideas' in the mind, be they sensations, feelings, complex ideas, etc.. 'Consciousness', on the other hand, is the perception (by the self) that this activity is happening:

> Consciousness is the perception of what passes in a man's own mind. (Locke *Essay* II,I,19)

> Every man being conscious to himself that he thinks; and that which his mind is applied about whilst thinking being the ideas that are there,...(Locke *Essay* II,I,1)

'Ideas', in Locke, is a notoriously broad term, but insofar as 'thinking' covers all occurrences of 'ideas' it is equally broad. As indicating the class of such mental states as sensations, emotions, abstract ideas, etc. it indicates in general everything which makes up 'inner sense', to use Kant's term. This all-inclusive aggregate of mental activity is what the empiricists especially, as well as others (including Kant), referred to as the 'flux of thoughts'[59] which, as conscious beings, we 'observe' by introspection. Locke, for example, says (*Essay* II,XIV,3-4):

> It is evident to anyone who will but observe what passes in his own mind, that there is a train of ideas which constantly succeed one another in his understanding, as long as he is awake.

The distinction between primitive and articulated thinking can also be observed in Kant's pre-critical works, and especially the lectures on logic, which Kant continued to use well after writing the first critique. Kant usually uses the term 'cognition' for the primitive meaning of 'thinking' I have been developing. In a seven-stage hierarchy of types of cognition he describes the lowest three stages as forms of presentation which are pre-conscious. Consciousness, or cognition proper, (*cognoscere* as opposed to *noscere*), enters at the fourth stage.[60] Kant allows that animals participate in the lower stages of presentation, but they are not *conscious*:

> To be cognizant with consciousness, that is, to cognize (cognoscere). Animals also are cognizant of objects but they do not cognize them. (Kant 1974b: 71)

Elsewhere in the Logic Kant defines consciousness in this way. "Actually, consciousness is a presentation that another presentation is in me." (Kant 1974b: 37).

This doctrine is not lost in the critical philosophy. We may here note the famous passage at A320 of the Critique of Pure Reason (Kant 1965):

> The genus is representation in general (Repraesentatio). Subordinate to it stands representation with consciousness (perceptio).

This distinction between thinking and consciousness could be explored in much more detail, but I hope the general point is clear. A commonplace tendency in Enlightenment psychology is the distinction between two aspects or levels of human awareness: (1) an inner flow of mental states, the 'presentations' of our thinking; and (2) Consciousness of this presented mental content, achieved by 'reflection' or attention to the present mental states.

It is against the background of this general distinction between primitive and articulated thinking that the claim that language is necessary for thinking arises. For what this claim means more precisely is that language is necessary for articulated thinking, for consciousness. Put slightly differently, language is necessary for the transition from primitive to articulated thinking to take place. This argument is operative in Humboldt, as I showed earlier. He says that language is necessary for the formation and preservation of 'thought-units'. To clarify the logic of the argument however I must begin by noting some general features of how the terms 'idea' and 'concept' are used in this period.

2.4.2 The argument for the necessity of language in articulated thinking.

Parallel to the problem of the relationship of thinking and consciousness is some seventeenth century discussion of the terms 'idea' and 'concept'. There is a broad meaning of 'idea' by which it indicates any mental state, any constituent element of the 'flow of thoughts', as it were. But there is also a more restricted meaning of 'idea' where it picks out a particular part of that flow of thought and refers to it, whether that part is now 'in' our thinking or not. Thus in the broader sense an 'idea' is that which (those things which) are, at any given moment, the presentations making up my thinking. In the narrower sense the 'idea' may exist in my thinking at the present time, but it also may not; it has so to speak an ideal or self-subsistent existence.

This distinction may be explained, then, as a tension between what I will call the 'subjective' and 'objective' meanings of 'idea'. We may call the current contents of our thinking 'ideas', in the subjective sense. But we also want to say that the idea of 'justice' which I was pondering a week ago, and may think about tomorrow, continued to exist in some fashion in the interim. Any locution such as 'he is thinking about the same idea as I am' assumes the objective meaning. To put it another way, the distinction is between 'idea' as an 'act of thought' and as that which is 'thought about'.

Although 'idea' generally came to have only the latter, 'objective' meaning, (as 'concept' had right along), this two-fold usage is still prevalent in the Enlightenment. It is nowhere more prevalent than in Locke, whose all encompassing usage of 'idea' is probably the largest source of confusion in his work. Ian Hacking (1975: 27), in trying to explain Locke's treatment of language against the background of his theory of ideas, cites Armstrong's list of the possible meanings of 'idea' in Locke. They include:

a) sense-perceptions (sense impressions);
b) bodily sensations (such things as pains or tickles);
c) mental images;
d) thoughts and concepts

Ryle similarly distinguishes five significantly different ways in which the word 'idea' is employed by Locke.[61] Both of their lists could, I think, be subdivided into instances of 'subjective' and 'objective' meanings of idea. (E.g., in Armstrong's list (a-c) are 'subjective' meanings, and (d) the objective.) Locke himself clearly has the 'objective' sense in mind occasionally, for example in his very first definition of 'idea', as:

> ... whatever is meant by phantasm, notion, species, or whatever it is which the mind can be employed about in thinking; (Locke Essay: Intro, sect 8).

Descartes and Leibniz were both well aware of this confusion in the use of idea, and guarded against it. Neither wishes to include under idea, for example, images, which Locke allows.[62] In the Reflections on Knowledge, Truth and Ideas (1684) Leibniz clearly states the two alternative uses of 'idea':

> In order to see clearly what an idea is, we must guard ourselves against a misunderstanding. Many regard the idea as the form or the differentiation of our thinking, and according to this opinion we have the idea in our mind, in so far as we are thinking of it, and each separate time that we think of it anew we have another idea, although similar to the preceding one. Some, however, take the idea as the immediate object of thought, or as a permanent form which remains even when we are no longer contemplating it. (Leibniz 1951: 327)

Essentially two problems arise with 'ideas' in the objective meaning. How do they exist when they are not actually part of the stream of thinking, not 'in view', as Locke puts it? How do we form or construct 'ideas' out of the material presented in thought, if an idea is going to be considered something over and above those presentations?

The first problem is glossed over rather than really solved, by Locke, by simply placing out-of-view ideas in 'the memory'.[63] Leibniz does not really have the same problem because he defines ideas or concepts as a disposition or power to be able to think about something on an occasion.[64]

The second problem is rather more serious, particularly for Locke and his French followers. If one does not begin with a doctrine of innate ideas or a definition of ideas as dispositions, then some explanation must be given as to how ideas (beyond the images, feelings, etc., in primitive thinking) are constructed and retained. The more radical the form of empiricism the more serious this problem becomes. Hume's difficulty with the concept of the 'self' is famous, but the problem is more general. Cassirer's note (1951: 128) on this is to the point:

> Berkeley, Hume, and Condillac consider a concept merely as a shower of impressions, that is, as a simple summation or the symbol we use for such a summation. No independent significance can be attributed to this symbol; it only represents indirectly for the memory that which was concretely given in perception.

The problem is, however, already present in Locke. All the elements in our primitive thinking are, for Locke, 'simple ideas'. Since Locke begins with commonsense assumptions about memory and a 'self' which is attending to the presented images (unlike, e.g., Hume and Condillac) he has little difficulty with the construction and retention of simple ideas. I recognize this red shape as the 'same' as that which appeared a while ago, etc.. But how do we derive and retain a complex idea from this stream of presentations; for example, that of a man, a car chase, betrayal? Locke must say that all complex ideas are 'made up of' simple ideas, whether of sensation or reflection. These complex groupings of simples are derived by the conscious activities of combination, comparison, and abstraction (Locke _Essay_ II,XII,1).

Our complex ideas, however, whether sensual or 'general' (e.g., 'man' or 'beauty') are obviously not just summations or concatenations of simple ideas; they have an immanent bond, or they would not have been so constructed in the first place. So, for Locke, to have a 'complex idea' in mind cannot _only_ mean to have in mind a certain string of simple ideas. (We can, of course, always 'define' our complex ideas in this way.) To have complex ideas in mind is more than having an aggregate of simple ideas in mind. In short, the immanent unity of that aggregate must also be in mind, or 'in view', presented in the stream of thinking. But the 'presentation' of that unity in thought, the presentation of the complex idea _as a unit_, as opposed to its simple constituents, obviously cannot be accomplished by a mere re-presentation of any among those simple constituents, or even of all of them.

Locke recognized, admittedly in an undeveloped way, that for complex ideas, as such, to be presented in thought, they must have a signifying symbol, a 'name'. Assigning a name to the complex aggregate of simple ideas is an essential step in the construction and presentation of the complex idea in its own right:

> Ideas thus made up of simple ones put

> together, I call complex; such as are beauty, gratitude, a man, an army, the universe; which, though complicated of various simple ideas, or complex ideas made up of simple ones, yet are, when the mind pleases, considered each by itself, as one entire thing, and signified by one name.
>
> (the complex idea) ... has its unity from an act of the mind, combining those several simple ideas together, and considering them as one complex one, consisting of those parts; and the mark of this union, or that which is looked on generally to complete it, is one name given to that combination. (Locke Essay II,XII,1)[65]

2.5 Résumé

I have tried to suggest here two general and related themes in Eighteenth century philosophical thought which Humboldt was familiar with and which form (I believe) the most helpful context in which to understand his treatment of the 'psychological' function of language. Thought and consciousness are not identical; rather the latter is a reflective attention to the former. This reflective consciousness can not be explained without conceptualization, forming concepts or 'thought-units' out of the ongoing presentations, the flux of sensual images, emotions, feelings etc. which constitute primitive thought. The claim that a doctrine of 'signification' is necessary for conceptualization, however, is not as widespread as this psychological scenario within which it arises. Descartes and Kant, with a few exceptions, do not have much to say about language.[66] Leibniz, although much more interested in language, does not seem to have regarded it as a necessary accompaniment of conceptualization. He did, however, regard a system of signs as very helpful in human reasoning.[67] Locke and his successors, for whom the problem of conceptualization was perhaps more difficult, show a tendency to argue that language is necessarily involved in the construction and retention of concepts. Humboldt stands within this problem area. He operates from the general standpoint of a distinction between primitive consciousness and conceptual consciousness. Conceptualization, the construction of 'thought units', is a necessary condition for articulated thinking, and language is a necessary condition for the construction of concepts.

CHAPTER THREE
HUMBOLDT'S THEORY OF DESIGNATION

3.1 *Introduction*

In discussing Humboldt's treatment of designation I have here in mind primarily the problem of the relationship between the manifest language, namely, words or sentences, either spoken or written, and that which is 'designated' by those words or sentences. There are two main themes which I would like to emphasize in this section. (1) Although Humboldt in many ways follows earlier writers on language by taking the 'naming' function of nouns to be paradigmatic for linguistic designation in general, he consistently distinguishes between the designation of objects and concepts, on the one hand, and the designation of grammatical relationships on the other. This distinction between 'lexical' and 'grammatical' designation is a central philosophical motive in Humboldt's defense of the inflectional superiority thesis, as I will show in Chapter seven. (2) In several of his essays Humboldt claims that the choice of certain sounds to designate certain concepts is not purely arbitrary but rather is motivated by 'sound-symbolism'. This is the case with respect both to 'lexical' and 'grammatical' designation. The doctrine of sound-symbolism is relevant to Humboldt's discussion of the influence of 'national character' on language, which I discuss further in Chapter six, and to his poetics.

The three basic elements in the relationship of linguistic designation are usually considered to be the *word*, the *thought* or *idea*, and the *object* or *referent*. These constitute the 'basic triangle' given in Ogden & Richards *The Meaning of Meaning* (1923), and are still the jumping off point for most 'referential' theories of meaning.[68] There are significantly different approaches to meaning; for example, the treatment of meaning as 'use' pioneered by Wittgenstein. For the purposes of this discussion of Humboldt, however, I shall stay within this referential model, since it has much in common with Humboldt's own views.

Humboldt's discussion of designation may initially be approached by noting that it follows in many ways the approach popularized, although not originated, by Locke in Book III of the Essay on Human Understanding (1691). Nevertheless, Humboldt will diverge from this approach in important respects.

For the sake of convenience I will refer to Locke's approach as that of 'representational semantics'. Language is considered not as an interconnected system of signs and rules of usage, but rather primarily as an aggregate of words. Further, the 'words' focused on, and taken as paradigmatic for the nature of linguistic designation, are those which function like names.[69] Two basic claims of representational semantics are that words (or at least 'naming' words like nouns) designate directly ideas, and that ideas (at least some of them) designate objects. Thus linguistic designation of 'objects' occurs in a mediate fashion when the idea designated by the word designates in turn an object.[70]

The guiding intuition of representational semantics is that language represents thought. The elements of a sentence are representations of what is present in the thought which that sentence is meant to express. The 'designation' relation is basically the same as the representation relation. The difficulty in defining the representation relation more closely is that it is not exactly clear what counts as an element of the sentence. If we limit these to the words in the sentence then we risk ignoring the syntactic aspect of language. A word designates (re-presents) a concept, and perhaps indirectly designates a physical object. But what of the grammatical organisation of the thought? As part of the thought should it not also reappear in the linguistic expression of the thought, i.e., be represented?

As has been often pointed out, the shortcomings of Locke's semantics become immediately evident when one endeavors to find an explanation of the formal or grammatical aspect of language within his theory. Aside from some brief attempts to base the meaning of such grammatical operators as particles upon his standard representational model, Locke avoids discussion of grammar. This is one important respect in which Humboldt's consideration of designation diverges from the 'picture theory' approach typified by Locke. Humboldt distinguishes consistently between two complementary types of 'designation' which constitute language;

namely, the designation of (1) 'things' and 'concepts', and (2) the grammatical relationships which interconnect these things and concepts:

> There appears a two-fold designation in language: that of concepts through words, and that of syntax through the structuring of words, through specific words, or through other means now to be examined. (GS VI/2 361)[71]

The latter, grammatical designation, neglected by Locke and his followers, is given equal if not predominant treatment by Humboldt. These two kinds of designation do not differ as designation, however, but only with respect to what is designated. Humboldt retains the representational perspective in that he treats even grammar as something which is present in the thought and represented in language. The shortcomings of the representational approach, already evident in Locke, become even more evident in Humboldt's attempt to treat grammatical designation within this framework. Nevertheless Humboldt's attempt is at least cognizant of the necessity of considering the formal dimensions of language.

I shall here explore Humboldt's treatment of designation by following his own division, just mentioned, between factual or conceptual designation (which I shall call lexical designation), and grammatical designation.

3.2 Lexical designation

The first point to consider here is the disjunction in the first type of designation, namely, that of 'facts or concepts'. For the most part Humboldt treats words as designating concepts.[72] Often, however, words are said to designate objects, or sometimes facts (Sache).[73] Occasionally both 'object' and 'concept' designation seem to be present and almost indifferently equated:

> In the whole area of things to be designated in language one can distinguish two species essentially different from one another: the individual objects or concepts and such general relationships as are connected with many of the former, partially for the designation of new objects or concepts, partially for the interconnection of discourse. (GS VII: 78)[74]

We are not yet specifically concerned with the second type of designation mentioned here, that of 'general relationships'. This would bring us already into the consideration of different kinds of concepts (individual, general, etc. as mentioned above in Chapter two) and of grammatical designation, which I will take up later on. Rather I here want only to note the ambivalence, in the first type of designation, between object and concept as that which is designated by a word.

The best way to resolve this ambivalence is precisely parallel to the way Kretzmann (1968) explains the same problem in Locke, where words are said to signify both ideas and objects or things.[75] With respect to Humboldt's terminology then we would say that words always designate concepts, and some concepts, in turn, designate objects.[76] Thus it is also true that some words designate objects, but they do so in a mediated fashion via the intervening concept.[77] Perhaps a terminological distinction can make this matter clear. I shall say that concepts 'represent' objects, and that words 'directly designate' concepts and 'indirectly designate' objects. Many concepts, of course, do not represent objects at all, and in these cases the word simply designates the concept without a further 'indirect' designation taking place.

Many words, of course, do not designate physical objects but rather designate abstract or, as Humboldt usually calls them, 'intellectual' concepts. Thus within the framework of the designation of concepts by words we may more specifically separate the kind of concepts which words designate into 'individual' and 'general'. The distinction of designation into 'conceptual' and 'grammatical' thus receives a further determination in that the side of 'conceptual designation' is subdivided:

> It is the same in the inner, intellectual part of language as in the case of the phonetic form, where the designation of concepts and the laws of syntax appeared as the two principal aspects. With respect to designation the distinction here appears, as there, as to whether the expression seeks out completely individual objects, or whether it is supposed to represent relationships which are applicable to a large number of individuals, collecting these equally into a general concept, so that, properly speaking, three cases are to be differentiated. The designation of concepts, under which the

> first two belong, constitutes with the phonetic the word formation which corresponds here to the conceptual formation. (GS VII: 89)[78]

Here we have the following kinds of designation in language.

I. Designation of concepts
   A) Individual concepts
   B) General concepts
II. Designation of grammatical relationships

The distinction between 'sensual' and 'non-sensual' or 'intellectual' concepts also appears, with respect to designation. This is a division of concepts "according to their origin".[79] Thus we have concepts of sensual things and of non-sensual things. In Humboldt's psychological orientation, of course, all concepts are 'non-sensual' in the sense that they are <u>mental</u> things, not physical things, and the terms 'sensual-' and 'non-sensual concepts' are short-hand phrases indicating the difference in kind of object which the concept represents.[80]

Having sketched Humboldt's general views on what words designate, we may next consider the question of <u>how</u> they designate.[81] That is to say, how does designation work? What is the relation between a word and a concept such that when one hears a word the corresponding concept comes to mind? It has often been said throughout the history of speculation about language that the relation between word and concept is arbitrary, established and maintained by convention. Thus when one hears or sees a word the corresponding concept comes to mind because one has learned the conventional association of this word with this concept.

Humboldt ultimately does not have much new to say on this topic. His feelings however are, evidently, that the signifying relationship is not completely arbitrary in all cases, but rather that there are 'more or less clear' motivating relationships between sound and concept. Compare his remarks:

> In the choice of sounds for concepts language is naturally guided by the more or less clear relationships which the senses and the imagination, according to the individuality of the nations, find among them. (GS V: 416)[82]

Humboldt immediately admits that, whatever these

relationships may have been historically, in the formative stages of a language, we shall rarely be able to discover them now. Phonetic and conceptual change and evolution over the years make it impossible for us to explore and reconstruct an 'original' rationale for any particular sound-concept designation. Nevertheless, granting that practical point, it is still not very clear what sort of 'guiding relationships' Humboldt has in mind even in principle. Several passages in Grundzüge and in Einleitung offer some clarification on this. In Grundzüge Humboldt indicates a three part distinction of designation:

> Originally this designation (which actually is such only with respect to the hearer, but is rather an apprehension with respect to the speaker) lies in every word; in those which imitate natural sounds in the tones of the objects, in others, for corporeal things in different properties of the thing, for intellectual things in the metaphors chosen for their indication. (GS V: 426)[83]

The first case mentioned here is that of words designating an object by reproducing the sounds which the object produces; the case of onomatopoeia. This case constitutes an insignificantly small part of the total lexicon of a language, however, even if only substantive type words are considered.

The latter two cases presumably are meant to cover all of the other cases, i.e., all other words (and concepts) in the language. We can see Humboldt employing here, as elsewhere,[84] the division between 'sensual' and 'non-sensual' concepts. Words designating (indirectly) a physical object do so by indicating a 'property' of the object; words designating 'intellectual' things utilize a 'metaphor', presumably drawn from some other 'sensual' designation.

This seems to help very litle, of course, in explaining more clearly how the relation between word and concept in the latter two cases is not arbitrary. The question simply recurs: how does the word-sound designating a physical object relate (non-arbitrarily) to the 'property' chosen from an object to designate that object? How is a metaphor chosen (non-arbitrarily) for the designation of 'intellectual' or 'non-sensual' objects? Humboldt seems to have hardly made a first step here.

A similar discussion of the word-concept relationship in his last work is not much more enlightening, but may help us to see at least what the general strategy of designation is which Humboldt is trying to suggest, even if the details remain obscure.

Once again, in Einleitung, Humboldt asserts that there is a connection beteen the sound and its significance, but that the character of this connection remains for the most part a theoretical enigma and an historical mystery.[85] Nevertheless Humboldt attempts to sketch out, so to speak, the parameters within which the 'natural' naming relation has its being. He distinguishes, for this purpose, between three forms of name-meaning relation. We can perhaps give the sense of this three-fold distinction by a brief quote describing each part: (GS VII: 76-78)[86]

> (1) Pictographic designation
> The first is the directly imitative concept, in which the tone that a resounding object brings forth is reproduced to the extent that articulated sounds are capable of reproducing unarticulated ones. ... Just as the picture represents the manner in which an object appears to the eye, language depicts the manner in which it is perceived by the ear.
>
> (2) Symbolic designation
> The second is the indirectly imitative designation, which shares in a property that is common to the sound and the object. ...It selects sounds to designate the objects which, inherently and in comparison with others, produce for the ear an impression similar to that of the object upon the soul.
>
> (3) Analogical designation
> The third is designation based on phonetic similarity in accordance with the relationship of the concepts to be designated. Words whose meanings closely approach one another become endowed with similar sounds; however, in contrast to the designative bracket just considered, emphasis in this instance is not upon the character inherent in these sounds themselves.

The first of these types of designation, 'pictographic', is, like the first case mentioned in the passage quoted from the Grundzüge, the case of onomatopoeia, in which a word copies a sound which its indirectly designated 'object' makes.

The second case, 'symbolic' designation, evidently intended to be much more sweeping, is also more elusive in character. For the 'property' which is common to the object and the sound is not some 'physical' property, in the way that, for example, having two legs is a property of a man. It is hard to imagine what 'physical' properties a word could have in common with a physical object except that of a common sound, covered already in case (1). So by the 'impressions' an object produces Humboldt here has in mind not a physical property but rather a certain quality of the designated object, like hardness, hollowness, elusiveness, etc.. His examples make this clear:

> For example _stehen_, _statig_, _starr_ give the impression of fixity; the Sanskrit _li_, 'melt' or 'disperse', suggests melting away; _nicht_, _nagen_, _Neid_ sharp severence. In this way objects that produce similar impressions obtain words with predominently the same sounds, such as _wehen_, _Wind_, _Wolke_, _wirren_, _Wunsch_; in all of these the restless motion confusedly passing before the senses is expressed by the letter _w_, hardened from the letter _u_, which is inherently dull and hollow sounding. (GS VII: 76)[87]

So this sort of 'symbolic' designation in the phonetics of the word is amenable not just to designation of physical objects, but also, apparently, to many more intangible 'objects' as well. With respect to the examples here suggested by Humboldt we could say that 'envy' or 'wish' are not physical 'objects' like 'wind', which is in turn a less tangible object than a tree, a stone, etc..

One is tempted intuitively to feel that such 'symbolic' designation is indeed still essentially arbitrary, and that Humboldt is grasping at straws. Empirical evidence for this would be radical differences between various languages with respect to the phonetic designation of the same, or the same kind, of objects. For if what Humboldt is saying were true, then each language should approximate, at least with respect to some objects, to the same phonetic designation, an implication which Humboldt realizes full well.[88] This seems intuitively to be an easily falsifiable implication, given the evident variation of languages; so much so that modern linguistics has had little interest in pursuing the matter of sound-symbolism.[89] It is not my purpose here, however, to pass judgment upon Humboldt's position, but rather only to clarify the nature of what he is suggesting.

This leaves the third type of designation, 'analogical', to be considered. Here, unlike the first two cases, the relationship between the word and the concept is considered rather than that between word and object. The basic point that he wants to make is that once a certain word becomes established in a given language as designating a certain concept then subsequent variations or additions to that concept will be designated by words formed out of the same phonetic base, producing certain phonetic-conceptual families. It is evident that we have here basically a suggestion about the <u>inter</u>-relationship <u>among</u> different word-concept units rather than about the <u>intra</u>-relationship (if I may so put it) between each word and the concept which it designates. This point, of course, does not touch the problem of the arbitrariness of the relation between a specific concept (or object) and the sign that designates it. The 'analogical' aspect of designation merely points out that similarities between concepts may become manifest in correlative similarities between their respective phonetic names. A modern formulation of this same point is made in a concise article by T.V. Gamkrelidze (1974):

> The phonetic closeness of such kinship terms as Eng. father-mother-brother, or Fr. <u>pere-mere-frere</u>, is a phonemic allusion to the semantic proximity of the corresponding signata standing in definite relationships to each other. Thus certain relations at the level of the signata are manifested at the level of the corresponding signantia by definite relationships of phonetic character specific for the plane of expression.[90]

Thus, to summarize, if Humboldt is attempting to suggest, in these passages, a non-arbitrary basis for word-formation, it seems to boil down to this. (1) Some words may be related to the physical objects they indirectly designate by sound-similarity (onomatopoeia). (2) Some words may, more generally, employ a sound-symbolism in designating both physical objects and abstract concepts. In the passages I have considered here Humboldt seems to regard this sound-symbolism as linguistically universal, but in other passages he regards it as varying and language-specific. (Cf. further discussion in Chapter six.) (3) Once some concept-word units <u>are</u> established (whether arbitrarily or not) further word-formation will develop in a non-arbitrary 'motivated' fashion by retaining and employing these previously established sound-concept associations.

These suggestions, despite their generality and evident shortcomings, nevertheless constitute the most direct comments Humboldt makes on how the designative relationship between concept and word-sound is established.

3.3 Grammatical designation

My primary concern here is limited to showing that, and how, Humboldt's treatment of grammar gives an acount of grammar which incorporates it into the representational approach. The main points to be made are as follows. Grammar is viewed as something which is represented or 'designated' in language. What is designated are grammatical relationships. These relationships constitute a means of interconnecting concepts and forming 'thoughts' Thus Humboldt may be seen as having a two-fold designative system; isolated (and hence indeterminate) concepts are connected to one another by various grammatical relationships, and both concepts and relationships are designated in the spoken or written sentence.

I have already mentioned above that Humboldt differs from earlier versions of 'representational semantics' by including extensive consideration of the grammatical structure of language within his account. But we should avoid from the beginning the tendency to blend 'grammatical' and 'lexical' designation together, as if the former could be explained as a subset of the latter. This tendency may have been characteristic of Locke and earlier versions of representational semantics, but Humboldt consistently separates these two aspects of language:

> In all the cases here drawn together there lies in the inner designation of the word two things whose completely different nature must be carefully separated. There is, associated with the act of designation of the concept itself, a product of the intellect placing it into a determinate category of thought or discourse, and the full sense of the word stems at the same time from that conceptual expression and this modifying indication. But these two elements lie in

completely different spheres. (GS VII: 109)[91]

Humboldt's most comprehensive treatment of grammar is found in the essay Von dem grammatischen Baue der Sprachen (1827-29). At the very outset he points to the difference which he sees between lexical and grammatical designation:

> Words represent for the most part corporeal objects. What grammar designates is nothing corporeal, nothing visible, never coming into the external world, only suspended, as an incorporeal form, in the things, insofar as a representing force takes them up, consisting throughout in intellectual relationships. (GS VI/2: 337)[92]

In his earlier description of the 'origin of grammatical forms' he clearly separates grammatical 'forms' from grammatical 'relationships'. The former are the "means of designating" the latter.[93] The question of what constitutes a grammatical 'form' becomes complicated, and will be considered in Chapter seven. Nevertheless an initial characterization of 'grammatical form' defines it very generally in terms of the designation of a 'grammatical relationship':

> That which, in a language, characteristically designates a grammatical relationship (so that it always recurs in the same situation) is for it a grammatical form. (GS IV: 295)[94]

The initial point to be made, then, is that explicit grammatical signs in the spoken or written language designate a certain class of 'relationships', i.e., 'grammatical' relationships. A second point, already mentioned, is that Humboldt clearly wants to view these relationships as separate from the concepts which words themselves designate. It is the combination of 'conceptual' and 'grammatical' designation which constitutes discourse.[95]

This suggests a general outline of Humboldt's theory of designation. A word designates a concept, either of a physical object, activity, property, etc. (e.g., 'tree'. 'run') or with more abstract or intellectual content (e.g., 'justice', 'compromise'). The word receives an addition or change (for example, an ending or prefix, vowal alternation, etc.) which itself designates a certain grammatical relationship. This then makes the concept more determinate, adding to it the relevant additional meaning which will relate it to other concepts in the thought (other words in the sentence), or even make it more determinate in isolation. For example 'have' is changed to 'had', adding the meaning of past tenseness to the basic meaning of the verb 'to have'. Or an adjective may be altered to indicate case, as in changing 'mein Vater' to 'meinem Vater'. The ending -em adds the meaning of the dative case, characterizing 'my father' now as the recipient of some action; 'to my father' or 'for my father'. The same addition is designated in English by the addition of separate grammatical words, i.e., 'to', 'for', etc..

The basic thrust of Humboldt's view here may be crudely characterized as attributing to words a certain conceptual 'core' of meaning, which becomes more definite (i.e., designates one or another of the possible alternative variations of its core meaning) through the accretion of grammatical relationships which also may be designated in the spoken or written word. (Of course they become more definite in other ways as well, such as by consideration of the over-all semantic context, motivations of the speaker, etc.. But in the present context we are only concerned with the role of grammatical designation in increasing the determinateness.) Humboldt seems to have this view in mind, for instance, when he says things like:

> For the expression of varying thoughts the speaker must use the same words. He must then divest these signs of individual concepts from that which only belongs to the determinate connection. In that he must in this way distinguish the persevering concept sign from the changing connective sound, ... (GS VI/2: 360)[96]

Grammatical designation by means of altering individual words can account, however, for only part of grammatical indication; that is, the part traditionally called morphology, as opposed to syntax (which indicates grammatical relationships in the sentence as a whole, sometimes by means which transcend the manipulation of a single word; for example, word order). Humboldt is aware of the need for a distinction like this. In his work on Chinese as well as elsewhere he draws a distinction between "two separate parts of grammar"; 'etymological' and 'syntactic'. 'Etymological' grammar basically means that grammatical designation which is accomplished within an individual word, so that analysis of that word (a 'grammatical etymology') could etablish its meaning, apart from any consideration of the context. In Chinese this is not possible; the designation of grammatical relationships occurs only by 'syntactic' means, as Humboldt says:

> The grammar of other languages has two separate parts, an etymological and a syntactical part, but in the Chinese grammar we can find only the latter. ...One must immediately appeal to the dictionary for help and give the construction of the sentence only on the basis of the meaning of words, the arrangement, and the sense of the discourse. (GS V: 310)[97]

This conception of syntax, however, seems a rather impoverished one. And in his later essay on grammatical structure Humboldt uses the term 'syntax' to refer to any grammatical relationship which deals with the sentence as a whole, as opposed to isolated words. Designation of such relationships, even if localized in single words, are thus 'syntactic':

> The grammatical formation of words (the so-called etymological part of grammar) is only the preliminary preparation for the connection of discourse. This itself is determined first by the laws of construction (the syntactic part of grammar). (GS VI/2: 378)[98]

At this point Humboldt helps us to visualize a bit more clearly just what sort of relationships constitute the class of relationships which are 'grammatical'. He gives a list of aspects of the simple sentence which grammar "has to determine".[99] They are, not surprisingly, rather traditional categories of grammar, and include the following:

a) The use of the individual parts of speech.
b) The grammatical concordance of the elements which belong together in the same function in different parts of the sentence, (e.g., adjective agreement).
c) The relationship of the parts standing in different functions in the sentence (e.g., on the one hand, as effecting and governing, on the other as effected and governed).
d) The indication of species, to which the whole sentence belongs, insofar as a specific one is required (i.e., whether it is declarative, subjunctive, interrogative, etc.).

Most of Humboldt's more specific discussions of particular relationships concern matters which would fall under these headings. In Entstehen he discusses, for example, the concept of the 'infinitive' as it is designated in many languages. An essay from 1827, Ueber den Dualis, considers the general nature of the dual and the forms by which several languages designate it. In Vom gram. Baue he mentions, for example, the general relationship of the active voice, and some specific ways of designating it:

> The grammatical relationship is not always apprehended in its pure generality. If something particular remains in it, then there arises probably a series of forms in the place of an individual one. This is the case when the active is designated by insertion of the pronominal accusative into the verb. (GS VI/2: 376)[100]

It remains to be noted that Humboldt also feels here, with respect to grammatical designation, just as we earlier saw with 'lexical' designation, that some type of motivation may exist between particular relationships and their phonetic designation. Although the signs for grammatical connection often may be purely conventional, they may also arise as if by some 'feeling' about the grammatical purpose:

> But they can also have arisen quite properly out of the feeling of the grammatical purpose which they serve, and thus become 'symbolic'. ...The symbolic usually lies in such an alteration, as e.g., in reduplication as a characteristic of the past; but they can also depend on the nature of the letters, and there thus arises, as in the case of words, an analogical connection between the concept and the sound designating it. (GS VI/2: 371-72)[101]

This problem could be further explored by reference to some other passages and examples given by Humboldt, but since it is parallel to the discussion above concerning 'lexical' sound motivation I shall not pursue the matter further.

In his recent work Tilman Borsche (1981) has suggested that Humboldt came to regard the distinction between 'lexical' and 'grammatical' elements of language as valid only from a theoretical standpoint which

Humboldt had already surpassed. According to Borsche, the distinction is valid only from the standpoint of 'wissenschaftlichen Sprachbetrachtung', and Humboldt eventually achieves a higher perspective than this, a perspective from which "... language itself is distinguished from the conditions of its investigation" (Borsche 1981: 251). The division of language into lexicon and grammar "... as useful as it may be for scientific reflection, does not stand up to this particular intention under reflection. In discourse designating (lexical) and connecting (grammatical) elements can not be separated from one another." (1981: 255).

It is certainly accurate to say, for Humboldt, that grammatical and lexical elements cannot indefinitely be considered and investigated separately. He joins the two under the general topic of 'designating' elements of language, considering both grammar and lexicon as 'designating' elements. In this respect it is misleading to imply, as in the last passage quoted from Borsche, that the distinction of lexicon from grammar for Humboldt ever corresponds to a distinction of 'bezeichnende' elements from 'verknüpfende' elements. It seems, therefore, an exaggeration to say that Humboldt eventually surpassed or sublated this distinction. From the beginning he regards the lexicon / grammar distinction as a dualism _within_ the designative function of language, and it is a dualism which he continues to find appropriate and useful throughout his writings, as the various texts I have discussed in this chapter clearly show.

CHAPTER FOUR
GENERAL ASPECTS OF LANGUAGE VARIATION

4.1 Introduction

In the first several chapters I have explored aspects of Humboldt's theory of language that are universal in scope. That is, the role of language in thinking and the problem of designation are themes which concern language in general, in all men, and not just this language or that one. Yet Humboldt is perhaps most often remembered as someone who stressed the <u>variation</u> of languages, and indeed not merely the 'surface' or phonetic variation, but also the 'inner' or conceptual variation. The aspects of his theory taken up so far may treat of the way language works in all men, but they do not provide an explanation of the variation of languages. The description of language as a necessary medium for forming or 'articulating' thought does not, by itself, explain why men articulate their thoughts in different ways. General features of how designation in language works do not explain why in fact the concepts which are designated vary from language to language.

Although the thesis that languages differ from one another at the conceptual level, as well as with respect to the sounds and syntactic rules which they use, is an old and much-debated idea, discussion of it has often focussed on what the extent of this variation is and what the implications of it are, for example, with respect to translation from one language to another. Modern consideration, for example, Whorf's investigation of time concepts, and Lenneberg's investigation of color recognition and codification,[102] concentrate on establishing <u>that</u> conceptual variation exists, and to what extent it exists. In Humboldt's works, however, we find a different orientation to this problem. For the most part he takes it for granted that languages differ conceptually, and is more concerned to explain how this variation came about. Why is it that all people do not develop equivalent understandings of the world in which they all live? Why is it that languages, considered as conceptual systems of understanding, do not all correspond exactly to one another, allowing, for example, for exact translation from one to another? Humboldt's theory of the production of language(s) focusses particularly on the causes of linguistic variation.

In the following chapters, accordingly, I will take up several aspects of Humboldt's philosophy of language which bear on the problem of the variation of languages. Two causes of variation that Humboldt discusses are the differing 'perceptions' which people have, and the differing 'national characters' of nations. In Chapters five and six I take up these two matters in turn.

Before turning to those subjects, however, I would like to consider some more general aspects of Humboldt's treatment of linguistic variation. In the present chapter therefore I discuss the following topics: (1) The ways in which languages vary, according to Humboldt; (2) Humboldt's views on universal grammar, which will function as a restriction on the extent of grammatical variation, and (3) The terminology which Humboldt employs in describing various parts of language.

4.2 Different kinds of language variation

Humboldt divides the variation of languages into several kinds. They vary with respect to the actual sounds used, with respect to syntactic rules, and with respect to conceptual content. In vergl. Sprachstudium he distinguishes variation in terms of the 'world-view' of a language from the diversity of 'sounds and signs':

> Their (language's) variety is not one of sounds and signs but rather of a diversity of world-views. In this fact is the reason and the ultimate purpose of all investigation of languages. (GS VII: 27)103

Apparently referring back to this essay in Nationalcharakter he says:

> In one of my earlier academic lectures I have sought to direct attention to the fact that the variation of languages consists in more than the mere variation of signs, that

> the words and syntax at the same time form and determine the concepts, and that, considered in regard to their connection and influence on knowledge and sensation, the several languages are in fact several world-views. (GS IV: 420)[104]

In the chapter "Innere Sprachform" in Einleitung Humboldt says that not only do languages differ with respect to the 'Lautform', but also with respect to the 'intellectual' part of language:

> With respect to the sound form an infinite multiplicity, not to be reckoned with, is conceivable. ... But that which, like the intellectual part of language, rests only on spiritual self-activity, appears to have to be the same in all men, with respect to the similarity of purpose and of means; and to be sure this part of language preserves a greater similarity. But even in it there arises from several causes a significant variation. (GS VII: 86-7)[105]

Under the variation of the 'intellectual part' of language Humboldt seems to understand both the variation of words and syntax. Later in Einleitung he says:

> But the intellectual variation of nations is evident far more in the syntax (Fugungen der Rede) than with respect to the individual words, ... (GS VII: 192)[106]

From the passage from Nationalcharakter. we may infer that the conceptual content of each language is different as well, and that this conceptual variation is what Humboldt means by calling different languages different 'world-views'. The grounds for the inference that languages differ conceptually would be: (1) that words and syntax 'form and determine' concepts; and (2) that words and syntax vary from language to language.

We might say, from the above passages, that Humboldt viewed languages as varying with respect to the following categories.

1. sounds
2. words
3. syntax
4. concepts
5. world-views

These are, of course, general categories of linguistic variation. That is to say, under each heading Humboldt will distinguish more specific types of variation. For example, he argues that the syntactic variation of languages falls into three areas.[107] As a further example we can note how he sub-divides conceptual variation:

> This influence of the national peculiarity in language is noticed in two ways: in the structure of the individual concepts and in the relative wealth of the language in concepts of a given type. (GS VII: 91)[108]

In the following sections I will restrict myself to those aspects of Humboldt's treatment of language variation which seem to me most philosophically significant and relevant to a systematic presentation of his views. I begin with a brief consideration of his orientation towards universal grammar. The claim that languages vary syntactically is prima facie in conflict with the tradition of thought which claimed that there were certain syntactic features present in all languages. Then I turn to the problem of clarifying the meaning of Humboldt's claims that languages vary in terms of concepts and world-views. The meaning of these claims can be clarified in a preliminary way by considering Humboldt's terminology, and getting clear about which terms refer to an area of variation and which not, and how these terms relate to one another. This discussion of terminology occupies part (4) of the present chapter. After these preliminary clarifications of Humboldt's views on variation I will concentrate in Chapters five and six on the matter of the conceptual variation of languages, and on Humboldt's attempts to explain how such variation came about.

4.3 Humboldt's treatment of universal grammar

Humboldt's views about language universals are not an essential part of the systematic inter-connections which I have described in this book. Nevertheless it should be noted that he did occasionally assert that certain features of language (more specifically, features of grammar) exist in all languages. Although this is not of central importance to the present study, it may be desirable for several reasons to provide a brief account here of Humboldt's views on universal grammar.

First, it is important simply to recognize and document the fact that Humboldt did accept and assert the existence of language universals. He is remembered and discussed primarily as a thinker concerned with the variation among languages. While this is a justified emphasis, any final evaluation of his views on the extent and influence of language variation must be tempered by an appreciation of what he regarded as common to all languages. In this respect this section is meant as an antidote to the Humboldt literature, which has given particularly poor treatment to the issue of universal grammar in Humboldt's thought. A noteworthy case in point is the chapter on language universals in Roger Brown's book (1967). Although polemic is not my main intention here, the many problems in Brown's treatment can not be passed over, constituting as it does one of the few discussions of the matter.

Second, in addition to pointing out deficiencies in the literature, I hope to correct that deficiency at least in a preliminary way by taking up the following questions. What did Humboldt mean by such phrases as 'universal language type' (allgemeiner Sprachtypus) and 'universal grammar'? How did he relate these to logic? What would examples of universal grammar be, in his view? The examples of what would fall under universal grammar, although only tentatively outlined, help to make his intentions clearer. He argues, for example, that the gerund is a form "justified according to concepts of universal grammar, and presented as necessary":

> Thus the gerund is not merely a form in certain languages, but also justified according to concepts of universal grammar, and presented as necessary. As a member intermediate between the pure infinitive and the verbal substantive it even needs its own name. (GS IV: 393)[109]

In examples like this Humboldt appears to be appealing to a conceptual deduction, so to speak, of certain grammatical forms on the basis of others. A form 'B' conceptually intermediate between forms 'A' and 'C' (as in the above quote), or the logical opposite of 'A', can be defined independently of the investigation of any actual natural language. I shall discuss this example and others like it further below after looking more generally at the meaning of universal grammar for Humboldt.

Brown's discussion suffers from several faults. He spends a great deal of effort considering what the influences on Humboldt in this regard were, but actually doesn't say very much about Humboldt's own views on universa' grammar. Whether the various sources he cites actually influenced Humboldt much is an open question, since Humboldt rarely cites or even mentions other thinkers. Roberta Ross (1970: 285-86) has argued that various of the alleged influences on Humboldt which Brown discusses, in particular that of the French school of grammarians, are not in fact very significant influences. She herself suggests that Kantian universal categories of perception and understanding may have influenced Humboldt here, as Brown also maintains (1967: 96).

Aside from these questions of emphasis, however, Brown's treatment is marred by vacillation over whether or not Humboldt changed his position over time, omission of consideration of significant texts, and misleading translations.

After assuming, at least implicitly, that there is a fundamental conflict between advocating linguistic universals and linguistic relativity, Brown (1967: 96; and cf also 103, 107) suggests several times that Humboldt's views on universal grammar underwent considerable change:

> Amongst other things, Humboldt's view of language universals changed considerably over the years: a rather pronounced belief in the existence of important language universals which is found mainly in papers written in the first two decades of the nineteenth century was later replaced by an emphasis on the fundamental differences between languages. Even so, traces of Humboldt's earlier position are still to be found in his later treatments of the problem.

Nevertheless the qualifier at the end of this passage is echoed several times when Brown finds discussions of universal grammar in various of Humboldt's later writings (1967: 103). In addition, significant discussions of universal grammar in Grundzüge and Vom gram. Baue are much in the same spirit as earlier discussions of the matter, as I will show below, but Brown completely ignores these writings. Indeed there seems so little basic change in Humboldt's viewpoint over time that the value of basing an interpretation upon an assumption of such change is questionable at the very least.

In addition, Brown suggests that Humboldt sees little danger in imposing the grammatical forms of familiar languages upon those of unfamiliar languages, and that, further:(1967:102):

> In the opening words of this essay, Humboldt appears confident that a change of terminology is sufficient to accommodate exotic languages within the framework of universal grammar. (Brown 1967: 102)

Humboldt, quite to the contrary, was very conscious of the grave dangers inherent in assuming that any one language (e.g., Latin) could be used as a standard for studying and describing other languages. In Entstehen he cautions against such dangers at some length (GS IV: 286-290), citing numerous mistakes resulting from this approach. In the essay from 1822, cited by Brown, Humboldt also regards these mistakes as easily incurred and as producing grave misrepresentations of foreign languages. Brown's point is supported only by a translation which reverses the meaning of the original.[110]

However, the real need here is not to become consumed by details of historical influence or points of translation, but rather to present Humboldt's own views. To this task I shall now turn.

Humboldt's view of language universals lies squarely in the tradition of the so-called 'speculative grammar' of the middle ages and the general or 'philosophical' grammar of the Renaissance and Enlightenment period, perhaps best typified by the Port Royal grammar of 1660. The guiding intuition of this tradition is that there are some grammatical structures which can be found in all human languages. In extent, then, these aspects of language are universal. Further, however, this universality was not usually regarded as a contingent fact (historically explicable, as it were, on the basis of the evolution of all languages out of one original 'Ursprache'). Rather, the existence of language universals was usually explained as a reflection or manifestation of universal features of the human mind, of certain thought structures or rules of thought common to all men. Thus, despite efforts by Aarsleff (1974: 94 and 111) and others to regard the origin of language controversy as having the same goals as universal grammar, the two approaches have a distinctly different orientation, as expressed well by Diderichsen (1974: 287):

> Universal grammar consequently was a sort of comparative grammar, but as it principally was concerned with universal semantic concepts, it was not interested in the diverg-

> ing forms of the particular languages, regarding these as pure variants of a general system, not as descendants of a common Ursprache.

Whenever Humboldt discusses universal grammar he links it to the universality of certain aspects of thought. In Grundzüge he says:

> What is common to all grammar (das Gemeinsame in der Grammatik) in itself and in its procedure, can only proceed from the nature and essence of language, the laws of thought, and the properties of the speech organs, and only the first two allow of derivation from pure concepts. (GS V: 450)[111]

> The similarity of the laws of thought produces what is shared by the grammar of all languages, by means of which each can be related to the universal grammar and to each other. Every grammatical form may, in some way or another, be pointed out in every language, ... (GS V: 453)[112]

Similarly in the long essay Von dem grammatische Baue der Sprachen he speaks of universal grammar as a Kanon to which every language may be related, because it includes and develops that which "... by means of the unity of the laws of thought and the essential nature of language, is shared by all tongues."[113]

Universal grammar is not the passed down product of an Ursprache but rather the manifestation of an abstract conceptual system which becomes instantiated in varying ways as soon as it enters into particular languages.[114]

Mention of the phrase 'laws of thought' raises the question of the relationship between universal grammar and logic. For at least in some traditional formulations, logic is concerned to formalize and interrelate the 'laws of thought', such as the law of non-contradiction, the laws of implication, etc. in a fashion independent of their expression in any particular language. If universal grammar is constituted by those aspects of language which reflect the 'rules of thought' and are present in every language, is it then the same as logic?

Both in Grundzüge and Vom gram. Baue Humboldt is drawn to consider this question and to try to state the difference between universal grammar and logic. The passage in the latter work is in fact in large part a literal repetition of the text from the earlier essay, a practice quite common in Humboldt's writings. Universal grammar and logic are, he says, very similar enterprises but they must be very carefully distinguished. Both deal with certain 'ideal' relationships, with the separation and connection of concepts, but they deal with them in different ways; compare Humboldt's statement:

> The basic determinations of grammar are already contained in the universal rules of thought. ... In this area universal grammar falls together with logic to a certain extent, but both doctrines must be carefully held within their proper borders, even with respect to that area in which they actually touch. The logical judgement and the grammatical proposition stand, through all their species and subspecies, in precisely the same area. But logic treats these ideal relationships merely in and for themselves, in the area of possibility, of absolute being. Language fixes them at a definite moment, and represents the subject, as (also) the predicate, as active or passive, in itself devouring or repelling (reizend oder zurückstossend). Thereby the dead relational concept, as it were the connective sign of mathematical equivalence, is brought to living movement. (GS VI: 345-6)[115]

At least one thing that is clear from this is that Humboldt conceives of both universal grammar and logic as concerned with a certain set of relationships between concepts. While the distinction between the logical and grammatical treatments of those relationships is less clear, we may at least say that by 'universal grammar' Humboldt means a certain set of grammatical relationships which represent, in language, corresponding laws of thought. Since these laws of thought presumably hold for all men, the relationships must be expressed in every human language, and are, hence, universal.

We may place here several characteristic claims which Humboldt advocates against the background of these statements. First, he does not view the evident multiplicity and variation of grammatical systems as conflicting with or refuting claims about universal grammar. There is a difference between the relationships (or at least those which are universal) and the varying ways in which they are designated in different languages:

> The grammatical relationships must be recognizable in some way in all languages. ... But the way in which this requirement is satisfied is not the same in all languages. (GS VI: 340-1)[116]

The variation of grammatical systems Humboldt customarily describes as occurring at three levels: that of a general grammatical viewpoint (Ansicht), that of technical means of designation, and that of phonetic variation.[117] This has already been discussed in the previous chapter, on designation. It should be emphasized however that what Humboldt means by the 'ideal grammatical view' of a language is quite different from universal grammar. The former varies from language to language, the latter does not. This point is made clearly in Vom gram. Baue.[118] My present concern however is not with what varies but with what remains unchanged.

A second claim characteristic of Humboldt which should be associated with his advocacy of universal grammar is his distinction of explicitly designated grammar and 'silent' grammar, which is 'added in thought'.[119] This distinction of 'express' and 'silent' grammar is not meant to differentiate whole grammatical systems from one another, in the sense that one language has a completely silent grammar, another a fully designated grammar. This may sometimes appear the case, as with Chinese. Humboldt however stresses that the distinction arises within each language:

> In the grammar of each language there is an expressly designated part and a part which remains silent, being added in thought. (GS V: 319)[120]

The view that grammatical relationships can be 'silently' present, without explicit designation, goes back at least to Entstehen (1821), where Humboldt clearly says that grammatical relationships depend on the intentions of the speaker, and they "adhere less to the words than they are added in thought (hineingedacht)".[121] The relevance of this here is that when Humboldt claims that certain grammatical relationships are 'universal', or present in every language, he is also allowing that they may not be expressly designated. Lack of explicit appearance of a relationship in some language need not refute a 'universality' claim, because, according to Humboldt's view, one could still recognize the intentional presence of this relationship and perhaps point out where it is added in thought. Thus he says in Grundzüge:

> When a grammatical form possesses no designation in a language, it is nevertheless still present as a guiding principle of the understanding of those who speak the language ... (GS V: 469)[122]

Having briefly explored what Humboldt means by universal grammar I will now give some examples of what he included in universal grammar. That is to say, if universal grammar is defined as the class of relationships which reflect 'laws of thought' and are, in some way, present in every language, then we may ask which relationships are members of this class. Some, including Brown and den Ouden, have suggested that by 'universal characteristics' of language Humboldt means, for example, the Sprachvermögen, the capacity that all men have to learn to speak.[123] But it is evident that what he means by universal grammar is much more specific than this, both from what he says about it in general and from the fact that he does give specific examples, although they are not always very clear.

In Grundzüge Humboldt clearly cites the case relationships holding between nouns, pronouns and adjectives and other words in the sentence, or at least the nominative, dative, genitive and accusative cases, as necessarily present in all languages. His reasoning here is illustrative of his general explanation of what universal grammar is. Some cases, such as the instrumental or locative, are not universal since they depend upon the contingent development of, and grammatical employment of, concepts like instrument or tool, and spatial location. But the four main cases just cited are, he suggests, necessary variations of the category of relation, and hence not dependent on the contingent conceptual development of this or that language. The point seems to be that relationships defined by logical opposition or reciprocal determination are present in every language (even if not explicitly designated) since they reflect only the immanent possibilities present in the *relata* themselves and not the further possibilities engendered by intruding additional factors, which would vary from language to language. Other examples Humboldt cites are the logical opposition of active-passive voices, the conditional, as necessary opposite to the indicative mood, the plural as necessary opposite to the singular:

> Thus (for example) the first four cases of declination flow necessarily and by them-

> selves from the category of relation, and to this derivation may be added a fifth (case), that of reciprocity. The instrumental and locative on the other hand first arise through the intrusion of the concepts of tool and place. A similar distinction can be found between the conditional, as necessary opposite of the indicative, and the optative, in addition to which many other (contingent) modes of obligation, necessity etc. could be cited; between the passive, as necessary contrast to the active, and the ninth and eleventh conjugations of Arabic, which are related only to certain objects, colors, physical defects, etc; between the plural, as necessary expression of multiplicity, and the dual, which contingently introduces a form for a particular determinate number; and so on. (GS V: 452-3)[124]

Humboldt is not, of course, claiming that the first four cases, for example, will be explicitly designated in all languages. The point is merely that the syntactic relationships named by these cases will be employed in every language, and if they are not indicated somehow in the surface structure of a language they must be "added in thought".[125]

A similar example is Humboldt's treatment of the gerund in the essay on Sanskrit verbal forms, first published in 1823. In this essay he explores the nature of the gerund as occupying a position between the infinitive of a verb and a verbal-substantive. Since, in his opinion, there is a clear logically intermediate position between these two, we have a grammatical form (i.e., the gerund) justified conceptually, apart from its appearance in this or that language (GS IV: 393).

It is not necessary here to go into Humboldt's long discussion of the nature of, and differences between, the infinitive and the verbal substantive. By these examples I hope merely to indicate that Humboldt viewed grammar as having certain immanent self-determined relationships, such as logical opposition (e.g., active / passive voice) or logical intermediacy between two opposites (e.g., infinitive / gerund / verbal substantive). These relationships can be explored conceptually without recourse to empirical examination of various natural languages. This exploration is apparently what Humboldt regards as universal grammar. Further, however, he seems to feel a need to view the grammatical forms posited in this way, i.e., by conceptual analysis, as present in all languages, whether 'explicitly designated' or only silently 'hineingedacht'. We may well wonder at this further claim. Does Humboldt mean that all languages actually employ the grammatical relationships which can be logically derived, or just that they are 'potentially' available to any language? He seems to mean the former, although this is not completely clear.[126]

At any rate, it is clear that he believes that there is a class of grammatical relationships which all languages employ ('universal' grammar), and the reason why there is such a class is because there are certain logical relationships inherent in thinking itself. These relationships may be investigated purely conceptually; there is no need for an empirical survey of existing languages to discover or verify what grammatical relationships are universal. In any case an empirical survey could not prove that any grammatical relation was in fact 'universal' in the strong sense since a particular contingent non-universal form (Humboldt's example, the dual) might in fact be (contingently) present in all languages.

A more concrete bottom line to these brief comments on universal grammar in Humboldt would be as follows: Humboldt did believe that there were some aspects of grammar which are common to all languages. He allows that they may not necessarily be explicitly evident or designated in particular languages, but if they are not they must be considered to be 'added in thought' by the users of that language when they are needed. Examples of syntactic forms which Humboldt cites as 'universal' are the first four cases, the active and passive voices of the verb, the singular and plural numbers, and the infinitive, gerund, and verbal-substantive forms of the verb. To this list we might tentatively add the list of grammatical tasks which, in Vom gram Baue, he suggests must be solved in every simple sentence (GS VI: 379).

4.4 The Terminology of Language Variation

The terms I have indicated below are all used, with varying degrees of frequency, in Humboldt's works from 1820 on. They are all closely related and easily confused with one another. To begin, then, I would like to sketch out in a schematic fashion the meaning each has in Humboldt's theory.

	Universal (present in all men)	
(1)	Sprachvermögen	(linguistic capacity)
(2)	Sprachsinn	(linguistic sense)
	Relative (vary from nation to nation)	
(3)	Sprachanlage	(linguistic tendency)
(4)	Charakter der Nation	(character of nation)
(5)	Charakter der Sprache	(character of language)
(6)	Form der Sprache	(Form of language)
(7)	innere Form	(Inner form of language)

(1) Sprachvermögen
(2) Sprachsinn

Sprachvermögen and Sprachsinn are terms found throughout Humboldt's linguistic writings, and seem to denote only the capacity which man has to possess language, and not any specific realization of this capacity. We may distinguish here between the mere possession by something of a capacity for a certain development or achievement, and a positive tendency (one might say 'urge' or 'impulse') to realize that development or achievement. A house, for example, has the 'capacity' to be inhabited, but not the 'tendency' to be inhabited. An acorn has both the capacity and tendency to become an oak. It is in the sense of mere 'capacity' that I think the terms Sprachvermögen, Sprachsinn, as well as some others less often used (e.g., Sprachkraft, Sprachfähigkeit) should be understood. They are present in all men in the same way, although perhaps not always to the same degree.[127] They do not <u>differ</u> from nation to nation, and thus can not be a cause of the variation of languages. In <u>Dualis</u> Humboldt distinguishes between the "purity and vitality of the Sprachsinn and the particularity of its view (Ansicht)" (GS VI: 23). In <u>Grundzüge</u> he says that "each man possesses a striving ... to bring forth the whole language gradually" (GS V: 382). This Sprachkraft is 'human', not 'national' (GS V: 384). Similarly in <u>Einleitung</u> the 'Sprachfähigkeit' is part of human nature (GS VII: 66).

All men, then, possess a basic capacity or ability to produce language. This will even be true of those people who never actually develop a language, or at least an explicit vocal language. We can understand in this way the persistent appearance in Humboldt's writings of comments on the linguistic capacity of deaf-mutes. Even they possess an "inherent capacity of articulation" (beiwohnende Articulationsvermögen)[128] which can be developed.

This terminology of a capacity present in all men

to produce language seems an uncontroversial if somewhat empty doctrine. That all men can learn a language follows rather safely from the fact that almost all men do learn one (or more). This claim by itself is not however related to the problem of the variation of language. Humboldt also wanted to claim that men possess a tendency to learn a certain language, and (which is a somewhat different but related point) that nations possess the tendency to develop their language in a certain direction.

(3) Sprachanlage

I have used 'tendency' as a translation for Humboldt's 'Anlage'. While this is perhaps too strong for ordinary German usage it does, I believe, capture the real strengthening of meaning over Vermögen (etc.) in Humboldt's usage. Perhaps 'disposition' would be better but this should be saved for Stimmung, which in any case seems used by Humboldt as synonymous with Anlage.[129]

The claim that men possess a tendency to learn a particular language, or at very least a particular type of language, runs counter to observed fact. This is probably why this aspect of Humboldt's theory of language is now either ignored or dismissed (cf. Baumann 1971: 7ff). Humboldt recognized this objection and discussed it. Although it can hardly be said that he alleviates the difficulty, his comments indicate clearly the distinction of Anlage from Vermögen. In Einleitung he says:

> Against this the objection could be raised that before they learn to speak children of every people, when displaced from their native linguistic ambience, will develop their speech capacity (Sprachvermögen) in the foreign tongue. This incontrovertible fact, it could be averred, proves distinctly that speech is merely a reproduction of what has been heard, and, without consideration of the uniformity or variability of the being, depends entirely upon social intercourse. In cases of this kind it has been hard to observe with sufficient exactitude how difficult it was to overcome the inherited tendency (Stammanlage), ... Even disregarding this, however, we can say that the power of genealogy (Abstammung) over language lies clearly enough before our eyes in their distribution according to nations. (GS VII: 58-9)[130]

Nor can it be said that Humboldt came to consider this problem only in this, his last work. Very much the same attitude towards it appears in the Grundzüge fragment ten years earlier.[131] The 'intellectuelle Sprachvermögen' also recognizes a certain tendency, a 'stammartige Anlage' (GS V: 386) which varies from nation to nation.

Humboldt doesn't give any closer explanation of how these Anlagen are constituted, or any examples of what they are and how their effect in language is visible. He does, however, do this with respect to the term Character of nation and language. Character is also something which varies from nation to nation and has an effect on language. I surmise that the two terms are roughly synonymous and fill the same slot in Humboldt's theory. That which can be said about Character seems also appropriate for the occasional places where he uses Anlage. Without more ado then I pass to Humboldt's usage of Character.

(4), (5) Charakter der Nation / Sprache

Although I will consider what Humboldt means by Character of a nation or of a language in much more detail in Chapter six below, a few remarks here can place it in the over-all perspective of Humboldt's theory.

The term Character emerges as one of Humboldt's favorite, if somewhat enigmatic, terms fairly early in his writings. Usually it is used in connection with aspects of the character of nations, and occasionally linked to consideration of language.[132] It becomes a central concept in his philosophy of language by 1822, in the essay Ueber den Nationalcharakter der Sprachen, and is progressively developed and enriched, receiving its final treatment in the long chapter "Charakter der Sprachen" in Einleitung.

The Character of a nation is what we might call a guiding emotional perspective, a 'mood' of an entire national community which becomes manifest in various ways, e.g., in customs, dress, morals, and in language. As such it must, I think, be regarded as something simple, as a guiding principle on the basis of which the most diverse appearances exhibit a common tendency. Humboldt often speaks of it as a principle or as a source of unity in diversity. To be contrasted to character, then, is the emptier universal Sprachvermögen, which itself injects no particular direction into the development of language, and the richer complex structure of any actual language (which he will call the 'Form' of the language). The 'Form', the structure of a language (whether by this one means the syntax, the conceptual structure, or the phonetic structure) will be the diversity or multiplicity which throughout is effected by, and thus reflects, the character of the nation. 'Character of language' refers to the way this character of the nation comes to bear on language, i.e., to a principle which determines, at least partially, the way grammar developed, concepts interrelated, etc.. The 'Form' of a language, then, is in no way to be confused with the 'Charakter' of a language. These points will be documented and considered in more detail in Chapter six.

(6) Form der Sprache
(7) innere Sprachform

It is not my intention here to deal extensively with Humboldt's concept of the 'Form of language' or even with the more specific term 'inner form of language'. The meaning of form in Humboldt's philosophy of language is difficult to pin down because it is used so often and in so many ways in his writings. The difficulty with 'inner form' is just the opposite: it occurs only five times in Humboldt's work, all in his last essay, Einleitung. Despite these facts both terms have been a favorite focus for a great deal of interpretation of Humboldt. Eigenbrodt (1968) reviewed sixteen differing interpretations of innere Sprachform, and his own genetic investigation accomplishes very little towards adjudicating between these.[133] Here I will begin by looking at some more recent discussion of 'Form' in Humboldt, and then present my own views.

I begin with Chomsky's claim that the Humboldtian concept of 'form of language' anticipates the theory of 'deep structure' developed by transformational grammar. Chomsky (1966: 26-27, and cf. 22-24) regards the notion of the 'Form of language' as the set of rules, both syntactic and semantic, which govern sentence production in a given language:

> As noted above, the form of language, for Humboldt, embraces the rules of syntax and word formation as well as the sound system and the rules that determine the system of concepts that constitute the lexicon.

Chomsky's work has spawned a new series of articles on the notion of form in Humboldt, perhaps the most instructive of which is Coseriu's (1970). He criticises

Chomsky's view, that the form of a language is a set of generative rules, on the grounds that, for Humboldt, 'Form' always has an active or dynamic sense, rather than the sense of 'that which is formed':

> In fact, 'Form' in Humboldt means always only something 'which shapes' (gestaltet) something, the forming thing (das Gestaltende) in respect to the 'formed thing' (das Gestaltete). (Coseriu 1970: 53).

Further, since Humboldt is concerned with the production of languages, and not that of sentences within an already established language, Chomsky's 'rules of production' (or deep structure) cannot be a Humboldtian 'form':

> The so-called 'rule-governed creativity', the 'production of new sentences', i.e., the mere employment of the particular language in speaking was indeed, in the Humboldtian understanding of language, not creativity at all, not language production, not properly activity or 'Energeia'. Chomsky's rules of production would therefore belong, for Humboldt, precisely to the produced things, not to the production. (Coseriu 1970: 55)

What this little controversy points out fairly clearly with respect to Humboldt's use of form is that, in Coseriu's terms, 'Form' means in general 'a forming thing'. Chomsky (1966: 22-23) himself has pointed out that Humboldt's usage of 'form' comes out of the discussion in the romantic period of the distinction between 'mechanical form' and 'organic form'. Gipper similarly has related Humboldt to the distinction discussed by Goethe between 'forma formans' and 'forma formata'; Humboldt's 'form' must not be seen as a static 'ergon' or product such as a system of grammatical rules, but rather as a 'forming force' (Formkraft).[134]

Regarding 'Form' as meaning primarily a 'forming force' or 'organic principle of formation' does not, however, neatly solve the problem of form in Humboldt. For this would imply that by 'form' Humboldt could never mean a static or dead product within language. Yet it is clear that he does use the word in this sense as well. Despite what Gipper says, in the passage just mentioned, Humboldt does, by 'form of language' mean at least the grammatical structure of the language. It comprehends the grammatical structure and the rules of word formation, although it includes more than this:

> It is already self-evident from the foregoing exposition that by the expression 'form of language' I do not mean merely its so-called grammatical pattern. ... The concept of the form of languages extends far beyond the rules of syntax, and even beyond those of word formation. (GS VII: 49)[135]

At least one thing more which 'Form' means is an urge to impart some particular point of view to a language by an individual or nation (GS VII: 47). This sense of 'form' is the same as that of 'character' as indicated briefly above.

We can also see different usages of 'form' in Humboldt's essay on grammatical form. 'Form' is used for, among other things, general types of grammatical designation, such as inflection, incorporation, etc., (GS IV: 285), particular grammatical formations (e.g., the infinitive, personal pronouns, etc.) (GS IV: 288f), and even individual words which have been put into a certain form (GS IV: 300).

We must rest content, in other words, with giving 'form' many different specific meanings within Humboldt's theory. Merely viewing form as being in general 'dynamic' instead of 'static', a 'principle' of formation rather than a 'product' of formation, does not rule out very many of these alternatives, nor should it, because 'form' is a relative term in Humboldt's system, as in that of many thinkers. 'Form' is whatever stands in a forming relation to some matter or substance. And that which plays the role of 'form' and 'matter' may vary, even within a theory of language. For example, in Humboldt's theory, a grammatical rule (say, formation of the past participle in German, for regular verbs, by attaching a prefix <u>ge</u>- and ending -<u>t</u> or -<u>et</u>) is a 'principle' or 'forming thing' with respect to its 'product' (e.g., 'gesagt', with the 'matter' here being perhaps the stem or infinitive of the verb). But this same grammatical rule may be regarded as the dead product, or 'formed matter' of some other prior principle (e.g., designate grammatical relationships by inflecting word stems or roots, etc.). And this principle in turn may be seen as 'formed' by yet a different principle ('indicate grammatical relationships by modifying individual words', rather than by word order, etc.).

The fact that what constitutes 'form' may vary from time to time is evident from Humboldt's use of the word. In addition he makes the point quite explicitly, in Einleitung:

> Admittedly, a matter (Stoff) stands in contrast to form. However, to find the 'matter' of the form of language, the bounds of language must be transcended. Within the limits of language something may be regarded as 'matter' only relative to something else; for example the primary word in relationship to the declension. In other respects, however, what is here matter is again recognized as form. ... Considered absolutely, there cannot be any unformed matter within language, since everything in it is directed towards a definite goal, the expression of thoughts. (GS VII: 49)[136]

In light of Humboldt's varying uses of form under this one guiding meaning, any effort to identify the meaning of 'form' by pointing to some particular location in Humboldt's theory is doomed to failure. Chomsky's identification of 'form' with the grammatical system is not completely wrong, just too narrow a view. Similarly the three senses of 'active forming principles' which Coseriu outlines are all present in Humboldt's theory, but none has an exclusive claim to the term. Indeed even the meanings which Coseriu assigns to the term can be regarded as 'products' of formation, as 'systems' of rules or principles for further formation. This is true even of the third, most general meaning of 'form' which Coseriu (1970: 54) mentions, the meaning of 'form of language' which was employed in the traditional task of language typology.

> Finally, the same concept (Form) can always be related to the inner linguistic relationship between the individual appearances of each language and the principles underlying them; in this respect the language-form (Sprachform) is the shaping-principle (or the system of shaping-principles) of each language; each language has a determinate form; that is, it contains the principles of its own production and further production. In the most precise sense the concept of a form of language in the third sense can be identified with the legitimate -but unfortunately often misinterpreted- traditional concept of a 'language type'.

If there is any specific place in Humboldt's theory where 'form' of language retains its 'organic' force as a simple guiding principle penetrating into all of the other aspects of languages, such as phonetic structure, syntactic structure, and conceptual structure, (which can of course be regarded as systems of principles in their own right) this place is Humboldt's discussion of the 'character' of nations and languages.

While 'form' is used in many ways by Humboldt, 'character' is used basically only in this last mentioned meaning of a guiding principle penetrating all the other aspects of the language. Further, Humboldt does not develop extensively this meaning, that of a simple active principle stemming from the nation and penetrating the whole language, under the rubric of 'form', but rather under that of 'character'. In his last work in particular, the chapter on "Charakter der Sprachen" is explicitly set apart from the earlier sections on "Form der Sprachen" and "innere Sprachform". It may be true that in the essay *Nationalcharakter* Humboldt had not yet made a distinction between 'Charakter' and 'Form' der Sprache, as Steinthal (1882: 208) suggested.

Given these facts it is simply perverse to focus on all the meanings of form in Humboldt, trying to locate the 'correct' one, as much of the secondary literature has done, right up to the present time. This will only produce and perpetuate the dispersal of interpretation which Eigenbrodt documents well enough. It is equally perverse to ignore his discussion of character, or pass over it briefly (as Chomsky (1966: 27) does, for example, confusing character with a certain kind of *usage*), since we have abundant discussion of this term in Humboldt, the exploration of which will clarify at least one of the central meanings of 'Form der Sprachen'.

I propose, accordingly, to arrange Humboldt's terms in the following fashion. This arrangment is somewhat of a simplification, but it is not in conflict with any of Humboldt's usages, and it allows us a quick systematic overview of his theory. I begin by noting Verburg's (1974: 215) helpful if somewhat sparse schema.

The terminology of language variation

Reality in ordered perspective	<--	*'innere form'* of national language	<--	representative mind of national community

This schema can be retained but expanded to illustrate the respective relationships of the terms I have discussed above.

Reality in ordered perspective
↑

---

	outer form.....	Phonetic structure
Form of	inner form.....	grammatical structure
language	inner form.....	conceptual structure

↑
Character of language
Character of nation

Notes on the schema

We are dealing here with what may be called Humboldt's theory of language production. The highest level of the schema, 'reality in ordered perspective', lies outside of language. Nevertheless I include it here (as presumably Verburg does) to indicate Humboldt's view that the form of language which a nation develops has an influence on the way it orders and understands the world it lives in.

I emphasize, here, Coseriu's point, against Chomsky, that Humboldt is not basically concerned with the rule-governed creation of sentences within a language. Thus there is no arrow between the 'outer form' and the 'inner form', as if the former were Chomsky's 'surface structure', i.e., actually produced utterances. Rather, the phonetic structure is the system of rules by which the phonetic form of utterances is produced, much like what Chomsky (1968: 125) calls phonetic transformation rules, or the rules of phonetic representation, which assign phonetic interpretations to surface structures. Humboldt views the underlying active principle ('character' of a language), which has an effect on the whole 'form' of a language, as coming to bear on each aspect of the form of language independently, and not, for example, on the phonetic structure via the syntactic structure, etc.

To regard the force of the arrows as indicating a complete production of the subsequent stage by the preceding would be too strong for Humboldt's intentions. The force of the arrows is merely that of having a partially determining effect on, in each case. Thus, for example, the character of a nation can not have just any sort of effect on the phonetic structure, since certain intrinsic relationships between sounds will also have an effect on the sound structure a language uses. Humboldt notes the necessity of distinguishing between sound peculiarities lying in "the nature of sound itself", and those lying "in the national individuality":

> Not all phonetic properties of languages, however, can be brought under the euphonic principle, ... They fall into two classes, namely into those which the nature of the sound itself brings about, and those which lie in the national individuality. (GS VI: 383)[137]

We might say, in modern terminology, that some sound relationships are universal while others are language-specific.

The force of the arrows must further be considered only as 'partially effecting' since, insofar as the 'character' of a language has an 'ongoing' effect on the form of a language, its effective force will be restricted by the already present form:

> In the course of development of languages, two mutually restrictive causes collaborate. They are the principle originally determining the direction of the language, and the effect of the material (Stoff) already brought forth, ... (GS VII: 160)[138]

The inclusion of both 'character of nation' and 'character of language' in this schema may seem redundant. Humboldt uses both terms, and sometimes a combination of the two, such as 'Nationalcharakter der Sprache'. Occasionally he seems to use the two terms interchangeably. Nevertheless I think that a distinction should be made here, and both terms maintained, for the following reasons. The character of the nation is not specifically linguistic; it is a national mood or disposition which has an effect on many aspects of the community, such as dress, religion, laws, and language. The character of the language is the specific manifestation of this national character as a principle influencing the formation of the language. Now, if there are no outside forces operating, then the character of the language would be identical with the character of the nation. In Humboldt's terms, nation A, with a 'sensual' character, will express this character in its language, and thus language A also takes on a sensual character. In this case the character of the language is identical with the character of the nation. Suppose, however, that nation A develops its language as a combination of an older vernacular with a foreign language (like, e.g., the development of the romance languages under the influence of Latin). In this case the character of the resulting language will be a combination of the vestigial character imbued in the foreign language with the local national character. Thus language A may have, say, a character half sensual, half spiritual, although the character of the nation is only sensual. For this reason I believe we need to retain both terms and not confuse them with each other. I have not had much to say about the term 'innere Sprachform'. Given the paucity of times that Humboldt actually uses this term, interpretation of it is necessarily quite speculative. Despite the great variety of interpretations which Eigenbrodt mentions, the most common and ultimately most helpful way to take it (as I have here) is as just indicating in general the syntactic and semantic organization of any given language.[139] More particularly, the concept of 'inner Form' has been interpreted by linguists as pointing out a program of research into the 'meaning' or 'content' structure of languages. This program has, to some extent, been carried out by the theory of 'semantic fields' developed in this century by Jost Trier and Leo Weisgerber, among others. The illustration and development of Humboldt's concept of 'innere Sprachform' by semantic field theory has been reviewed, with examples, by Basilius (1952: 95-105) and more recently by Lyons (1974: 250-69). This general interpretation of 'innere Sprachform' seems basically correct to me, and I shall have little more to say about it here. The term will have to be considered further when I consider Humboldt's linguistic doctrines in greater detail.

The general schema sketched above is meant to clarify the meaning of several of Humboldt's key terms with respect to one another. More specifically, it enables us to locate more closely the place and significance in Humboldt's theory of his discussion of the 'character' of languages. I will return for a closer look at his treatment of national character and its effect on language in Chapter six.

CHAPTER FIVE
LINGUISTIC VARIATION AND PERCEPTUAL VARIATION

5.1 Introduction

I think we can safely consider Humboldt's explanation of the production of linguistic variation under two headings: perceptual variation, and variation of 'national character'. While he has much to say about the latter, he has very little to say about the former. Consequently my discussion of perceptual variation as a cause of linguistic variation must proceed essentially as a reconstruction of what I take to be Humboldt's argument, on the basis of a few rather scanty texts. Nevertheless, it is important to make this attempt. Any doctrine that languages differ primarily because of originally differing national character is likely to meet an initial resistance by modern readers, and it is probably better to explore first the alternative sources of difference. It will turn out (at least in Humboldt's view) that perceptual variation ultimately cannot stand on its own feet but rather must involve an appeal to a further source of difference, i.e., national character. But it is preferable to show the necessity of Humboldt's turning to the latter rather than beginning with it.

I begin by sketching what I mean by the argument from perceptual variation and then turn to Humboldt's own formulations of it.

5.2 Perceptual variation

'Perception' is a philosophical term with a long career. Quite often the term has meant not only perception of external, physical objects but also awareness of inner mental states. We are concerned here, first of all, only with the former. Further, we are concerned not merely with a passive reception of sensual images, which some modern philosophers might call 'sense data'. That is, we are not concerned with mere 'sensaton' or sensual intuition. Perception is here taken in the richer sense of an understanding awareness: in Kantian terms, perception is of 'objects', and takes place as a combination of sensual intuition and 'conceptualization'. Although Humboldt does not often use typical Kantian terminology I think that the texts considered below will show the appropriateness of attributing this basically Kantian framework to him.

The argument that linguistic variation is caused by perceptual variation may be initially divided into two cases. Suppose two different communities (Humboldt's 'nations'), nation A and B, are in the process of developing languages. That is, they are in the historical process of initially forming their languages. Aside from the questions of phonetic and syntactic variation, why do A and B develop different conceptual systems, different 'world-views', as Humboldt would say? At present we limit the question to variation concerning the understanding of physical phenomena, and suggest two reasons for this variation. (1) A and B perceive different things. (2) A and B perceive the same things differently.

5.2.1 A and B perceive different things

This type of variation seems fairly straightforward, but will only be relevant to a small class of phenomena. It thus only accounts for a rather fringe area of variation. If nation A and B are located in geographically and climatically different areas, then they will each likely contain some concepts which the other lacks. A desert nation, for example, may have words for (and concepts of) hidden water sources, desert reptiles, sand storms, etc. which a nation in a tropical area of the earth does not have; and they may, similarly, have words (and concepts) which the former does not. In this sense the two languages would vary.

In an enrichment of this first case we could regard geographical and climatic location as creating not only a variation because some objects are present in one location but not at all present in another. The prevalent presence of some kinds of phenomena compared to their relative absence in a different environment will probably cause a difference in the way these phenomena are conceptualized by the two nations respectively. Here Whorf's (1956: 216) famous example concerning the Eskimo vocabulary for snow, compared to English and Aztec, comes to mind:

> We have the same word for falling snow, snow on the ground, snow packed hard like ice, slushy snow, wind-driven flying snow, whatever the situation may be. To an Eskimo, this all-inclusive word would be almost unthinkable; he would say that falling snow, slushy snow, and so on, are sensuously and operationally different, different things to contend with; he uses different words for them and for other kinds of snow. The Aztecs go even farther than we in the opposite direction, with 'cold' 'ice' and 'snow' all represented by the same basic word with different terminations; ...

The point here is that the presence of certain natural phenomena in different geographical and climatic locations varies not only absolutely (present / not present) but also varies relatively, to a greater or lesser degree. And, so the argument from perceptual variation goes, this greater or lesser presence will naturally produce varying conceptualizations of these phenomena by the people living in those diverse places. If (to use Whorf's example) nation A is an Eskimo or Arctic nation, its understanding of snow and cold will vary from that of nation B, temperate or tropical nation.

So far the conceptual variation of languages A and B has been explained as the inclusion, in one, of concepts which are not present in the other, and this variation is caused by the differing presence of the phenomena differently conceptualized. The speakers of the two languages perceive (in some cases) different things, namely in those cases where the thing is present in the environment of one community but not in that of the other. Here we can say that the two languages develop varying 'worldviews' because in a quite straight-forward sense they _do_ perceive different 'worlds'.

Still, it doesn't seem as though we shall get very far this way. At least two large problems arise.

(a) The explanatory principle is too narrow. The kind of variation discussed so far will concern only that class of natural phenomena whose presence varies greatly over differing locations. Thus it cannot account for conceptual variation concerning the many kinds of phenomena _common_ to all (or at least most) areas where people live, such as the human body itself, its parts, tools, the sun, moon and stars, food and clothing, etc.. (Perhaps one could stretch geographical and climatic variation into a principle of variation with respect to how these kinds of common phenomena are understood, as well, but this would be a rather more speculative process.) Further, it cannot account for variation concerning abstract concepts, such as man, anger, God, emotion, time, relation, thing, etc., which I have temporarily excluded from consideration.

It is true, of course, that people have extended the argument in an attempt to explain the variation of all types of concepts, and indeed the variation of cultures generally, by reference to environmental differences. The discussion of the relationship of environmental difference and cultural difference (including language variation) was a source of speculation well before the 19th century. Humboldt would probably have been familiar with this debate at least in the writings of Winckelmann, Montesquieu, and Herder. A good short summary of this background movement is given by Roger Brown (1967: 69-79), although he does not, unfortunately, get around to anything more than a preliminary discussion of Humboldt's own views.

(b) The application of the argument will only explain variation between certain languages, namely those which are in widely different geographical and climatic settings. Thus it will not come to bear on variation among many, indeed most, languages which share a very similar environment, which perceive very much the same 'world'. We shift, accordingly, to consider the second case, that different nations perceive the same things differently.

5.2.2 A and B perceive the same things differently

The basic intuition behind this second argument from perceptual variation to linguistic variation is roughly as follows. Different peoples, encountering the same natural environment, come to understand or conceptualize that environment in different ways because they 'see' that environment and the objects in it from differing perspectives of need or appreciation. These differing perspectives direct the attention in the case of one nation towards one feature of a phenomenon, in the case of another towards a different feature. Here I am discussing perception not as sensation but basically as concept formation concerning the things sensed.

The position that objects are conceptualized according to a <u>specific</u> feature or characteristic that they possess, rather than 'in their totality', so to speak, is an old doctrine, and was certainly present in

Humboldt's contemporaries. We may cite Kant and Herder.

Kant (1974b) says, in his lectures on logic, that we know things always only with respect to a certain 'feature' (Merkmal) which they have. Further discussion of the various kinds of 'features' which things may have is found in various places in the Logic. I quote here from the introduction (Kant 1974b: 63-64):

> Human cognition on the side of understanding is discursive, that is, it takes place through presentations that make what is common to several things the ground of cognition, thus through characteristics as such. We thus cognize things only through characteristics (Wir erkennen also Dinge nur durch Merkmale); and this means precisely re-cognizing, which comes from cognizing (Erkennen, welches von Kennen herkommt).
>
> A characteristic is that in a thing which makes up part of its cognition, or, which is the same, a partial presentation so far as it is considered as cognitive ground of the whole presentation. All our concepts therefore are characteristics and all thinking is nothing but a presenting through characteristics.[140]

Herder, in his Essay on the Origin of Language (1772), connects the 'first judgment' which we make about something, and the formation of a 'clear concept' of it, with the act of focussing on a specific 'distinguishing mark' of the thing:

> He (man) thus manifests reflection if he is able not only to recognize all characteristics vividly or clearly but if he can also recognize and acknowledge to himself one or several of them as distinguishing characteristics. The first act of this acknowledgment results in a clear concept; it is the first judgment of the soul; and through what did this acknowledgment occur? through a distinguishing mark which he had to single out and which, as a distinguishing mark for reflection, struck him clearly.[141]

Although Kant emphasizes the choice of a distinctive feature as part of the cognition of a thing, whereas Herder will link this choice to the 'naming' activity as well, the point is basically the same in both. In the perception of the thing some aspect, a 'feature' of the thing, is singled out and becomes the basis by which the thing is understood. The word designating the thing actually does so by designating not the 'totality' of the thing but rather by emphasizing a particular feature. This understanding of the thing is then passed down over time in the language as the meaning of the word. With respect to the cause of 'variation', then, we can say first of all that people speaking different languages have (if and where conceptual variation actually exists) picked out <u>different</u> features of a thing and emphasized them in their understanding of it.

This establishes, so to speak, a formal epistemological framework within which linguistic variation may be explained. It is the framework which Humboldt employs, as will be shown in the passages to be considered below.

Having pointed out the framework within which variation in conceptualization is explained, I return then to the argument from perceptual variation. We are now in the position of arguing that languages 'vary' conceptually because they understand the same things differently. And this is because now one, now another feature of the thing, is seized upon (by the differing nations) as the 'distinctive feature' in forming a concept of it. Previously I was trying to explain variation in conceptualization by reference to actual variation in that which is perceived, from one language to the next. The attempt was, so to speak, to put the blame for variation on the things perceived rather than on the perceiving person or nation. Is this any longer possible?

We may first consider <u>what</u> the different features of a thing might be, to get an idea of the kinds of variation in understanding it which might arise. Staying for the moment with common physical objects, we note that, to begin with, they may be perceived differently by the different senses. That is, they have a 'visual' feature, a 'tactile' feature, perhaps olfactory and auditory features, and probably a more or less definite taste. One (or more) of these may impress itself on our mind as more 'significant' than the others in terms of understanding that thing. Thus, for example, our concept of an orange emphasizes its taste and color more than its texture, or probably even its shape, whereas our concept of a soccer ball emphasizes the shape, (and perhaps the weight, buoyancy, etc.) rather than taste and texture. Variation based upon emphasizing one or another of sensual characteristics is, I suggest, hinted at in the following passage by Humboldt from <u>Nationalcharakter</u>:

> There arise here two quite remarkable differences among languages; one out of the degree of feeling of that inadequacy, and the effort to overcome it, the other out of the variation of dominating views in the mode of designation, since the many-sidedness of objects, connected with the multiplicity of organs of apprehension, allows an indefinite number of such views. (GS IV: 432)[142]

Aside from the purely physical characteristics of things, however (without delving here into the whole problem of 'primary' and 'secondary' properties), one could add a more abstract kind of variation among things. Namely, they are amenable to appropriation by humans in differing ways. A chair has not only a certain shape, but also an evident use; one can sit in it. This use may be regarded as deriving from its shape; nevertheless it can be regarded as a different 'feature' of the chair over and above its shape. More obviously a radio is understood in terms of its 'use' quite apart from its shape. Here perhaps one is tempted to say the radio is understood qua its 'auditory' feature; but the 'use' or functional definition of a radio is much more complicated than the mere fact that it emits noise (as opposed, for example, to an air raid siren). A radio is understood as 're-producing' noise, as in fact a medium of communication, not just as producer of sound.

All this is apropos of trying to extend the notion of 'distinctive features' of a thing beyond the merely sensual characteristics of a thing. Likely candidates seem to be features relative to the human person perceiving the thing; e.g., use possibilities, aesthetic value, religious significance. And the possibility seems quite open that different perceivers of the thing could find in it differing such features, leading to different 'understandings' of the self-same object.

The final point to consider in the argument from perception would be, now, whether the emphasis upon one or another of the distinctive features of a thing can be blamed upon the thing itself, or whether the choice must be viewed as stemming from the perceiving person, and thus not really a 'perceptual' variation at all. (We could say of course that the choice is dictated by the perceiver's <u>language</u>; and indeed that is part of the 'linguistic relativity thesis' to be discussed in chapter eight below. That claim, however, already presupposes existent and varying languages which could exercise such an effect. Here we are only considering, as emphasized earlier, how such variation among languages was originally produced in the formation of the languages, and not the subsequent effect of that variation.) Before addressing that matter, however, I turn to some passages from Humboldt to show that the argument from 'perceptual variation' to linguistic variation is indeed present in his own writings.

In the chapter on Humboldt's theory of designation I have already briefly made the point that designation, for Humboldt, of external physical things, by a word, is always accomplished via the intermediate designation of the concept of the thing. To review; (1) the word designates a concept, which in turn designates or 'signifies' the thing. (2) Further, the concept never captures, so to speak, the thing in any neutral or total fashion, but rather emphasizes some feature(s) which are regarded as 'essential' to the thing when the concept is formed. Thus the word designates the thing by designating (in its concept) some particular view of the thing. The more general point is, in Humboldt's words:

> For language never represents the objects, but always the concepts actively constructed by the intellect in the course of language production. (GS VII: 90)[143]

The more specific point is:

> For it (the word) foists upon the idea a form (Gestalt) and abstracts, in the case of the corporeal object, from the totality of its reality, in that it holds it fast in one feature (an einem Merkmale fest hält), and designates it, in this feature, by something foreign to it, a tone. (GS V: 428)[144]

Because the object becomes understood or conceptualized in the mind with respect not to its 'totality' but only one or some among its several features, the object is always represented in a "thereby modified fashion":

> The object, whose appearance in the mind always accompanies an impression individualized by language and constantly regularly recurring, is also represented in itself in a thereby modified fashion. (GS IV: 23-24)[145]

These aspects of designation in Humboldt seem to implicate the general framework of cognition and concept formation briefly mentioned above with respect to Kant and Herder. Humboldt however utilizes this framework as an explanatory device for the variation of concepts from language to language. The modified fashion in which an object is represented will vary from language to language:

> Thus, in the period of language formation in several (different) languages there arise a number of expressions for the same object. There are just as many properties under which it has been thought and whose expression one substitutes in its place. (GS VII: 170)[146]

> Therefore there arise in the synonymous words of many languages varying representations of the same object, and this property of the word leads chiefly to the fact that each language imparts a specific world view (eine eigne Weltansicht). (GS V: 420)[147]

These passages, drawn from various of Humboldt's works, all illustrate, albeit in a quite general and undeveloped form, what I have called the argument from perceptual variation to linguistic variation. Probably the most developed discussion of this matter in Humboldt's works is in Grundzüge (GS V:417-420), a passage which is terminated by the last quote given above.

Humboldt, then, holds that our view of things (here: external objects) is always a partial or incomplete one, in the sense that it does not encompass the 'whole' of that thing. We might note here that he does not indicate any necessity to this incompleteness, as if we could not conceptualize the thing in terms of all of its aspects. Müller-Vollmer states the position in this stronger fashion,[148] but there seems to be no forceful claim like this in Humboldt. Rather, we simply do always understand a thing via emphasizing one or another of its features. I suggest that this is part of the psychology of understanding which Humbldt accepts from his contemporaries as an adequate account of how the human mind does work; and he is not terribly concerned with whether or not it is necessary that it so work.

What remains is to consider the limitations of the approach to linguistic variation through perceptual variation, for they are formidable indeed. To begin with, we restricted our attention to 'outer objects', since the whole point of the argument from perception is to find a source of linguistic variation, which does not assume or exploit a difference or variation already somehow existing in different individuals or nations. Thus the argument cannot, from the beginning, offer an account of conceptual variation with respect to all kinds of inner and abstract objects. But even with respect only to external things the argument seems to reach an impasse.

The epistemological framework which Humboldt seems to employ to account for conceptual variation is fairly clear. Different people emphasize different distinctive features of a thing in their conception of it. Now the question becomes: what governs the choice of emphasis? Why do different peoples or nations emphasize different aspects of a thing in their understanding of it? Can this variation of choice be blamed on the thing, or must it be seen as a manifestation of a preexisting variation in the peoples or nations involved, a difference of 'national character', as it would have been expressed in Humboldt's day?

Although we can easily allow that physical objects do indeed have many different 'features' in the sense discussed above, it is not at all clear how the choice of one or another of these features may be regarded as dictated in some way by the object itself.

Given that humans are all basically the same physically (i.e., with respect to sense organs) the various sensual features of objects may be assumed to be equally available to all perceivers, other conditions being equal. Thus the (different) choice of one or another feature as a focus of emphasis, by different nations, does not seem amenable to a physiological explanation. Still less is the choice of more abstract features such as use, aesthetic value, or symbolic value attributable to physiological explanation.

We may conclude that the emphasis on one or another feature of a thing is, then, a reflection not (or at least not only) of the environment or the thing itself, but of the context of interests, needs and other factors which the perceiving person brings to the thing. Where significant conceptual variation occurs between two languages, concerning the same thing, it does not seem explicable on mere grounds of 'perceptual variation'. There must be a motivation stemming from the perceiver to choose this or that emphasis in his understanding of the thing.

Now with respect to physical objects and events, what we might call the realm of 'nature', conceptual variation is not likely to be all that significant between various languages. In focussing on this realm in the above I have sought to reconstruct Humboldt's thoughts about the causes of conceptual variation, so to speak, in the most minimal case, i.e., with respect to that class of concepts whose 'variation' from language to language seems most amenable to explanation without reference to the perceiver. Weimann (1965: 504) uses this distinction in the following paraphrase of Humboldt's views:

> The words for ideas of individual properties and things mediate an equivalence (if also not a precise reflection) of the natural environment. In the words for higher species concepts a stronger arbitrariness of combination and conceptual limitation already makes itself felt.

That even the natural environment may be conceptualized in significantly different ways is clearly Humboldt's view. In Einleitung he says that even for "external, corporeal objects which can be frankly perceived by the senses ...":

> the word is not the equivalent of the object hovering before the senses, but is rather the conception thereof by the speech production at the very moment it creates the word. This is a particularly important source of the multiplicity of expressions for the same object; ... (GS VII: 89)[149]

In Dualis Humboldt notes similarly that the 'intellect' (Geist) exerts an effect on the "sensual intuition of the world" and on the "inner realm of thoughts":

> A language carries traces that have been produced in its development, especially from sensual intuition of the world or from the inner realm of thoughts, where that world intuition was already influenced by the intellect. (GS VI: 23)[150]

It has not been my intention here to probe very deeply into the relation between language and perception. The issues I have brought into consideration can not be so quickly dealt with as my brief consideration may unfortunately suggest. Nevertheless for the present purpose at hand, namely to indicate the relevant philosophical background of Humboldt's discussion of language variation, this brief treatment may be adequate.

He himself discusses the notion of national character and its effect on language at some length. In order to appreciate his felt need to do this I suggest that it is helpful to explore alternative sources of linguistic variation which he obviously considered himself but found inadequate. Whether we might also, on further examination, find them so inadequate is an open question, but somewhat beside the point here. It is, accordingly, time to examine his treatment of the theme of differing national character.

CHAPTER SIX
NATIONAL CHARACTER AND LANGUAGE

6.1 Introduction

In chapter five I have discussed a number of key terms which Humboldt uses in his account of language production and variation. It may be recalled here how the term 'Charakter' fits into that terminological context. The character of a nation is a tendency towards a certain mood or disposition. It has an effect upon, among other things, language, producing the character of the language. This in turn has an effect upon all aspects of the 'form' of the language. In the present chapter I will examine Humboldt's drawn out attempt to make the concept of national character more determinate, to give examples of it, and of its effect on language.

Two general difficulties in discussing the concept of the character of a nation (or of its language) may be mentioned here in advance. First, there is the problem that, with regard to this matter, one encounters much prejudice and little argumentation. Often in interpretation of Humboldt the concept of character of language is mistakenly equated with 'inner form' of language, and there are, to be sure, a great many interpretations of this latter term. Nevertheless the two concepts are different, although related in a quite straightforward way. Insofar as character of language is considered in its own right, there is very little discussion of the matter. When the matter is raised it is usually to criticise Humboldt. Maurice Leroy (1967: 29ff), for example, sees Humboldt as a precursor to a racial psychology which reached its peak in the Nazi era. Hans-Heinrich Baumann (1971: 8-9) has interpreted the notion of character of language as a claim that the ability to learn specific languages is innate and inherited:

Humboldt's view in this manner is today

> rather unacceptable, as it has been rather conclusively shown that any child can equally learn any language, placed in the proper environment.

The mentioned criticisms carry some force. The difficulty in general is that in Humboldt's time the hypothesis of various 'national characters' which affected language was much more popular, viewed at least prima facie with much less suspicion than it is today. Humboldt regarded his own opinions in this area as generally accepted views, and indeed quite commonplace.[151] In what follows I hope to avoid as far as possible prejudging this issue, attempting basically only to present Humboldt's view of the character of languages and to show how it operates in his theory with respect to other aspects of that theory.

A more serious problem which must be mentioned here is what I shall call the 'priority' problem. That is, Humboldt often claims that each language exerts a certain effect on the nation speaking it, and in fact is itself a cause of differing national characters. He says, for example:

> In itself however that which is attained out of the influence of language expresses itself in two ways, as an elevated linguistic ability, and as a characteristic world-view. (GS IV: 428)[152]

Elsewhere, he asserts:

> ..., it is certain that the development of language first conveys national differences into the clearer region of the intellect. (GS VII: 171)[153]

In her genetic account of Humboldt's views in his writings before 1820 Roberta Ross (1970: 295) claims first that Humboldt gives complete priority to language as a cause of national diversity. Nevertheless in her subsequent exploration of those writings it becomes clear that Humboldt by no means gives the priority to either side. As a result, Ross prefers to say that Humboldt remains 'ambivalent', an opinion also voiced by Roger L. Brown (1967: 82).[154] I will suggest that the priority problem is too complex to view as an 'either / or' situation. Nevertheless it is clear from her attempt that a genetic account will not solve this problem. What I intend to discuss in the following is precisely the converse claim, namely, that national character is a cause of linguistic variation. This represents however a one-sided approach to Humboldt's position. A more accurate although complicated account of his position will have to explain how he can claim both that national character determines language and that language determines thinking. Humboldt himself saw this reciprocal nature of the relationship. His stock phrase is usually to call the power of man over language 'dynamic' and the power of language over man 'physiological'.[155] What I have sketched out in this section, therefore, is only the first half of the story. The other half, the reverse effect of language on the intellect, will come to the fore in a later chapter on the so-called linguistic relativity thesis, and there the integration of Humboldt's claims into one coherent theory will be evident.

6.2 Humboldt's early discussion of character.

In this chapter I will emphasize the following points. (1) Humboldt's interest in national character developed very early in his writings, and is linked with language from the beginning. (2) Nevertheless his fullest description of national character, and its effect on language, is found only in his last work. (3) National character is not to be regarded as identical with national customs, dress, religious and moral temper, language, etc.. These exhibit its effects, but it lies hidden behind them, as a simple albeit subtle emotion or instinctive 'mood' which intrudes into these products of the nation. (4) Thus national character for Humboldt might be described as having the philosophical status of a 'postulate' or explanatory hypothesis for national variation, although an extremely justified one in his opinion. At one point he calls it the "highest and ultimate explanatory principle."[156] (5) Any particular national character can be described as an emphasis either on 'inner mentality' or on 'outer reality' (GS VII: 180), or as some combination of these two, as a point on a spectrum between them, so to speak.

Humboldt's early discussions of differences in national character stem primarily from his study of classical Greek culture, although they were undoubtedly stimulated by his extensive travels in the 1790s and early 1800s as a Prussian diplomat. In Ueber das Studium des Altertums (1793) he first sketches out four ways in which the 'character of an individual nation' is preserved in the products which it leaves behind, and then examines ancient Greek culture with respect to these areas. Although language per se (as distinct, for example, from 'intellectual products themselves' such as historical writing, poetry and philosophy (GS I: 266)), is not extensively considered as a manifestation of national character, he nevertheless recognizes and briefly mentions the value of language as indicative of national character. Deviations will arise in a language because of the individuality of the speakers in three different significant ways. (1) By the borrowing of words or idioms from foreign languages; (2) by the way in which 'general and abstract' concepts are designated, either by newly formed words or powerful use of existing expressions, and (3) by reflection on the nature of language in general, by the members of the national community themselves. Humboldt feels here that the character of a nation, as expressed in its language, could be clearly studied by analysis of the language:

> Individual examples with respect to the development of words, of inflections and connections could show here the agreement of the language of the Greeks with their Character. (GS I: 265)[157]

In <u>Latium und Hellas</u> (1806) Humboldt again is preoccupied with trying to describe the character of the classical Greeks, the "einzelnen Eigenschaften des Griechischen Geistes ...", or "Das Charakteristische der Griechischen". This is investigated via art, poetry, religion, morals, customs, public and private character and history (GS III: 142). Here, however, he also is led to consider the effect of character on language. The study of language teaches us, aside from the actual use of language, "... the analogy between man and the world in general and with respect to each nation in particular, ...". (GS III: 167)[158]

This leads him to a brief consideration of "the nature of language in general". We need not pursue this further here except to note that Humboldt attempts to distinguish between 'subjective' and 'objective' effects on language; those that stem from 'man' and from the 'world' respectively. "Language must, therefore, take up the twofold nature of the world and of man," (GS III: 168). Humboldt means by this that the way the world is understood will always be a mixture of what it is, in reality, and the way man perceives it. This is applied to two kinds of objects; 'sensual' and 'non-sensual'. Even the former (although especially the latter) are perceived differently by different nations. This is the subjective element, and because of it even the words of various languages which refer to the same physical objects will have different meanings:

> Thinking never treats an object isolated, and never uses it in the whole of its reality. It merely skims off relationships, conditions and viewpoints, and interconnects them ... and it may therefore justifiably be said that even with respect to completely sensuous objects the words of various languages are not perfect synonyms, and that those who say hippus, equus, and Pferd do not say throughout and completely the same thing. (GS III: 170)[159]

We can also note, for later reference, that Humboldt resists strongly in this essay the temptation to treat national character as only developed and formed over time and not also 'original'. He recognizes a question raised against him, namely: how does the 'character' of a nation arise. It would, he says, be a wasted effort to try and derive the national character "... as it were mechanically from the gradual influence of individual circumstances." (GS III: 164)[160] There are two objections against viewing character as a 'product' of the successive circumstances that the nation is in:

> ..., that the very things whose influence they insist on are for the most part themselves only the results of the character which they are supposed to explain; and that other nations under the same circumstances have taken a different turn of character. (GS III: 164)[161]

Thus we are left with asserting the existence of an 'original' character of the nation. This is a definite stance with respect to the priority problem. At this stage of his writing Humboldt seems comfortable in asserting that the character of a nation exists prior to its language and exerts an influence upon the formation of the language.

There are, of course, great difficulties with this approach. It is not even clear that a 'nation' can be defined as something which goes back to some historical point prior to all the circumstances through which it develops. And even if one could make sense of such an ahistorical definition of 'nation', one would be left with no means (i.e., no historical material) to study the 'original' character of the nation. Further, this viewpoint may imply that character is an 'innate' property of the people who constitute the nation, and that it is transmitted down through the generations. This latter point in particular seems implied by Humboldt's views on language acquisition in children.

Problems like these can be seen to weigh rather heavily on Humboldt himself in his later discussions of national character, and perhaps because of them he progressively avoids describing character as 'innate' or original. This, however, will lead him into other difficulties.

In general, then, Humboldt's early essays are often concerned with national character, and occasionally relate it directly to language variation. Although a general distinction of 'subjective / objective' contributions to language qua understanding is hinted at as a criterion for determining national character(s) Humboldt gets no further than a rather literary treatment of character which seems partly stimulated by his classical studies and partly by his encounters with the Romantic debate over aesthetic theory. His role in the latter has been examined at length by Müller-Vollmer (1967, 1976).

Similar brief, general, and not very revealing discussions of national character and its relation to language occur in Humboldt's writings throughout the early 1800s.[162] It is not until the 1820s however that he devotes his efforts primarily to language, which brings as one consequence a sharpening up and more extensive consideration of the influence of national character on language itself, with respect to its own structure (phonetic, syntactic and conceptual). Here Humboldt goes significantly beyond the Romantic concerns with poetry, philosophy, literature and other intellectual products, to question the effect of national character on the very medium in which those products are conceived and realized. There are here two important texts to consider: the essay <u>Nationalcharakter der Sprachen</u> (1822), and the chapter "Charakter der Sprachen" in <u>Einleitung</u> (1836).

6.3 <u>Discussion of character in Humboldt's later writings</u>.

The fragmentary essay <u>Ueber den Nationalcharakter der Sprachen</u> was written in the period 1821-22, and intended as the third lecture in a series presented before the Prussian Academy of Sciences, the first two lectures in the series being vergl. Sprachstudium and Entstehen. Nationalcharakter, however, was never completed nor presented. Its first publication was by Steinthal in 1882 with a brief commentary (Steinthal 1882). The present title was supplied by the editors of the Gesammelte Schriften. Steinthal had suggested a slightly different title; "Ueber den Charakter der Sprachen und dessen Zusammenhang mit der Nationaleigentümlichkeit".

It is clear that in Nationalcharakter Humboldt had not yet worked out a clear position on the relationship between language and national character. The most immediate evidence for this is the fact that the essay was not completed and delivered as were its two earlier companion pieces. Also, Humboldt himself bears witness to his troubles with this problem via the several cautionary remarks, sprinkled through the essay, warning us of the difficulty and obscurity of the problem. He says, for example, that to a certain extent the individuality of languages "... is only sensed and cannot be represented" (GS IV: 421). The character of a nation (and of a language) is described in this essay as a certain 'force', and Humboldt warns us (and himself) of the difficulty of studying what this force is, while yet holding out some hope for its elucidation:

> A correct view of living forces must to be sure renounce the hope of representing the effect of such forces in their individual character. One can however come so close to a sketch of it, whose outlines to be sure remain impossible to describe, observe so many points which determine its direction, that that which opposes exact portrayal nevertheless may be to a certain extent sensed and surmised. (GS IV: 423)[163]

Despite the admitted obscurity of the subject matter and the incompleteness of the essay, several points in it anticipate his later discussion of the problem. (1) With respect to the 'priority' problem, Humboldt is very hesitant in this essay about assigning an original causal status either to national character, causing the character of language, or vice-versa. (2) The character differentiation of languages is linked to the idea of a 'force'. This force, further, is described as a tendency in the nation to inject into its various products (including language) an emphasis either on 'sensual intuition' or 'inner spirituality'.

6.3.1 The priority problem

Humboldt does not, in this essay, posit an original national character which exercises an initial and ongoing effect upon a language. Rather, he regards the question as, historically speaking, beyond investigation, since the connection of languages and nations in general goes back earlier than recorded history. Although this fact does not keep him from speculating here and elsewhere on the nature and source of variation among languages, it does make the question of original causal priority, the question about the first determining source of variation, impossible to solve. It is a question about pre-historical development. Unlike many of his predecessors, Humboldt regarded the origin of language problem as an historical question and not a philosophical question. In actual investigation we always deal with the conjunction of a language and nation, both of which have a particular character. Thus Humboldt speaks in this essay of the 'double' influence on the character of a language: the influence of its own already determined character and that of the nation which begins to speak it. To attempt to get at the initial production of character of a language would take us into the "darkness of the past":

> If one joins together the nation with the language, a more original character in the latter is unified with one received from the nation. Indeed one can not here assume an as it were fixed point, and least of all historically, where a nation receives its language at its initial development, since the origin of the nation itself is only a transition in a constant series, and it is as hard to imagine a beginning point of a nation as of a language. Our historical studies in no way justify the assumption that a nation could ever be present before its language, or, in other words, that a language would ever be developed only by its nation. Accordingly there also lies in each language an original particular character and type of influence. Yet this connection of a double character, in languages whose origin goes back into the darkness of the past, appears an indifferent one since we can no longer get at the original situation. (GS IV: 424-425)[164]

Although we cannot achieve an historical clarification about the origin of the character of a language in its initial formation, there is an historical parallel which allows at least the process of the interaction of already existing national character and language character to be studied: that is, the development of new languages out of old ones. In this essay and elsewhere Humboldt emphasizes the value of the development of the romance languages out of Latin as a locus for the study of the effect of influences which determine the character of a language.[165]

Despite the fact that the actual influences acting upon a language in its formative period are usually historically inaccessible, Humboldt is quite clear in saying that a language does receive a particular character from the influences acting upon it, and that this becomes '... its own character':

> Language receives, through the influence acting upon it, an individual character (eine Individualität) which also quite essentially becomes its own character (Charakter) insofar as it (language) in turn also has an effect upon that (character) and insofar as it may easily be used only within the limits of that character. (GS IV: 424)[166]

This brief passage already indicates a resolution of the priority problem. The character of a language is the result of influences acting upon it in its formative period, prominent among which is the national character of the speakers who form it. This position is not in conflict with the position that languages exercise an effect upon their speakers and each determines and maintains a certain 'Worldview'. The formation of language comes first, its reciprocal formative effect is felt subsequently. Hence the effect of national character on language is most likely already viewed by Humboldt at this time as 'prior' to the effect of language on national character. The essay breaks off before this is clearly stated, however. The doctrine of a 'double character' then is relevant not to the initial formation of languages, but only to the subsequent evolution of new languages out of old ones. Schematically this might be represented as follows.

Double character influence on language

```
     Prehistory                  Historical Period

     Language A -------> ------\ Language A
                                \ (with char. A)
Influences (including             ------Language B
  nation A, with                 Influence of character
  character A, etc.)             of nation B
```

Here language B, an off-shoot of A, has a character which is influenced both by the residual character of language A and the new influence of national character B. And this is not in conflict with saying that language B also exercises an effect upon its speakers, nation B. The schema is overly simplified in the sense that much language branching is prehistorical. Trying to trace back the development and influence of the 'character' of various languages would be an even more difficult task than the reconstruction of pre-historic phonetic evolution. It is the historical difficulties which underly both Humboldt's cautionary warnings and the notion of a 'double character' in this essay, not a philosophical ambivalence on his part concerning the priority of influence.

6.3.2 The concept of force

It remains to be seen, however, what can be said towards defining the concept of the character variation of languages more closely. In Nationalcharakter Humboldt makes several tentative suggestions in this regard. The first is to link the character to the 'force' (Kraft) which "produces the thoughts by means of language" (GS IV: 430). Although Humboldt does not develop the notion of 'force' here, it is a clear anticipation of his description of character as a sort of impulse (Drang) in Verschiedenheiten (1827-29). Also we can recall from the literary essays that force for Humboldt is never just a universal Sprachvermögen, but rather a tendency (Anlage) in a certain direction. He says in Latium und Hellas (1806) that force "... is never conceivable without some kind of direction ..." (GS III: 165)[167] In the essay Ueber Goethes Hermann und Dorothea (1798) he is already quite definite on this general point:

> There is no free and forceful expression of our capacities without a careful preservation of our original natural dispositions; no energy without individuality. (GS II: 118)[168]

Although this description of character as a force is not further explicated by Humboldt in this essay, he does give a few further suggestions as to how languages may vary in character. The most interesting of these is the suggestion that one nation (or language) will emphasize more the aspect of 'sensual intuition'; another more 'inner spirituality', and so on. Compare his statement:

> Notwithstanding the infinite variation of them, there lies in every language, in that it is comprehended by one nation, something common to the appearance that is communicated to the word, as a sign. One can probably characterize this, in broad terms, as (the fact) that the words of one language possess more sensual intuition, those of another more inner spirituality, a third more sober presentation of concepts, and so on, ... (however) None of these mentioned peculiarities stand by themselves, and where they also are found in common to various nations, they are in none the same. (GS IV: 432-33)[169]

Although one could use this text as a jumping-off point for exploring Humboldt's suggestions, they remain here, as in the whole essay, rather vague. The distinction between 'sensual' and 'spiritual' emphasis, however, is a clear anticipation of Humboldt's much richer discussion of national character in _Einleitung_ (1836). It will be easier to explore these ideas by reference to that more developed treatment.

Before turning to _Einleitung_, however, it is worth paying brief attention to another stage in Humboldt's development of his position on this matter. The long essay _Ueber den Verschiedenheiten des menschlichen Sprachbaues_ (1827-29) is often regarded as only a practice run for _Einleitung_. And it is true that many passages are taken over verbatim to the later book. Nevertheless the long third section, "Sprache und Nation", contains many discussions _not_ taken over into the later work, and especially interesting in the present context. There is, for example, a lengthy consideration of the relation (if any) which exists between racial differences and language variation. Humboldt concludes that there is no connection whatsoever (GS VI: 196). This text seems generally overlooked by those who accuse Humboldt of linguistic racism.

More immediately relevant to the present context is Humboldt's attempt to clarify the concept of a 'nation' by contrasting it to the terms Volk and Staat:

> If one regards the words Volk, Nation, and Staat as separated from one another by strict limits, then the first is related to the geographical location, and the social life (das Zusammenleben), the second to the genealogy (Abstammung), the last to the social conception (bürgerliche Verfassung) ... But 'Nation' is used especially as designation of that particular unity of the 'Volk' upon which all the various circumstances have an effect; but one need not already commit oneself here to deciding whether genealogy or language are, within this unity, the same, or have the same extension. Thus one speaks of the French nation, without regard to (i.e., without excluding) the linguistically separate Volk of lower Britanny, of the Spanish without regard to the Basques, Valencia and Catalonia, of the Swiss, aside from the fact that their genealogy and language are common with the Germans. (GS VI: 187)[170]

The problem Humboldt is explicitly addressing himself to here is the need to define 'Nation' more closely so that he can go on to discuss the relationship holding between a language and the nation that speaks it. To this end he defines it in terms of a particular unity of the people. By this he presumably means to define the nation as a group of people united by some common feature. But what kind of feature does he have in mind here as defining the nation? In the passage quoted above it is that particular unity "upon which all the various circumstances have an effect". This may mean that the unifying feature is either or both: (1) produced by a combination of the various circumstances in which the people live, and / or; (2) influenced in an ongoing way by the changing circumstances in which the nation subsequently finds itself. We might ask what kind of circumstances Humboldt has in mind here.

Although he does not go into this extensively, he does say that influences on the nation 'as a whole' include genealogy and language, social conditions (das

Zusammenleben) and similarity of morals, a particular social constitution (Verfassung) and the national history and literature (GS VI: 188). Nevertheless the unity of the nation is not merely the aggregate of all these influences, but rather a national 'feeling' (Gefühl) which they all combine to create and influence. Humboldt describes this effect as the production of a "particular way of thinking, sensing and acting":

> In this sense a nation is a part of mankind such that various causes, in themselves neutral and determined by others, have an effect upon it, so that in it is thereby developed a particular way of thinking, sensing and acting. (GS VI: 188)[171]

Although, as just mentioned, language is one of the influences <u>on</u> the formation of the nation as a whole, Humboldt also here clearly states that the variation of languages is an 'expression of' the national variation. The language receives its form from the 'coinciding tendencies' of all the individuals who make up the nation:

> The actual variation (of nations) always expresses itself also in variation of language, even if it is only one of dialect, ... (GS VI: 188)[172]

> Language lives and moves in nationality, and the mystery of its essence is indicated especially in the fact that it develops out of the apparently chaotic mass of individuals, among whom no specific individual need be pointed to. It receives its whole form out of this dark natural effect of unconsciously coinciding tendencies, ... (GS VI: 189)[173]

It would seem as if Humboldt is ambivalent here on the priority question. Indeed he admits that language and 'national peculiarity' (Eigentümlichkeit) are so intertwined that "it would be a difficult task to precisely separate where it determines and where it receives determination" (GS VI: 191). But this would be true only if he were making claims about an initial or original direction of formative influence between national character and language. Nowhere here, however, does he pose the question in this way. Since he seems concerned to explore only the continuing or ongoing relationship of influence between language and national character, there is no ambivalence in stating that the influence may work in both directions. It is merely a recognition of the complex and reciprocal nature of the relationship. Thus Humboldt's position here seems much the same as in Nationalcharakter. The question of the original direction of influence recedes to the background, and with respect to the continuing relationship between language and national character Humboldt says, in effect, that the influence works in both directions.

What is gained in Verschiedenheiten over Nationalcharakter is a closer consideration by Humboldt of the term 'nation', and a clearer tendency to describe the meaning of national character or particularity not in terms of the various ways in which it becomes manifest, but rather in terms of a guiding principle or leitmotif which itself is simple, a 'unity'. Further, this unity is described in basically emotional terms: it is a national 'feeling' or 'impulse' (GS VI: 188-89, 249).

Humboldt's last treatment of national character and language is the chapter entitled 'Charakter der Sprachen' in Einleitung. In this chapter some of the earlier tendencies in his reflections on this theme surface in a clearer and more committed manner. I shall consider three aspects of his discussion: (1) The concept of character of language is quite definitely separated in principle from the grammatical and lexical structure of language. (2) Humboldt appears more committed to a resolution of the priority question, asserting that 'national character' exerts an original effect upon language, and is not itself completely a product of language. (3) The description of 'national character' as an orientation towards, on the one hand 'sensual' or, on the other, 'spiritual' aspects of things is here more clearly suggested, accompanied by a discussion of the character of Greek and Latin as illustrations of the suggestion.

In the earlier chapters of Einleitung Humboldt has dealt with the nature of language in general, and with general issues of phonetics, syntax and word construction. These concerns are what he refers to in his chapter headings, somewhat vaguely to be sure, as the outer and inner form of language. ('Outer form' refers to the phonetic structure of the language, and 'inner form' to the syntactic and semantic structure.) At the beginning of chapter 20, however, entitled "Charakter der Sprachen", he clearly indicates a different direction of interest:

With the grammatical structure, as we have

> considered it up to now as a whole, and with the external structure of language in general the essence of language is however by no means exhausted. The actual and true character of language rests on something more subtle, more concealed, and less accessible to analysis. (GS VII: 165)[174]

Humboldt emphasizes that the distinction between the 'form' of language and its character is an abstract one. In actual investigation of a language we must study its character by means of the way in which it is _manifest in_ the form of the language. That is, we must examine the peculiarities of a language's sound structure, syntax and vocabulary in order to formulate a description of its character. Nevertheless in setting forth the general theory of language production Humboldt, trying to be clear about what he _means_ by character, stresses the distinction.

> Thus in order to pursue the interweaving of the intellect with language more precisely, we must distinguish the grammatical and lexical structure as the fixed and external attribute of language from its inner character which, similar to a soul, resides in language and produces the effect which every language produces peculiarly upon us as soon as we begin to master it. But it is in no way meant by this that this effect is foreign to the outer structure. (GS VII: 165-166)[175]

It is clear then that by character of a language Humboldt means something quite different than the structure or form of the language. The structure is a complex aggregate of rules and relationships operating in different areas (phonetic, syntactic, lexical) as well as across areas, coordinating them. The character however remains the same, a principle having an influence throughout the structure.[176] In terms of linguistic variation we would say that at least one reason why languages have different structures is because the 'characters' which influence them are different. It is also clear that the character of a language is, in Humboldt's view, an immediate reflection of the national character of its speakers. I will turn in a moment to his attempts in _Einleitung_ to define this concept of character more concretely. First, however, it is worth noting for future reference that in _Einleitung_ Humboldt appears committed to regarding national character as an original cause of (as well as an ongoing influence on) the variation of languages, and not just as a subsequent result of such variation. The relationship of 'Sprache' and 'Geist' arises historically at a time inaccessible to us. Nevertheless he says:

> Without wishing to decide upon the priority of either the one or the other (Sprache or Geist), we must consider as the real explanatory principle and as the true determinative ground of linguistic variation the intellectual power of nations, because only it stands before us in an animated, self-subsistent way, while language is only connected to it. (GS VII: 42)[177]

We must not, he says, rest content with any lower Erklärungsprincip of languages than this:

> ..., that the structure of languages in the human race varies because and to the extent that it is the intellectual idiosyncrasy of nations themselves. (GS VII: 43)[178]

Elsewhere Humboldt speaks of the "original tendency of national peculiarity" as reacting upon language, as well as changes in this peculiarity having a continuing effect on language during its development (GS VII: 174). The character of languages is a "natural result of the continuous effect of the intellectual peculiarity of the nation."[179] The color and character of a language is produced by the thought and sensations of a people, and these effect the language already "from its earliest beginnings."[180]

It is also significant in this regard that, in a rough description of the sources of national character Humboldt does not here explicitly include language:

> The national character is supported and intensified by the common dwelling place and by common activities, and, indeed, to a certain degree it is produced by them. Actually, however, the national character is based on the uniformity of natural tendency (Naturanlage), which is usually explained by the common origin of the people. (GS VII: 170)[181]

This description can be contrasted to the parallel passage in <u>Verschiedenheiten</u> where <u>Abstammung</u> and

Sprache are mentioned together as influences on the nation (GS VI: 188).

One passage in Einleitung seems to recall, however, the double character doctrine seen in earlier essays. Humboldt says that the character of a language originates from the uniform feature common to the nation, and from "the stimulation native to each particular language" (GS VII: 170). This doctrine is rare in Einleitung however, and can still be interpreted as concerned not with the initial production of a language but rather with a later development of a new language out of an older one.

With regard to the question as to what, more specifically, is meant by the term 'national character', Humboldt makes some further suggestions in Einleitung which are similar to the tentative remarks earlier in Nationalcharakter. The character of a nation is a particular mood or attitude towards reality which is formed in the people of a nation early in its history by influences already discussed above. This mood will be an emphasis on either 'spiritual' or 'sensual' aspects of things; an emphasis either "toward the intimacy of the mind or toward external reality" as that nation develops its understanding of man and the world. These two emphases are perhaps only rare extremes; Humboldt seems to suggest that a scale of intermediate positions, between the two extremes and formed by different combinations of them, would better represent the character orientations of various nations.

Humboldt presents this theory by partially using a metaphysical terminology of matter, force, and activity to describe the kinds of character a nation can have. Although this is interesting in its own right I shall quote here only what seems to me to be the general idea he is proposing:

> Now, if we pursue the total internal and external activity of man to its simplest terminal points, we discover it in the way he relates to reality as an object he picks up or as matter which he molds, or even how he plots courses for himself independently thereof. How deeply and in what way man becomes rooted in reality is the original characteristic mark of his individuality. The various types of the foregoing association may be innumerable, depending upon whether man attempts to separate the reality and the internality, neither of which is capable of getting along entirely without the other, or whether he combines

> them in various degrees and directions.
> ... If the character of a nation is revealed by everything truly peculiar to it, which we cannot doubt, it is especially apparent in its language.
> ... The feeling for the distinction between the material which the soul absorbs and produces, and the power motivating and attuning this two-fold activity-- that is, the distinction between the effect and the effective being, or the correct and relative evaluation of both and the more or less clear presence of what is uppermost in our consciousness-- does not pervade every national peculiarity equally.
> ...Between these two extremes is found an innumerable quantity of intermediate stages. The prevailing direction of these is either toward the inner realm of the mind or toward external reality (nach dem Inneren des Gemüths und nach der äusseren Wirklichkeit).
> ... The great dividing line here also is whether a people instills more objective reality or more subjective internality into its language. (GS VII: 179-180)[182]

Although Humboldt's manner of expressing his ideas is often obscure, his basic proposals here may be condensed to the following. By 'national character' we mean an emotional orientation or mood which is to a great extent common to all the people of that nation. This mood, moreover, is a tendency either to emphasize on the one hand the mental activity of man, i.e., to intellectualize, to abstract away from the immediate presence of sensual consciousness, to understand things in terms of abstract Merkmale, or perhaps to understand them in terms of symbolic significance. On the other hand the national character may be a tendency to emphasize immediate perceptions, and, further, to understand the perceived world more in terms of how man can pragmatically utilize and manipulate it. The phrases from the above passages which Humboldt uses in trying to capture this distinction can be grouped as follows.

A	B
Sensual character;	Spiritual character;
emphasis on:	emphasis on:
l. reality	l. internality

2. material which the soul absorbs and produces.	2. power motivating and attuning this activity.
3. effect	3. effective being.
4. more or less clear presence of what is uppermost in our consciousness	4. evaluation of what is present.
5. external reality	5. inner realm of the mind.

Humboldt suggests of course that we should view actual national characters as some mixture of these two emphases, as an intermediate position on a spectrum between them. It is, then, this kind of composite tendency which Humboldt suggests is operating as a guiding principle manifest in the various activities and products of the nation, including its language. We can see the application of this concept of character in the following passage:

> The character is a natural consequence of the protracted effect of the intellectual peculiarity of the nation. Because the latter always picks up the general meanings of words in the same individual way and accompanies them with the same collateral ideas and emotions, and because it produces ideological combinations along the same lines ..., it imparts a peculiar coloration and shading to language which fixes these peculiarities and thus reacts along the same track. (GS VII: 172)[183]

It is not evident how far this treatment of national character could actually be applied in classifying nations by examining their languages (as well as other national products, one assumes). Humboldt himself, as is evident from the various cautionary remarks I have mentioned, does not seem to have been very optimistic about concrete investigation of national character. He does, to be sure, give some examples of what he has in mind, and even when these seem in themselves unclear or contentious they do, nevertheless, illustrate further the speculative theory of character which is sketched out above. Speaking of the ancient Greeks he describes their thought as directed:

> ... especially toward what things are and how they appear, not unilaterally toward the

use to which they could be put in the realm of reality. Its direction was therefore originally internal and intellectual. (GS VII: 181)[184]

PART TWO

THE LINGUISTIC DOCTRINES

CHAPTER SEVEN
THE INFLECTIONAL SUPERIORITY THESIS

7.1 Introduction

Humboldt, like many other students of language at the beginning of the 19th century, claimed, in many of his essays, that languages using a certain type of grammatical method, i.e., 'inflection', are superior to other languages. Inflection is defined in principle by Humboldt as grammatical designation by means of by themselves 'meaningless' affixes or vowel changes attached or 'fused' to the main or radical word element.

The superiority which Humboldt attributed to inflection over other grammatical techniques is less easy to define. The inflectional superiority thesis (hereafter IST) became less fashionable by the 1850s and today is an issue of interest primarily only to historians of linguistics. The reasons why Humboldt and others advanced the thesis that inflected languages are superior became gradually forgotten as interest in the thesis itself waned in the late nineteenth century. Bopp, in 1856, was still well aware that the motivation for the thesis in earlier writers rested upon the view of inflection as employing 'bedeutungslosen Sylben', although Bopp (1856: 203) himself defended the thesis on other grounds. The tendency in many modern accounts of the IST is to view it as a cultural or literary prejudice. Sapir, in 1921, regarded the IST as simply a cultural prejudice arising out of the fact that linguists of Humboldt's generation were more familiar with the highly inflected classical languages than with other language types. He said (1921: 123):

> The vast majority of linguistic theorists themselves spoke languages of a certain type, of which the most fully developed varieties were the Latin and Greek that

> they had learned in their childhood. It was not difficult for them to be persuaded that these familiar languages represented the 'highest' development that speech had yet attained and that all other types were but steps on the way to this beloved 'inflective' type.

Richard Hönigswald (1970: 110-111) similarly attributed the IST to 'cultural dispositions' (kulturellen Stimmungen) prevalent in the early 1800s . R.H. Robins (1967: 181) more recently has attributed Jacob Grimm's admiration for inflectional morphology, and especially the ablaut (vowel gradation) method of inflection, to Grimm's 'national feeling' about the German language. The guiding intuition behind this kind of explanation of the IST is that Humboldt, Friedrich Schlegel, and others regarded the cultural products of the Greeks and Romans as superior to other cultures, and by conscious or unconscious extrapolation they extended this claim of superiority to the grammatical method of the languages themselves.

These efforts to view the IST as a result of nationalism or cultural ethnocentricity have, I believe, tended to obscure the original systematic motivations for the thesis, which are philosophical. To correct this tendency I will concentrate here on Humboldt's defense of the IST. It is not my intention to try to resurrect the IST as a legitimate thesis but rather to resurrect the original context within which the thesis was advanced and to show that it followed fairly consistently from several philosophical assumptions that were axiomatic for Humboldt.

I will proceed in three sections. In section 7.2 I briefly place the discussion of inflection against the general background of language typology. In section 7.3 I clarify more specifically what Humboldt meant by 'inflection'. These two sections establish <u>what</u> Humboldt attributed superiority to although not yet <u>why</u>. In section 7.4 I argue that Humboldt advanced the IST primarily because of certain views about designation and the nature of thinking which I have discussed in Chapters two and three. Some of the connections I will follow up here have in recent years been adumbrated in various respects in scattered articles. Most worthy of mention here are those by Verburg, Weimann, Hartmann, and especially Coseriu.[186]

7.2 Language typology

The general background against which Humboldt's treatment of inflection must be viewed is the beginning of language typology in the early 19th century. Although I am not here concerned with either language typology in general or with Humboldt's contribution to it, the meaning which inflection had, for him as well as his contemporaries, can best be clarified in a preliminary way by looking briefly at the early history of language typology.

Although the study of inflection as a grammatical method goes back into earlier classical philology, the use of it in sweeping divisions of languages into general categories begins essentially with Friedrich Schlegel's immensely influential book Ueber die Sprache und Weisheit der Indier (1808). The IST is already present in this work and indeed predates Schlegel in such earlier linguists as Johann Christoph Adelung (1732-1806).[187] Schlegel distinguished two broad types of language, two 'Hauptgattungen der Sprachen': Those which indicate grammatical determinations of meaning by alterations of the root sounds (Flexion) or by adding on additional words (Affixa) which indicate those determinations:

> The additional determinations (Nebenbestimmungen) of meaning are indicated either through an inner alteration of the root sound, by inflection; or however in every case by a proper affixed word, which already in and for itself means plurality, pastness, a future ought, or other relational concepts; and these two most simple cases also designate the two main species of all languages.[188]

Schlegel (1975 (1808): 155) is fairly careful to note that this distinction may not always be clearly observable. For example the 'appearance of inflection' (Schein von Flexion) may arise when the affixed words ultimately lose their own meaning and "melt into the main word".

August Wilhelm Schlegel (1971: 14-16), in 1818, expanded Friedrich's two part system into a three part one. Whereas Friedrich had lumped all non-inflecting languages into one 'affixing' class, August Wilhelm, recognizing that 'affixing' does not properly describe the procedure of languages which do not in fact join together words in ways which indicate grammatical relationships (e.g., Chinese), added a third category of languages, those 'without any grammatical structure'. This latter group became commonly designated, by Humboldt and others, as 'isolating' languages. The intermediate 'affixing' group are also sometimes called 'compositing' or 'agglutinating' languages. To a large extent early typology operated only on the basis of these broad, rather indistinct, differences. Not only was there indistinctness in the sense that many concrete examples could not easily be decided as between 'composition' and 'inflection', but also there was still a considerable amount of confusion about what 'inflection' meant in principle. Humboldt is generally considered to have subscribed to a three part typology of 'inflecting, compositing, isolating' languages, or to have added a fourth category to it.[189] In fact, although Humboldt used these terms, as we shall see below, he seems neither to have definitely advocated a three-part typology nor added a fourth class. The confusions over his views on language typology in general are documented and corrected by Coseriu (1972), and I shall not further concerned with the matter here, since it is merely 'inflection' which is the present concern.

7.3 The meaning of 'inflection' for Humboldt

I shall try here to clarify the meaning which 'inflection' had for Humboldt in several ways: by showing how he distinguished himself from Schlegel and Bopp on this matter; by looking at his explanation of what constitutes a 'true' or 'genuine' grammatical form (especially in *Entstehen*); and by documenting his consistent distinction between 'meaningful' and 'meaningless' (bedeutsam and bedeutungslos) signs, and identification of inflection with the use of the latter. In order to have a preliminary characterization of Humboldt's definition of inflection in mind consider the following passage from *Entstehen*:

> If a language arose through an actual convention the addition and insertion of meaningless word elements, and the alteration of vowels and consonants, would be the most natural and suitable means. It is the true inflection, in contrast to composition, ... (GS IV: 296)[190]

It should first be made clear, as an aside, that when Humboldt speaks of inflection, composition, etc. he is interested primarily in them as grammatical methods, and is only secondarily, or not at all, interested in the classification of languages which could be based on these methodological distinctions. In Vom gram. Baue he says:

> I speak here with great care always of methods, and do not, without special reason, confuse this expression with that of languages. For it can probably easily be shown that there is probably no language which does not use all or most of these methods at the same time ... (GS VI: 387-8)[191]

We may further locate Humboldt's concern with inflection by separating several different kinds of concern with grammar, roughly as follows:

(1) Grammatical relationships per se (e.g., case, voice, tense, mood, number).

(2) General means of creating grammatical relation designators (e.g., inflection, word order, composition).

(3) Language-specific grammatical rules (e.g., how to form the present perfect in Greek, the past definite in French, etc.).

(4) Individual word-forms (e.g., sing, sang, sung).

Humboldt's concern, when discussing inflection, composition, etc., and indeed when arguing for the IST, is level (2) here. He suggests this kind of distinction himself at several points, for example, in Dualis:

> Languages are grammatically different namely:
> (a) first of all in their apprehension of grammatical forms according to their concept,
> (b) then in the type of technical means of their designation,
> (c) finally in the actual sounds used for the designation. (GS VI: 21)[192]

The discussion of inflection concerns level (b) in this list.

A central aspect of the concept of inflection is that designation of both the radical meaning and the grammatical determinations of it occur in the same word. This aspect of inflection may be called the fusing criterion, and it was generally accepted by Humboldt and his contemporaries.[193]

During the early 1800s, however, a crucial difficulty in the meaning of 'inflection' as a general grammatical method was whether or not inflectional additions to the radical word, i.e., the suffixes, prefixes or internal changes, can have their own independent meaning. If the affix can have an independent usage then is the constructed, 'fused' word an example of 'inflection' or mere 'composition'? Friedrich Schlegel was unclear on this question, allowing that when words with independent meanings were 'fused' with other radical words the 'appearance of inflection' was produced (1975 (1808): 155). The distinction is clearly stated in retrospect by Robins, although there is less reason than he assumes to attribute a clear understanding of it to the Schlegels. According to Robins (1973: 15):

> A.W. Schlegel, like his brother, made the point that the difference between affixing and inflecting languages was not simply a matter of whether serially placed affixes were used or not in the surface morphology, since a good many affixes were found in the inflecting languages. What was relevant to the distinction was whether the affixes themselves had a definable and isolatable meaning or whether as affixes they were devoid of identifiable content in themselves and only served to form a complete inflected word unity with its totality of specified meaning.

Franz Bopp, a close friend of Humboldt, ultimately sought to explain all grammatical designation by inflectional changes as parasitical upon the original meaning of the inflectional affixes. As Verburg points out (1974: 451):

> For Sanskrit and its related languages Bopp finally thought, as we saw, that 'agglutination' (adopting Humboldt's terminology) was the universal structural principle. Of flexion in the old sense Bopp only recognizes reduplication in the Indo-European languages; this, however, is also an element of the word. Only, it has no previous pronominal independence, ...

Humboldt clearly separated his own views from the obscurity of Schlegel and the 'compositing' viewpoint of Bopp. In a letter to A.W. Schlegel in 1822 Humboldt confessed that he had never clearly understood what Friedrich meant by 'inflection' (Leitzmann 1908: 116-119). In correspondence with Bopp he takes issue with Bopp's attempt to understand all inflection (except reduplication, perhaps) as originally composition (Lefmann 1897: 51ff).

This point seems confused by Ross (1970), who sees both Bopp and Humboldt as advocating the formation of inflectional endings out of original composition.[194] While there is some evidence that Humboldt may at times have regarded this thesis as historically likely, he certainly regarded inflection in principle, and as practised in many languages, as quite distinct from composition. Once the original meaning has been lost, Humboldt would argue, the affix just is inflectional. In Einleitung he says clearly that the original independent meaning of suffixes is no necessary obstacle to the purity of genuine inflection.[195] Just like inner word change it fulfills the 'goal of inflection' (den Zweck der Flexion). There is no need to confuse an historical issue of etymology with a theoretical distinction of designative techniques.

Most decisively, however, Humboldt's own writings are quite clear on what 'inflection', in principle, meant for him. It meant the fusion onto, or into, a radical word (verbal or substantive) of affixes which have no meaning in themselves beyond designating grammatical determinations of the radical word.

This point may be demonstrated by noting Humboldt's characterization of grammatical designation as 'meaningless' (bedeutungslos), and his consideration (especially in Entstehen) of what he called a 'true' or 'genuine' form.

The first point emerges emphatically in Entstehen (1821) and remains evident throughout the rest of Humboldt's writings. True inflection, Humboldt says, if we were to posit it as chosen at some hypothetical invention of language, would utilize 'meaningless word elements':

> for the inflection, in itself completely meaningless, contains nothing but the pure concept of relationship. In the grammatical word there is, in addition to that, the complementary concept which is referred to the relationship in order to determine it, ... (GS IV: 304)[196]

In Grundzüge there is a general discussion of the use and value of 'bedeutungslose Laute' in inflectional grammar (GS V: 402). In Vom gram. Baue Humboldt gives a list of four types of grammatical devices which utilize 'meaningless sounds' (GS VI: 372f). This list, which indicates basically the possible types of inflection, in

Humboldt's view, includes: (a) attachment of a characteristic sound; (b) inner alteration of the basic word; (c) repetition of the basic word or part of it (reduplication); and (d) absence of all designation. These are the types to which all 'bedeutungslosen grammatischen Bezeichnungsmittel' may be reduced.

A further clarification of Humboldt's understanding of what constitutes inflection can be gleaned from his description, in Entstehen, of inflectional forms as 'true' or 'proper' grammatical forms. At the end of Entstehen Humboldt outlines a four stage progression of types of grammatical designation, moving from word order and the use of 'object designating words', through 'standardized' word order, the development of 'objective' words into (relation designating) affixes, and culminating in the stage of 'pure inflection and pure grammatical words' (GS IV: 305).

The central argument in Entstehen by which Humboldt distinguishes inflection from other means of grammatical designation is that by employing (in inflection) word elements which have no 'objective' designation, the resulting word is itself a unified whole, a designation of a certain concept in its syntactic relation to other parts of the sentence without the additional semantic presence of collateral concepts (Nebenbegriffe). The desideratum is a word which represents a true semantic unity, not an 'aggregate':

> But everything given here does not cancel out the distinction between true grammatical forms, like amavit, epoieisas, and such word or syllable arrangement which most primitive languages use for the designation of grammatical forms. It lies in the fact that the former expressions actually draw together into one word, and that in the latter the elements only appear serially linked to one another. (GS IV: 300)[197]

The same points are made in Humboldt's last work, Einleitung, where 'die Flexionsmethode' is connected with 'die wahre innere Festigkeit' of the word (GS VII: 108ff, 118, 155-56, 162).

This notion that inflectional grammatical designation promotes the 'unity' of designation in a word is Humboldt's version of the view that inflection is a more 'organic' method of grammar. Composition, word order, pronunciation, as used to designate grammatical status, are seen on the contrary as 'mechanical' methods. This terminology of 'organic' and 'mechanical' is commonly used throughout the period and is a metaphor which extends far beyond the study of language. In that not only Humboldt but also the Schlegels and others almost invariably regarded the 'organic' (i.e., inflecting) languages as superior,[198] using valuational terms such as 'true' or 'proper' forms, or 'more complete' (vollkommenere) forms for inflectional grammars, we are here already in the midst of the inflectional superiority thesis. What remains to be asked then is <u>why</u> an 'organic' grammar should be more highly valued than a 'mechanical' grammar. Why should the creation of a more 'unified' designation in the word be a criterion of linguistic superiority? After all (as Humboldt, at least, freely admits) (GS IV: 287) all languages manage to accomplish in their own way all the grammatical requirements. Why should the employment of 'meaningless' symbols (prefixes, etc.) for grammatical designation be more 'complete', more 'natural', more 'suitable' than the use of independently meaningful words or affixes for the same purpose? And besides, just what does it mean to call inflectional affixes 'meaningless'? If they designate some grammatical determination then isn't this their meaning?

With these questions we are at the heart of the matter. So far I have tried to clarify Humboldt's usage of 'inflection' by pointing out (1) that he insists on the 'meaningless' status of inflectional affixes, and (2) that in inflected words a true 'unity' of designation is achieved. When it is claimed, therefore, that inflecting languages are superior we may regard at least these two aspects of inflection as constituting its claimed superiority over other grammatical techniques. Why Humboldt would have viewed them as contributing to the superiority of inflection is the next question, and to that question I turn now.

7.4 <u>The arguments for the inflectional superiority thesis</u>

What are in fact the evaluative terms which Humboldt uses to state the IST? In a passage already quoted above (GS IV: 296) Humboldt calls inflection the 'most natural and most suitable' (das natürlichste und passendste Mittel) of grammatical indication. In <u>Vom gram. Baue</u> he speaks of the 'completeness and purity' (Vollständigkeit und Reinheit) of the grammatical structure of a language (GS VI: 363). The term 'completeness' (Vollständigkeit or Vollkommenheit) is the term most often used by Humboldt to describe the alleged superiority of inflecting grammars, and the term seems commonly used by others as well for the same purpose (Coseriu 1972: 115). In Entstehen Humboldt says that "It cannot be denied that only the grammatically developed languages possess complete adequacy (vollkommne Angemessenheit) for the development of ideas" (GS IV:310). Some languages have 'very incomplete' (unvollkommnen) grammatical forms (GS IV: 288ff). Similarly in Vom gram. Baue he speaks of the "... variation of degrees of completeness (Vollkommenheit) of grammatical structure in the existing languages ..." (GS VI: 355) and of those methods which have in common "a certain lack of sufficient grammatical designation ..." (GS VI: 366).

One thing which should be clear from this terminology is that Humboldt is not judging the relative merit of languages on the basis of the extent or richness of their vocabulary, or their literary and philosophical output, etc.. The IST is by no means so simple-minded a form of cultural ethno-centrism. He says clearly in Grundzüge:

> For the excellence of languages is not determined by the biased richness of images and concepts which they present to the soul, but rather through their effect on thinking and sensing in general. (GS V: 422)[199]

Similarly in Entstehen and Vom gram. Baue he emphasizes that the issue of the excellence of languages is a question of an interest in the 'pure form of thoughts' which cannot be promoted by a language which "is not accustomed to represent the form as such" (GS IV: 292, and GS VI: 382).

Certainly it is true that Humboldt himself never defends his evaluation of the differing merits of grammatical techniques by reference to Latin or Greek as paradigmatic 'superior' languages, or by reference to the 'superiority' of Greek or Latin culture. To the contrary, he says that the differing merit of languages "follows from the nature of thinking and discourse" (GS IV: 312). This general point is made by Coseriu (1972: 126), who says that Humboldt's criterion for the excellence of inflection is "the parallel between thinking and speaking: the expression by inflection would best correspond to thinking". Although Coseriu leaves the matter at that, this statement remains at best a formula, not explaining just what is implied by 'corresponding to thinking', or 'a parallel between thinking and speakingö which in some way motivates the IST. The secondary literature on Humboldt's writings on language has neglected to explore Humboldt's defense of the IST, or to explain what 'adequate' or 'complete' correspondence between language and thought meant for Humboldt. The only attempt to clarify this matter is to be found in an appendix to Peter Hartmann's Theorie der Grammatik (1963). Hartmann emphasizes, correctly, I believe, that the excellence of inflection, for Humboldt, lies in its ability to maintain at the symbolic (i.e., linguistic) level a distinction that exists at the psychological level, in thought. Hartmann (1963: 117-18) calls this distinction that between 'qualitative' and 'general' determination, or between naming and classifying. He states Humboldt's case incompletely, however, in that he overlooks a second essential argument for the IST, as I shall show below.

A brief summary may be helpful here. Inflection, for Humboldt, is a grammatical method which utilizes affixes or vowel changes to indicate the grammatical status of the word to which they are attached. These affixes, in themselves 'meaningless', fuse with the main word in such a way that the result is a true 'unity'; a concept determined in a certain fashion rather than an aggregate of concepts (composition). Languages which utilize this method are, Humboldt claims, more 'complete', 'adequate', 'suitable' than others for the expression of thought. For the sake of clarity I suggest the main motives for this claim be reduced to two points, which are, however, closely related.

(A) Humboldt argues that, as a symbolic system representing thoughts, language must be regarded as symbolizing two qualitatively different kinds of things: concepts (which may in turn designate objects, facts, events, feelings, etc.), and grammatical relations holding between concepts. For convenience I have called this viewpoint, stemming from various philosophical influences on Humboldt, the 'dual designation' doctrine.

(B) Although Humboldt makes a sharp distinction between the conceptual contents of thought and their grammatical interrelations, he does not hypostatize grammatical relations into concepts in their own right, but argues instead that such relations are always a function of some other concept. Thus, to express the point psychologistically, a 'thought' is a concatenation of conceptual building blocks, or 'thought-units' (Gedankeneinheiten), some of which are modified in accordance with the grammatical relationships intended by the thinker. 'Past-tense', for example, does not stand alone as an independent unit in the thought, but rather exists only as a modification of some other conceptual unit, e.g., a verb. Humboldt was led to this viewpoint via his approval of a philosophical - psychological account of thinking and concept formation drawn from his reading of Enlightenment philosophy.

To briefly express (A) and (B) one could say that Humboldt qualitatively distinguished between concepts and grammatical relations, but regarded the latter as always 'attached to' the former, never existing independently in thought. I have discussed (A) and (B) more extensively in chapters two and three. My present concern is to show how these doctrines functioned in Humboldt's theory as arguments for the inflectional superiority thesis.

(A)

The dual designation doctrine provides us first with an explanation of Humboldt's common description of inflectional devices (endings, vowel changes, etc.) as 'meaningless' (bedeutungslos). If we accept that there is in fact a clear qualitative distinction in a thought between the concepts involved in it, on the one hand, and the grammatical relationships linking those concepts in a particular way in that thought, on the other hand, then there should be a clear distinction in the way these two aspects of the thought are designated in the linguistic unit (word, phrase, sentence) which represents that thought. This, at any rate, is Humboldt's position.

The point to be appreciated here is that Humboldt seems to reserve the term 'meaning' for the conceptual content of thought, and remove the 'relational' aspect from the realm of 'meaning'. The grammatical designation, if it is done in such a way that <u>only</u> the grammatical modification of the concept is designated (as in inflection) is by that token a 'meaningless' designation, which is, as I have shown above, Humboldt's common description of inflection. 'Meaningless' here of course is not to be taken pejoratively. Quite to the contrary, it is precisely the <u>excellence</u> of inflection, for Humboldt, that it is a grammatical technique which succeeds in designating only relational determinations of a concept <u>without</u> adding any collateral conceptual 'meaning' (any 'Nebenbegriffe').

Although Humboldt does not define the term 'meaning' (Bedeutung) or indeed use it often, (except in the adjective 'bedeutungslos' employed as noted above) his restriction of it to conceptual content is suggested by passages such as this one from Einleitung.

> Since it (the inflectional method) takes every element of discourse in its two-fold value (Geltung), its objective meaning (Bedeutung) and its subjective relation (Beziehung) to the thoughts and the language, and designates this two-fold thing in its relative weight by phonetic forms directed to that purpose ... (GS VII: 162)[200]

Occasionally Humboldt seems to retract this terminological restriction of 'meaning' as well. But in these instances he is always careful to maintain the separation of the two kinds of meaning.

At the sixth and last stage of his sketch of grammatical designation in Vom gram. Baue Humboldt says that inflectional designation has no other meaning than 'grammatical significance' (Bedeutsamkeit) (GS VI: 386f). This should be contrasted to the third stage, where relationships are indicated by 'proper words' which have 'independent meaning' (selbstständige Bedeutung) and 'stand separated' (GS VI: 386). Similarly, in his discussion of the relative pronoun as a 'pure grammatical word', he emphasizes that it is so because "its meaning is directed exclusively at the connection of discourse" (GS VI: 380).

Despite these few instances of granting 'meaning' to relational designation, the overwhelming tendency in Humboldt is to label inflected word modifications as 'meaningless', as shown above. I suggest that in trying to describe Humboldt's position systematically we maintain the terminological restriction of 'meaning' to concepts or conceptual 'content', for this is his own persevering tendency, which motivates both the description of inflectional affixes as 'meaningless' and as (therefore) more 'adequate' or 'suitable' a method of grammatical designation than others.

In Entstehen the separation of the 'content' and 'relational' aspects of thought is explicitly linked to the superiority of inflection:

> The first and most essential thing is that the spirit requires of language that it clearly distinguish thing and form, object and relation, and not mix the two with one another. ... But this separation is first purely attained precisely only in the

> development of genuine grammatical form through inflection or through grammatical words, ... (GS IV: 308)[201]

Humboldt goes on to maintain that the true grammatical form:

> ... contains the expression of the relationship purely, and contains nothing substantial according to which the understanding could deviate, (thus) it notices therein the original word-concept altered, so it must apprehend the (grammatical) form itself. In the non-genuine form it can not do this, since it does not see the relational concept sufficiently defined in it, and is still dispersed through associated concepts. (GS IV: 308)[202]

> For the inflection, in itself completely meaningless, contains nothing but the pure concept of the relation. (GS IV: 304)[203]

These passages make clear that by 'pure formality' in grammar Humboldt means a method of designation which only indicates a grammatical relationship, and nothing more. Inflection satisfies this requirement best, and is in this respect the best method of grammatical designation. The inflected Greek pepeika, for example, designates by inflectional signs several grammatical determinations of the verb 'to persuade' (i.e., indicative, active voice, past perfect tense) which are designated in English by several separate words plus an ending on the verb: I have persuaded. Humboldt would argue that in the introduction of the auxiliary verb 'have', for example, 'Nebenbegriffe' are introduced which add more content than is necessary for the designation of the 'past perfect' determination of the verb.[204] In Vom gram. Baue he speaks of the promotion of 'thought unity' by the removal of factual content from grammatical designation:

> Negatively the presentation of the thought unity in language occurs through the removal of every factual concept (Sachbegriff) from the grammatical designation. The distinction here raised is visible through the comparison of languages which designate the

> tense of the verb through temporal adjectives, prepositions by parts of the human body, (back, front, etc.), and those which designate the former by endings, the latter by meaningless words. (GS VI: 362)[205]

The fact that inflection seems to best maintain, at the symbolic level, the separation of the 'content' and 'relational' aspects of thought motivates both Humboldt's description of inflectional affixes as 'meaningless' and as (therefore) more 'adequate' or 'suitable' a method of grammatical designation than others.

(B)

Hartmann, in his account of Humboldt's argument for the IST, emphasizes, correctly, that the excellence of inflection for Humboldt lies in its ability to maintain at the symbolic (i.e., linguistic) level a distinction that exists at the psychological level, in thought. However, Hartmann relies only on the first argument, that inflection is the optimal grammatical means of maintaining the 'concept / relation' dichotomy in thought which Humboldt accepts:

> Inflection attains the proper goal, a _bipartite_ characterization, by the unification of qualitative and 'general' determination (that is, of naming and classification) ... (Hartmann 1963: 118)

Nevertheless this argument alone is not enough to motivate the IST, I would suggest. For one could surely imagine a language in which grammatical designators are 'meaningless' in Humboldt's terms, i.e., indicate only the grammatical modification of a word, but yet are not attached to the radical word stem or root, that is, are not inflectional. Suppose, for example, that English irregular verbs such as _sing_, _sang_, _sung_ had their tense indicated not by an internal vowel change but rather by an external indication of the relevant vowel. Resulting forms such as: _I a sing_ (= _I sang_); _I u sing_ (= _I sung_); _we a drink_ (= _we drank_) would maintain the dual designation criterion without being genuine inflection. As strange as this may sound, my point is simply that requiring grammatical designators to have purely relational significance, without introducing _Nebenbestimmungen_, does not by itself require that the grammatical designators be _attached_ to conceptual designators such as word stems or roots. In short, the dual designation argument does not by itself support the fusing aspect of inflection, the union of conceptual and relational designation in one word. In that a non-inflectional language could still satisfy the requirement of clearly separating conceptual and relational designation, this requirement alone cannot be all that motivated Humboldt to describe inflection as the most adequate or complete method.

Because a grammatical relation is not a concept in its own right, but rather the modification of a concept, Humboldt would view the grammatical relation as attached to a concept, and not as an independent entity in a proposition. In the proposition 'I walked', for example, we do not have in mind three separate concepts ('I', 'to walk', and 'past tenseness') but rather only two, 'I', and 'to walk' modified as occurring in the past. I have already stressed above that Humboldt values inflection over other grammatical methods because, in his terms, the resulting word is a 'true unity' and not a mere 'aggregate'. This may now be partially explicated, I believe, by noting that, for Humboldt, in thought relational modifications attach to or 'belong to' conceptual units. They form together a single semantic unit, not an aggregate. Accordingly the most accurate symbolic representation of this semantic unit is one in which relational and conceptual designation occur in the same word. In brief, in thought relations attach to concepts, ergo in language relational designators should (i.e., it is a desideratum) attach or fuse to concept designators.

It is the combination of these two views; (A) that concepts and their grammatical modifications are qualitatively different constituents of thought, and (B) grammatical relations should not be hypostatized into concepts in their own right but rather always are attached to concepts, which motivates Humboldt's description of inflection as a more 'complete', 'adequate' or 'suitable' representation of thought.

According to this account there would be essentially two ways in which non-inflectional grammatical designation is inferior to inflection. Either grammatical designation is absent or insufficiently present, as in 'isolating' languages, such as Chinese, in which case the linguistic representation is 'incomplete' or 'inadequate to the thought', or the grammatical relationships are indicated by the addition of new conceptual content (compositing languages), in which case the linguistic representation is more than complete and, again, inadequate to the thought. Humboldt does not often put the matter as briefly as this, but the following texts are representative of the general position:

> The first principle (re: Inhaltes der Wörter) prevailing here is that a correct articulation of the thought matter by language ... contains everything which belongs to the completion of its concept, and nothing which is not essential to it, or depends on it only accidentally. (GS V: 424)[206]

> The thought receives clarity and determinateness only through language, and this effect is only complete when everything which is going on in the thought also gets an analogous expression in the language. Every language which leaves something to be added in this area finds itself at a disadvantage in this respect. (GS V: 323)[207]

> They (deviations from pure grammar) fall into two main classes; when the grammatical relation is not sufficiently indicated, and when it is not indicated with pure formality. (GS VI: 364)[208]

In Humboldt's opinion inflection is 'superior' because it is a method of symbolic designation which conforms more accurately to that which is symbolized (thought) than other methods do. Inflected forms, in which 'fused' affixes or vowel changes designate grammatical determinations, symbolize more precisely (in terms of quantity and form) the actual constituents of thought. Just as the grammatically determined concept is still only one thing, one 'thought-unit', so the inflected word is still one symbol. In Einleitung Humboldt argues that the sharpness of the 'articulation capacity' (Articulationsvermögens) and the purity of the 'inflectional sense' (Flexionsinnes) stand in a "reciprocally reinforcing connection" (GS VII: 117).

This claim is far removed from any judgement about the superiority or inferiority of the content or ideology of any thought or its linguistic representation. Nor does this claim have anything to do with a language's capacity as a medium of understanding and communication; Humboldt admits quite explicitly that all languages are basically complete and adequate in this sense (GS IV: 286f). The point is that the non-inflectional linguistic representation may not be 'adequate to the thought', i.e., correspond point by point, mapping out the thought in an isomorphic fashion, as it were, without containing too much or too little.

What we have in the IST is essentially a semiotic claim about the superior accuracy or completeness of one symbolic system over others which represent the same thing. I have tried in this chapter to highlight several aspects of Humboldt's views about thinking which motivated him to claim that inflection was a superior method of grammatical representation. It might still be argued that Humboldt's ready acceptance and use of these philosophical assumptions is itself a result of his cultural conditioning. In that case the IST would be the result of cultural prejudices in an indirect fashion. To explore the non-philosophical (e.g., cultural, emotional) reasons why a thinker may find certain philosophical views attractive, and use them in an axiomatic fashion, is a complex and subtle task, and limitations of space preclude my attempting it here. What I hope at least to have accomplished is the clarification of the explicit systematic reasons why Humboldt advanced the IST. This clarification should bring into question the common treatment of the IST as a manifestation of early 19th century nationalism and Indo-European cultural prejudice, and place it instead against the background of philosophical and psychological assumptions which early linguistics inherited from the Enlightenment.

CHAPTER EIGHT
THE LINGUISTIC RELATIVITY THESIS

8.1 Introduction

In this chapter I will examine some of the connections between Humboldt's philosophical views on thought and language and his version of the 'linguistic relativity thesis' (hereafter LRT). By the 'linguistic relativity thesis' I mean the general claim that thought is relative to language; that the way someone thinks is determined by the particular language which that person speaks.

With the LRT we are in a completely different historical context than was the case with respect to the inflectional superiority thesis. The claim that a person's language exercises an influence over how that person thinks is a thesis which has appeared in various guises throughout the history of philosophy and which continues to be an issue in the twentieth century. There are many versions of the thesis before Humboldt and during his period which he may have been familiar with, and many versions of the thesis after him which are influenced by him. To examine these myriad versions of the LRT insofar as they influenced Humboldt or are influenced by him may help to clarify the general issues at stake here, but ultimately an examination of the whole tradition, even a cursory one, would go far beyond the bounds of this book. I shall, accordingly, give only a brief review of the overall historical context here, and then proceed to a more detailed examination of Humboldt's views. In focusing on Humboldt's work I am particularly concerned to point out the way in which his basic philosophical views on thought and language, in conjunction with the 'national character' hypothesis, provide the psychological and epistemological framework within which 'linguistic relativity' can be given a more determinate description. That is to say, in explicating

Humboldt's philosophical orientation we get a clearer picture of how 'linguistic relativity' was seen to 'work', or take effect, by the philosophers and linguists of that period. Quite apart from questions about the variation of languages, the linguistic relativity thesis must imply, or make use of, whether implicitly or explicitly, some account of what thinking is when it claims that language has a determining influence on thought. In my discussion of Humboldt below I hope to clarify further this account of thinking, and its interaction with language, which is employed in his version of the LRT. This will, I believe, be helpful in understanding and evaluating the meaning of the linguistic relativity thesis in Humboldt's period, and perhaps in comparing it with the ways in which the LRT has been advanced in the twentieth century.

The above comments have already suggested one clarification of the LRT which I would like to stress at the very beginning. The linguistic relativity thesis has, in all of its various historical forms, always been a thesis about the relationship between thought and language in general; and not about the relationship between this or that particular language and thought. We should be careful to keep this general claim about language and thought separate from problems concerning the variation of language.[209]

It is true, of course, that some of the more interesting ramifications of the LRT stem from the additional fact that there are many different languages. If language determines thought, and there are different languages, there arise the interesting issues of translation. And, more generally, if a language has been influenced by national character, as Humboldt argues, then the language will tend to imprint this character back upon its subsequent speakers. The variation of character during the formation of languages, hence, will come home to roost as a variation in the way people speaking different languages think, if the LRT is true. For example, a nation with a 'sensual' character will tend to develop its language in a certain way, according to Humboldt. This character will have an effect upon the whole 'form' of the language, including its phonetic, syntactic and semantic structures. Subsequently, however, the language itself, so structured, will determine the thought of those people who learn the language, inducing them to think after the 'sensual' pattern which has gone into the production of the language. Whereas earlier (in Chapters five and six) I was concerned with influences on the production of linguistic variation, here with the LRT I am concerned with the influence which languages have back upon thinking, with the 'Rückwirkung', as Humboldt would say.

Despite the fact that many of the more interesting ramifications of the LRT follow only from the complementary factor of linguistic variation, the LRT as such is not related in any necessary way to the variation of languages. If everyone spoke the same language it might still be true (or false) that that one language had a determining effect on thought.

It is true that Humboldt himself was very interested in the variation of languages. This is indicated by just the titles alone of several of his essays. In chapters five and six I have discussed several features of his treatment of the causes of language variation. His associated claim that these different languages have a reciprocal influence over the way their speakers think, and thus function to maintain different 'worldviews', must depend, however, not just on a treatment of the variation of languages, but also on a more general account of how it is that any language (and, hence, every language) exercises an influence over thinking. Humboldt does, indeed, realize that this more general account is necessary, and I shall discuss below some passages in which the LRT is stated in its own right, apart from its conjunction with linguistic variation.

8.2 The historical context

It is often acknowledged that the general idea that language is somehow necessary for thinking, or even that thinking and language, or reason and language, are 'identical', was explicitly present in Humboldt's immediate predecessors, especially Hamann and Herder.[210] Hans Helmut Christmann, taking up the LRT as the claim that every language represents a certain world-view (Weltbild) which the users of that language share, traces the presence of this claim through many thinkers of the French, Italian and English Enlightenment. He uses a working definition of the Weltbild thesis drawn from Leo Weisgerber, as follows:

> So the possession of a determinate vocabulary and a determinate syntax means already the presence of an articulation (Gleiderung) of the world, an articulation which in no way is fixed in the things themselves, but rather precisely in the language. Every language represents an access to the world; ... (Christmann 1967: 4)

Christmann doesn't go into the theoretical underpinnings of the concept of language as world-view, nor attempt to examine the various philosophical assumptions and arguments which may be involved in it. He is content rather merely to indicate its presence in the works of a wide range of thinkers in the Enlightenment period. This historical survey alone, however, suffices to show that the general idea that language exercises an influence over thought was a widespread, if not commonplace, idea from the early Enlightenment right up to the present day, and was in no way the creation of any particular thinker or school of thought.[211]

Nevertheless the LRT as advanced by Humboldt's predecessors often seems to be a singularly vague claim, indeed little more than a platitude passed down from thinker to thinker. The language one speaks makes one think in a certain way, have a certain view of the world. What this means in terms of its relation to the epistemological and metaphysical issues of the day is rarely spelled out in any way. In Humboldt, however, some of these connections do become more visible, as I shall try to show.

After Humboldt the LRT seems to have lain dormant for about a hundred years. In the twentieth century, however, interest in it has again been evident. Two general schools of thought may be delineated. The so-called 'semantic-field' theorists, primarily in Germany, have been centrally concerned with the thesis that each language represents a particular way of understanding the world, and that this 'Weltbild' structures and influences the way its speakers think. The most important figures in this school are Leo Weisgerber (b. 1899) and Jost Trier (1894-1970), both of whom point to Humboldt as inspiration. Indeed this movement is often called 'neo-Humboldtian' linguistics.[212]

Anglo-American attention to the LRT has tended to focus on the formulations of it by Edward Sapir (1884-1939) and Benjamin Lee Whorf (1899-1941), the whole problem of linguistic relativity becoming known under the rubric of 'The Sapir-Whorf hypothesis'. A representative statement of it by Whorf is the following:

> It was found that the background linguistic system (in other words, the grammar) of each language is not merely a reproducing instrument for voicing ideas but rather is itself the shaper of ideas, the program and guide for the individual's mental activity, for his analysis of impressions, for his synthesis of his mental stock in trade.(Whorf 1956: 212)

A further development of the Sapir-Whorf hypothesis can be traced in the psycholinguistic research of the late Eric Lenneberg and others in the 1950s and later. Lenneberg was fascinated by the implications of Whorf's ideas, but felt that a crucial shortcoming of Whorf's work was his failure to escape a completely linguistic frame of reference. That is to say, Whorf merely pointed out certain striking differences between languages (especially Hopi and English) and concluded that the speakers of those languages thought in different ways, had a different 'conception of the world'. But to show that this is true, Lenneberg (1953: 453) argues, we must have some additional and independent evidence for the differing 'thinking' or 'world-conception' of the speakers aside from the differences of their languages:

> Underlying all of Whorf's theoretical work is the fundamental assumption that the individual's conception of the world (including perception, abstraction, rationalization, categorization) is intimately related to the nature of his native language. ... However, a demonstration that certain languages differ from each other suggests but does not prove that the speakers of these languages differ from each other as a group in their psychological potentialities.

Lenneberg pursued a series of experiments designed to correlate linguistic variation with non-linguistic evidence of 'cognitive variation' which could presumably then be explained as a <u>result of</u> the linguistic variation. Chief among these experiments was the attempt to correlate color coding and color recognition by speakers of different languages (or even of the same language) with the quantity and type of color terms in those languages. A good brief survey of the work of Lenneberg and others in this field is in Roger Brown's 1976 memorial tribute to Lenneberg (Brown 1976).

It is clear then that the linguistic relativity thesis is an issue which has had a long career and which has been taken up in a number of different ways. In limiting my remarks below to a consideration of Humboldt's views, then, I plunge somewhat arbitrarily into the middle of this historical development. Nevertheless this arbitrariness can be somewhat mitigated by pointing out exactly what it is which I hope to gain by turning back to Humboldt again.

8.3 Humboldt's philosophical grounding of the linguistic relativity thesis

Once we separate the linguistic relativity thesis proper from the phenomena of the multiplicity and variation of languages, as I have suggested should be done, the problems of defining what is meant by this thesis and seeking to confirm or refute it shift from the areas of empirical study and comparison of differing languages to the area of philosophical consideration of language as such. For, just as Lenneberg argues against Whorf, no amount of evidence documenting differences between languages (whether lexical or grammatical) will ever serve to prove or disprove that language (any language) determines the way its speakers think. For Lenneberg what was necessary was some independent non-linguistic investigation of thinking against which we could compare the lexicon and grammar of differing languages, to see whether a correlation can be established. For Humboldt, however, the relationship of language and thought is primarily a philosophical problem. It cannot be examined through the comparative investigation of many languages; it cannot be studied through psychological experiments. These activities themselves will necessarily be dependent upon a prior conceptual definition, (or at very least an implicit theory), of what thinking is, what consciousness is, and how language is related to them. Thus to argue the LRT cannot, ultimately, mean only to point out differences between, say, Japanese and English; or even to point out correlations between color terminology and color recognition. It must also, and most importantly, necessitate giving a philosophical theory of what thought and language are <u>such that</u> it makes sense to say that language determines thought.

The reduction of the LRT to a philosophical theory seems to be a rarity in the literature on it; in Humboldt's period and earlier the LRT seems often advanced either as a comment on the variation of languages or as lip-service to conventional wisdom of the day. In Whorf (1956: 65-68, 240ff) there are occasional indications of philosophical definitions of thinking and language, but for the most part he rests his claims only on the evidence of language variation. Lenneberg and his followers are more interested in examining particular cognitive phenomena (e.g., categorization, recognition), relying on behavioral experiments as evidence for an influence of language on thought in specific cases, without caring to formulate a general philosophical theory. What we stand to gain by looking again at Humboldt's own statements of the LRT, accordingly, is a chance to see what sort of philosophical account of thinking and language is involved in the linguistic relativity thesis. Whether his account is representative of the tradition, or only certain parts of it, is an open question, which I shall not try to deal with here. Nevertheless, examination of the interconnection between Humboldt's philosophical views and his advocacy of the LRT is one preliminary way to get at the philosophical background and motivations for a thesis which has endured now for at least several centuries.

I shall quote here several representative passages where Humboldt states the linguistic relativity thesis, and then proceed to try to clarify what he means by it and show how it is based on the account of thinking and language which I have discussed in chapter two above:

(1)

> In one of my earlier academic lectures I have sought to direct attention to the fact that the variation of languages consists in more than the mere variation of signs, that the words and syntax at the same time form and determine the concepts, and that, considered in regard to their connection and influence on knowledge and sensation, the several languages are in fact several world views. (GS IV: 420)[213]

(2)

> Each language, no matter what it may be, carries at every point of its existence the expression of all the concepts which at that time can be developed in the nation. Each is, further, at every point in its life exactly equal to the conceptual range of the nation at that time. Each ultimately, in each of its states, developes the totality of a world-view, in that it contains expression for all representations which the nation makes about the world, and for all the sensation which the world brings forth in it.
>
> This proposition rests on the identity of thinking and speaking: what one can think one also is able to say. (GS V: 433)[214]

(3)

... in the vocabulary of a nation lie the collected concepts (Gedankenstoff) of a nation. (GS V: 411)[215]

(4)

Thinking is however not merely dependent on language in general, but also, to a certain extent, it is determined by each individual language. (GS IV: 21)[216]

(5)

A people speaks as it thinks and thinks so because it so speaks, and that it so thinks and speaks is essentially grounded in its corporeal and spiritual dispositions, ... (GS VI: 344)[217]

First let us try to separate the claim or claims made in these statements into distinct manageable parts.

A central claim certainly is that thinking is dependent upon language. The words and syntax of a language 'form and determine' (bilden und bestimmen) the concepts, and have an influence (Einfluss) on knowledge and sensation (1). Thinking (Denken) is dependent (abhängig) on language in general, determined (bestimmt) in each individual case by the particular language (4). A people thinks as it does 'because it so speaks' (5).

A closely related claim is that each language represents, at any given time, the total conceptual knowledge which that speaking community has developed, or has available to it. This is what he here calls the 'conceptual range' (Gedankenumfang) (2), or the 'total thought-substance' (gesammte Gedankenstoff) (3) of the nation. The point seems to be that, if thinking is dependent on language, then the potential thought possible for the speaker of a language is equal to the total conceptual content of that language, i.e., all the concepts which have words in the vocabulary of that language. In brief (and probably too simplistically) the total lexicon at any given time represents the total available constituent elements for any potential thought of the speaker of that language. (This would have to be modified in the case of people who know more than one language, of course, but the main point would still hold. These people would simply have expanded their total available potential conceptual material beyond the limits of their native language.) This formulation has a strange ring to it for several reasons, which I shall take up shortly. Nevertheless I think that this is a first approximation of what Humboldt means by a language being the 'gesammte Gedankenstoff' of the nation.

In that the language represents the aggregate of all possible thought constituents of a speaker, Humboldt calls this totality the 'world-view' of the nation (1,2). Here this often cited and sloganized term finds its terminological location in Humboldt's system. The 'world-view' (Weltansicht) can be clearly separated in meaning from the Humboldtian terms 'character' and 'inner form' of language. To say that a language represents the 'world-view' of its speakers does <u>not</u> point to some guiding national mood or tendency which has a pervasive <u>influence</u> on the language ('Charakter' of language; cf. passage (5): "corporeal and spiritual dispositions,") or to the particular lexical and syntactic <u>structure</u> of the language (its 'inner form'), but rather to the total conceptual content of the language. Primarily I think Humboldt here has in mind the lexicon of the language more than its grammatical rules. Helmut Gipper, in his writings on the LRT, has made some very helpful distinctions between the meanings of Weltansicht, Weltbild, and Weltanschauung, pointing out that Humboldt does <u>not</u> have in mind the ideological implications usually associated with the latter term.[218]

There are, then, two subtly different ways in which these quoted passages claim that thinking is determined or influenced by language. The first claim is that thinking is dependent upon language in general. This implies that every individual instance of thinking is determined by language. The second claim would seem to be that what a person can think is limited to the confines of the total conceptual possibilities of his language, his 'world-view'. In this second sense thought is determined by language in the sense that it is confined by it to a certain conceptual extension.

This second claim as to the determination of thought by language, although closely related to the first, seems a somewhat weaker claim, using a less significant sense of 'determining'. We may say, to use a non-linguistic example, that what I do in my daily activities is 'determined' by the total aggregate of things which I know how to do and am able to do, in the sense that it is 'limited' to that aggregate. I cannot get up tomorrow, for example, and play Chopin's First Piano Concerto, because playing the piano is not, at present, a potential constituent element of my activities, not part of my 'gesammte Welttätigkeit', to coin a term. Let us try a linguistic example. The French language has a word, 'chez', which has no equivalent in English. Although we can say all of its various meanings in English, such as 'at the house of' and 'with respect to', we do not have one 'thought-unit', as Humboldt would say, which is the same as the French have in this case. (German 'bei' on the other hand is closer to 'chez'.) In this sense the English speaker (who does not know French) has a determinate limitation put on his thought by the exclusion of the thought-unit 'chez' from his 'gesammte Gedankenstoff'. The French Weltansicht in this case differs from the English.

I have attempted briefly here to delineate two claims in the meaning of the 'linguistic relativity thesis' for Humboldt. The second claim, which I have already commented on briefly, is that the thought of a speaker is determined by the speaker's language as a whole, in the sense that it must move within that language's potentialities, move within it as a 'world-view'. Much more could be said about this sense of the LRT, particularly as it relates to the notion of creativity in languages. Now, however, I would like to turn to the other aspect of the LRT which has been delineated in the passages quoted above; namely that thinking in each and every case is determined by, because it is 'dependent upon', language.

With this claim it seems to me that we have reached the real core issue of the LRT. I argued that the multiplicity and variation of languages as such is quite irrelevant to the central claim of the LRT. If the LRT is true, then it would still be true if there were only one language. It is just that everyone's thought would be dependent upon the same language; there would only be one 'world-view'. I suggested further that the 'world-view' aspect of the LRT advances basically a weaker sense of the thesis, and is itself dependent upon the other claim, namely, that thought is always and in general dependent upon thinking.

Having reached this point, it is now evident that we have come full circle back to Humboldt's philosophical positions on thinking, consciousness, and language treated in chapter two. Indeed the fact that the linguistic relativity thesis in effect reduces to a claim that thinking needs or is dependent upon language is clearly stated in passage (2) quoted above: "this proposition rests on the identity of thinking and speaking"). It may seem then as if it is quite pedantic to speak of the 'philosophical foundations' of the LRT, as if the LRT were in fact quite distinct from some philosophical theory which serves as its 'foundation'. In a sense this criticism is justified. Chapter two is itself devoted to explaining what Humboldt meant by saying that thinking 'necessarily needs', or is 'dependent upon', language, that there can be no conscious thought without language. I have no intention of repeating that discussion here. Moreover, merely exposing the linguistic relativity thesis as little more than a restatement of the claim that thought must utilize language for its very existence is not my primary aim here. For, as mentioned above, Humboldt's account may be seen as providing a description (philosophical, psychological) of how 'linguistic determination of thought' works, of what happens when language determines thought. It is in this sense that an interesting philosophical distance exists between the LRT and Humboldt's philosophical claim that thinking needs language. Although the former may ultimately reduce to the latter, one may still ask how Humboldt envisaged the _process_ of linguistic determination as taking place. The answer to this question must be phrased in terms of his psychological description of intellectual activity; i.e., the interplay of thinking, consciousness, and language.

I suggest that an account of how linguistic determination of thinking takes place, following Humboldt's philosophical views, would go roughly as follows. In the development of consciousness out of simple pre-articulated 'thinking' (a level of awareness which man shares with the other animals), the initially chaotic flux or manifold of sensations and ideas is 'articulated' into thought-units. This production of thought-units is basic to the establishment of the subject-object structure which essentially defines 'consciousness' as opposed to mere thinking (cf. _Ueber Denken und Sprechen_). Language, in Humboldt's view, as well as for some of his predecessors, plays a necessary role in the production of these thought-units.

The thought-units ('concepts') created are of various kinds and complexity, of course. Supposing an initial manifold of thought to include a mixture of various kinds of sensations, instincts, and desires, the concepts formed or articulated out of this manifold, once 'reflection' or 'attention' comes about and consciousness is attained, may include 'simple' ones and then more complex ones constructed out of these 'simples'. Suppose we try to construct an example illustrating this basic viewpoint. Some simple concepts might be: brown, red, pain, near, warm, shaggy, sharp, hunger, wet. Suppose some complex concepts formed out of simples, for example: danger (near, pain), fish (brown, wet, hunger), friendly (near, no pain), dog (friendly, brown, shaggy, warm), etc. Humboldt's psychological scenario holds that as this stock of concepts is built up (precisely parallel with the growth of language) the particular constitution of the concepts (especially those of more complex physical objects, e.g., mountain range, city, and of 'abstract' things, e.g., property, law, love, justice) will be affected by the geographical and perceptual circumstances and the 'Charakter' of the nation or speaking community, whose 'homogeneous subjectivity' has an effect on the articulation of concepts such that the language becomes a 'national' linguistic 'Weltansicht' (GS VII: 60-61). In Vergl. Sprachstudium Humboldt says:

> The expressions of sensible objects are probably equivalent (i.e., in different languages) insofar as in all of them the same object is thought, but, since they express the determinate mode of it which is presented, their meaning in each case may be different. For the effect of the particular view of the object on the formation (Bildung) of the word also determines, as long as it remains active, how the word recalls the object. (GS IV: 29)[219]

In other words, as the language becomes richer, the concepts formed have a particular content, which reflects the circumstances of their formation and subsequent development. All complex concepts have a particular make-up of constituent parts (their definition or 'meaning'). All subsequent users of the language, and in general all users of any language, are committed to the meaning of the concepts in their language, in the sense that they must use these meanings, or work with them in defining 'new' concepts. When I am thinking about 'justice', for example, Humboldt would regard my thinking as made up of various concepts associated with justice; e.g., rights, distribution of goods, fairness, honor, equality, etc. which in turn have their own constituent elements. I may, of course, change my concept of justice over time; and it is not as if everyone always means the same thing by 'justice' or 'honor'. There may be variation as to what particular concepts, complex and simple, we are committed to in an ethical sense; but on Humboldt's view of thought our thinking is always and necessarily composed of some concepts, and they always bring with them previous meanings and associations. Thus while we may always change the concepts we are thinking about, change what our thinking is committing us to, in a sense, we can never escape the commitment itself to some conceptual meaning. It is in this sense, I think, that we must understand what Humboldt means by saying that language determines thought. We must use language (taken broadly, by Humboldt, as the concepts denoted by the words, as well as the phonetic forms and grammatical rules)[220] in thinking, but in doing so our thinking is always committed to this or that conceptual content which we take up and appropriate but never completely originate.

8.4. The conjunction of linguistic relativity with linguistic variation.

So far in this chapter I have been careful to separate the general claim of the linguistic relativity thesis from the problem of linguistic variation. Now, however, I want to point out some implications of the conjunction of the LRT with the fact that languages differ from one another. Humboldt's own discussion of the effect of language on thought often involves the complementary factor of variation among languages.

First it should be clear what language influences according to Humboldt. In chapter six I mentioned the 'priority problem'. One could regard as an inconsistency in Humboldt the fact that he seems to claim both (A) that differing national characters produce the variation of languages, and (B) that language determines thought and hence produces differing national characters. The criticism seems to be: Humboldt should make up his mind about priority; does character variation produce language variation or vice-versa?

This question is, however, unjustified. Humboldt does not say that language determines national character. As noted in the passages discussed above, he says that thinking (Denken) is determined by language, that language exercises an influence on the 'knowledge' and 'sensation' (Erkenntnis und Empfindung) of a nation. The title of the 1821 essay Entstehen promises to investigate the influence of grammatical forms 'on the development of ideas' (Ideenentwicklung), and the title of Einleitung relates the variation of languages to its influence 'on the spiritual development' (auf die geistige Entwicklung) of man.

The error in the dilemma posed above about priority of influence, accordingly, is simply that Humboldt did not hold (B). We might formulate his position about influence as follows. National character influences the character of the language which in turn influences the structure (form) of the language. The language in turn influences the thinking of the nation. The 'character' and 'thought' of a nation are not identical. For Humboldt, the former influences language, the latter is influenced by language.

This interpretation of Humboldt, which I believe dissolves the priority problem, is reinforced by his common description of character as a tendency or disposition of the nation, whereas thinking is never defined in this way. It is further reinforced by Humboldt's tendency to call the influence of language on thinking not simply an influence but a 'reverse' influence, 'Rückwirkung':

> In the effect of language back upon the intellect (In der Rückwirkung der Sprache auf den Geist) the true grammatical form makes the impression of a form, even where the attention is not intentionally directed upon it, and produces formal development. (GS IV: 309)[221]

> In the preceeding therefore we have been attentive (of the fact) that the thought taken up in language becomes an object for the soul, and exercises an effect upon it as thus something foreign coming to it. But we have regarded the object especially as arising out of the subject, and the effect as proceeding out of that upon which it reflects back (zurückwirkt). (GS V: 388)[222]

The conjunction of the linguistic relativity thesis with the variation of languages implies the consequence that the character variation of languages will have an effect upon the thought of individuals using the varying languages. In Humboldtian terms, if language A has been shaped by a 'spiritual' national character, for example, then it will subsequently influence its speakers to think in a 'spiritual' way. It is, I think, precisely Humboldt's intention to investigate the way the character variation of languages has had a subsequent effect upon the variation of the thinking of nations and individuals.

What remains then is to determine more concretely what sort of variation of thinking would occur as a result of character variation along a sensual / spiritual spectrum. One way to approach this question is by characterizing the intellectual products of a nation, that is, its literature, philosophy, poetry, etc. as showing a sensual or spiritual emphasis. This seems to be Humboldt's intention in some of his earlier writings on Greek culture, and is still his intention in the 1821 fragment Ueber den Einfluss des verschiedenen Charakters der Sprache auf Literatur und Geistesbildung.

A different aspect of the influence of language on thinking which Humboldt often emphasizes is what he calls the enhancement of 'formality in thinking' as a result of a highly inflectional grammatical system. This theme is particularly evident in Entstehen, as in the passage quoted above (GS IV: 309). He says, more generally, that the absence of true grammatical forms in a language inhibits the 'development of ideas':

> If now the cases where the designation of a grammatical relationship does not precisely correspond to the concept of a true grammatical form are numerous, if they constitute the peculiarity and the character of the language, then such a language is still far removed from suitability for the development of ideas, even if one were in a position to express everything in it. (GS IV: 290-1)[223]

A similar discussion can be found in Humboldt's essay on the grammatical structure of Chinese, of 1826. Here he asks:

> What corresponds in the soul to this reverse effect of language on the thought content via a complete designation of forms, and what must therefore be missing in the intellect of the speakers where (as in Chinese) such an effect is lacking or is weak? (GS V: 322)[224]

The effect of a 'formal grammatical structure', Humboldt says, is dispersed throughout the whole thought system (Denksystem). He gives in this passage some further indications as to what kind of influence over thinking a highly formal grammatical system will have:

> These so insignificant appearing forms allow to the intellect a freer flight, in that they present the means to lengthen and to intermingle sentences. The thought, which develops an unbroken unity in the mind (in

> dem Kopfe), finds this stability again in a language which organically connects all words. (GS V: 322)[225]

Although Humboldt does not link the question of 'formality' in thinking, viewed as influenced by the grammar of a language, with his discussion of 'sensual' and 'spiritual' national characters, one could use this theme to illustrate the path of influence as I have described it above. One could describe a 'spiritual' national character as promoting 'formality' in the grammatical structure of a language, and this formality, in turn, as influencing the thinking of the speakers by its promotion of the development of ideas. This would be one way of spelling out more concretely how the conjunction of the linguistic relativity thesis with the hypothesis of national character would transfer the 'character' difference into a 'Rückwirkung' of language over thought.

CONCLUSION

In this study I have concentrated primarily on Humboldt's writings on linguistics and philosophy of language. Humboldt's interests and influence, however, went far beyond issues of language, ranging, for example, into political theory, aesthetics, education, and anthropology. In conclusion I will try to give a brief indication of this broader perspective of Humboldt's interests and influence. While the specific philosophical views which I have examined in the earlier chapters do not always play a significant role in Humboldt's other writings, it is possible to observe some common themes emerge throughout the many disparate interests which he pursued. For example, his love of the classical languages, and his fascination with the concept of character, both individual and 'national', color his views on matters far removed from language and linguistics. By indicating this wider context of interests I hope to define the contribution which I feel the present study can make to a better understanding of Humboldt's thought.

One of Humboldt's earliest and most enduring interests was the theory of poetry. In the 1790s and early 1800s he became involved in the debate then current concerning the nature of poetic creation and communication. He became close friends with key members of the Romantic movement, especially Goethe, Schiller, and Christian Gottfried Körner. His participation in the discussion of aesthetic issues can be found in his correspondence with these, and other, thinkers, and in two important publications of the late 1700s: Ueber Goethes Hermann und Dorothea (1798), and an essay entitled Essais aesthétiques, published in a French journal in 1799. Many concerns surface in these writings, including the distinction between epic and lyric poetry, the debate between subjectivism and objectivism in the definition of art, and the issue as to whether art is properly defined as an imitation, 'Nachahmung', of nature. Humboldt's contribution to these issues has been discussed at length by Müller-Vollmer (1967, 1976).

In Ueber Goethes Hermann und Dorothea Humboldt argues that art, including poetry, communicates more by influencing the mind or disposition, 'Stimmung', of the perceiver, than by being an accurate or appropriate 'imitation of nature'.

> But it (i.e., the 'Nachahmung' account) contains an indeterminateness that can only be avoided if one does not seek the essence of art in the property of its object (as one has too often done previously), but rather in the disposition of the fantasy. (GS II: 132)[226]

> But it is not the intention of the poet to do more than influence the mind. (GS II: 137)[227]

Both in the essay on Hermann und Dorothea and in the later Essais aesthétique Humboldt argues that the most essential way in which a poem communicates is by influencing the mental disposition of the reader. In explicating and defending his position he is led to identify poetic creation and understanding primarily with the imagination. This is true not only in these early essays but also in the remarkably similar discussion thirty years later in the chapter 'Poesie und Prosa' in Einleitung.[228] A central part of Müller-Vollmer's argument (1967: 102; 1976: 228) that Humboldt's poetics is crucially influenced by German idealism, and especially by Fichte, seems to be an inference that Humboldt treats artistic imagination as an extension of the productive function of the ego in general.

Humboldt's foray into aesthetic theory did not gain approval from his peers in the Romantic movement, despite his high hopes (cf. Müller-Vollmer 1967: 72-75). Although he cannot be considered to have exercised any major influence on poetic theory, a case can be made that in fact his writings were ahead of their time, and anticipate positions developed by Baudelaire and his followers (Müller-Vollmer 1967: 108-110).

Although it is not clear that Humboldt himself explored the relationship between aspects of his philosophy of language and his poetics, I think it is clear that a strong systematic complementarity exists between these two areas. His assumptions about sound-symbolism and the effect of national character on language can be seen to provide a grounding theory to describe how the 'Stimmung' account of poetic understanding works. Thus despite the chronological discontinuity between his early consideration of poetics and his later essays on language and linguistics, there is a strong systematic continuity between claims which he advocates in these two areas.

From February of 1809 until April of 1810 Humboldt served as the minister of culture and education for the Prussian government. His actions in this period, and the essays on education he produced then and later, exercised both an immediate effect on German educational institutions and a central influence on educational theory up to the present day. He was successful in implementing a number of practical reforms at every level of education, from elementary schooling to the universities. Humboldt was not alone in this effort, of course. Many of these reforms had been proposed and discussed within liberal circles over the previous decade, and such prominent academics as Johann Gottlieb Fichte, Friedrich Wilhelm Schelling, and Friedrich Schleiermacher, had not only discussed the idea of a new university in Berlin, but had already given lectures there.[229] Nevertheless, Humboldt's personal energy and the power of his position enabled him to push these ideas into reality.

A basic theme in Humboldt's educational theory, as in other areas, is the primary importance of development of the individual. An educational institution (indeed the state as a whole) should be designed to foster the realization of every individual's character and essence. Humboldt is careful to separate the idea of 'Bildung', education which develops the whole individual, from the concept of vocational training, education which develops a specific skill. At the turn of the century most German schooling was oriented toward preparing students for a vocation. Even the universities were primarily oriented toward the professional faculties of law, medicine, and public service. Research in the sciences (including, in the broader German meaning of 'Wissenschaft', philosophy, philology, etc.) was often confined to the Academies. Humboldt restructured elementary and secondary schooling away from vocational training towards a broader curriculum, stressing the classical languages, philosophy, music, mathematics, and the natural sciences. In so doing he adopted many principles from the work of Johann Heinrich Pestalozzi, whose theories were being tested at that time both in Switzerland and in Germany[230], defending them on the principle of the total development of the child.

> With respect to instruction the viewpoint does not proceed, as was previously common, on the grounds that the child only learns to read, write, count, etc., but rather that all the higher capabilities of his body and soul are developed and exercised as harmoniously as possible, whereby those other skills will then arise by themselves. (GS X: 210)[231]

Humboldt's desire to further a broad-based curriculum carried over into his restructuring of the German university system. He was in an ideal position to promote this end by participating in the organization of the University of Berlin, a concept discussed over the previous decade and mandated by the Prussian king in 1807 (GS X: 139). In his vision of the university the whole spectrum of humanist and scientific disciplines, as well as the traditional faculties, are joined in one organization rather than left separated into the species of scientific institutes, universities, and academies (GS X: 141). Further, the university professors, as well as the students, must be allowed to pursue research and teaching in an academic environment free from considerations of income, career development, outside censorship, and the pursuit of specific economic or political utility.[232] Humboldt's reforms of the Prussian educational institutions had long lasting implications for education not only in Germany but also in North America, when the model of the German university was transported there in the late 19th century.

These issues have remained under consideration in the theory of education up to the present time, and indeed Humboldt's writings have remained an integral part of the modern discussion, perhaps most notably in the work of Clemens Menze.

As influential as Humboldt's work has proven for educational theory, however, his greatest influence was indubitably on the study of language. Not all of the concerns which interested him have remained dominant, of course. His basic orientation towards a <u>comparative</u> study of language has often made his ideas seem outdated or obscure to the structuralist movement in the twentieth century, although Chomsky has more recently attempted to reclaim Humboldt. On the other hand, his ideas have continued to be very influential in the development of the so-called 'inhaltbezogene Grammatik' developed in the early part of this century by Leo Weisgerber, Jost Trier, and others, which remains under active discussion today, for example, in the work of

Helmut Gipper (1963). Moreover, his writings on language have often exercised a cross-disciplinary influence over such sister disciplines as psychology. His discussion of 'national character', for example, was a guiding force behind the development of 'Völkerpsychologie' in the later part of the 19th century by Heymann Steinthal and Wilhelm Wundt.

It is perhaps an ironic result of the many-sidedness of Humboldt's interests that he has so often suffered from the image of being an intellectual dilettante who dabbled in many areas but was master of none. For insofar as this image of the man has helped perpetuate an image of his work and thought as fragmentary, disorganized, and unsystematic, it does him a grave disservice. The tendency to study Humboldt's contributions to various fields in an isolated fashion reproduces on a higher plane the tendency to study his ideas on language as a group of separate, essentially unrelated, themes. There is ample evidence to indicate that Humboldt was in fact a systematic, highly consistent thinker and that the inner coherence of his views was clear to him and remained remarkably unchanged over many years. In the present study I hope to have shown that a system of closely related ideas is present in Humboldt's work on language. Although I have not sought to take up exhaustively the whole scope of his work on language, the interconnections shown here can, I believe, be taken as a basic schema into which more detailed investigation of specific themes can be placed. If I have been able to clarify the systematic structure of Humboldt's ideas on language in this study, it can also be taken as evidence, at least by example, of a wider unity of thought throughout all the writings of this author.

NOTES

INTRODUCTION

1 The view that Humboldt's thought is unsystematic (or even confused) has dominated much of the secondary literature since the 1800s (cf Benfey 1869: 527) and still persists. In a recent article, for example, Humboldt's final work, Einleitung, is characterized as follows. "Il s'agit, non d'un développement systématique, mais plutôt de l'énoncé d'un certain nombre d'idées générales servant d'introduction à une étude particuliere." Luce Fontaine-De Visscher (1970: 452).

2 Einleitung, 1836, GS VII: 53: "Ich nehme hier das Verfahren der Sprache in seiner weitesten Ausdehnung, nicht bloss in der Beziehung derselben auf die Rede und den Vorrath ihrer Wortelemente, als ihr unmittelbares Erzeugniss, sondern auch in ihrem Verhältniss zu dem Denk- und Empfindungsvermögen. Der ganze Weg kommt in Betrachtung, auf dem sie, vom Geiste ausgehend, auf den Geist zurückwirkt." This paragraph first appears in Grundzüge, 1824-26, GS IV: 374. except that the last sentence concludes: "... auf den Geist zurückwirkt, im Individuum, in dem jedesmal lebenden Geschlecht und in der Nation durch mehrere Geschlechtes hindurch." Cf. also Nationalcharakter, 1822, GS IV: 430 and Einleitung, 1836, GS VII: 44.

3 Dualis, 1827, GS VI: 23: "Die Sprache ist aber durchaus kein blosses Verständigungsmittel, sondern der Abdruck des Geistes und der Weltansicht der Redenden, ..."

4 Cf. especially Roberta Graber Ross (1970), and Wilhelm Lammers (1936).

5 Both Ross (1970) and Roger L. Brown (1967) oc-

casionally argue that Humboldt's viewpoint undergoes substantial change over time.

6 Cf. for example, Grundzüge, 1824-26, GS IV: 374; Verschiedenheiten, 1827-29, GS VI: 151-152; and Einleitung, 1836, GS VII: 53.

7 Volker Heeschen, (1972: 5): "So anregend und vielschichtig die Lektüre von Liebrucks sein mag, so glauben wir doch berechtigt zu sein, nicht nur aufgrund des Umfangs seines Beitrags, sondern ebensosehr auch wegen der Eigenart desselben durchgängig auf Auseinandersetzung und Erwähnung verzichten zu können."

8 Cf. Gipper (1965: 15; Seidler (1967: 438); and Mueller (1966: 103). Cf. also Gipper and Schmitter (1975: 536).

CHAPTER ONE

9 Humboldt does often give references, in his linguistic writings, to many non-philosophical sources, such as grammars, dictionaries, and many contemporary works on linguistics and philology. It is rather hard to use these as evidence for philosophical influence however. Brown (1967: 99-102) tries hard to pursue this avenue in his discussion of the Kantian background of the work of the grammarians Gottfried Hermann and August Bernhardi. It is clear that Humboldt knew Hermann's studies of Greek grammar and Bernhardi's Sprachlehre (1801-1805) well, as attested by numerous citations. These citations occur, however, in the context of Humboldt's discussion of Greek phonetics and grammatical structure, in griech. Akzent., 1821, and in a short comparison of Greek and Sanskrit grammatical categories in 1828 (GS VI: 58-76). While Humboldt obviously valued the works of Hermann and Bernhardi as linguistic resources, it is doubtful that any definite and significant philosophical influences were transmitted to him through these primarily technical sources.

10 Cf. Leitzmann's description of Engel, in Humboldt, GS:VII: 465ff.

11 Engels Vortr., 1785-86, GS VII: 467.

12 Leitzmann notes (GS VII: 458): "Auch Kants (Wirkung) wird nur vorübergehend bei der Lehre von der

Idealität des Raumes gedacht, ohne dass seine Kritik Einfluss gewonnen hätte; Humboldt hat hier noch keine Anregung zu ernsterem Kantstudium empfangen können ... "

13 Engels Vortr., 1785-86, GS VII: 429: "Ich fahre fort, Leibnizens Ideenfolge nachzuspüren, und ihn selbst reden zu lassen; weil die die leichteste art ist, diese schweren und dunkeln Materien auseinanderzusezen "

14 Engels Vortr., 1785-86, GS VII: 429: "Es giebt nicht angebohrne Begriffe, aber angebohrene Grundgeseze."

15 Engels Vortr., 1785-86, GS VII: 413: "Die zweite Frage, in Ansehung der Kräfte der Dinge, ist, ob sie beständig und ununterbrochen fortwirken, oder nicht? Leibniz behauptete es; Lokke aber suchte ihn zu widerlegen. Indess hatte der erstere ohne Zweifel Recht. Denn, nach dem Lokkischen System, müsste jedesmal, da eine vorher unterbrochene Kraft wieder zu wirken anfinge, eine neue Schöpfung angenommen werden. Auch streitet die Erfahrung wider Leibnizens Meinung nicht."

16 Engels Vortr., 1785-86, GS VII: 369: "Definition des Begriffs. Leibniz nennt die blosse Vorstellung perceptionem, das Bewusstsein apperceptionem; den Begriff also perceptionem cum apperceptione conjunctam." "... Die blosse Vorstellung, an sich, giebt noch keinen Begriff. Denn es fehlt ihr das, zum Begriff nothwendige Bewusstsein."

17 For example, in the distinctions of clear, distinct, and obscure concepts; cf. GS VII: 380-384. On Leibniz's classifications of concepts cf. Robert McRae (1976: 70-71).

18 Tagebücher, 1798, GS XIV: 483-487: "Metaphysical conference between Jacquement, Cabanais, Tracy, La Romiguiere, Le Breton, Sieyes on the one hand, and Perret, Brinkmann and me on the other." (GS XIV: 483)

19 Tagebücher, 1798, GS XIV: 486: "Aller Philosophie liegt die reine Anschauung des Ichs, ausser aller Erfahrung, zum Grunde; entweder ausdrücklich, so dass man von ihr direct ausgeht, wie Fichte thut, oder nur stillschweigend, das man zeigt, die Erklärung der Phänomene führt auf so etwas, wie in Kant. Die Französen kennen dies schlechterdings nicht, haben weder Sinn dafür, noch Begriff davon, und so waren wir immer in zwei verschiednen Welten."

20 Tagebücher, 1798, GS XIV: 444-449, 479-481, 502-505, 509-511.

21 Tagebücher, 1798, GS XIV: 446: "Hier aber zeigt sich der grosse Fehler, dass alles als Erscheinung erklärt wird, dass die eigentliche Selbstthätigkeit, die nicht mehr erklart werden kann, überall verkannt, ... ist." See, similarly, 504, on the Traite des sensations: "Der Hauptfehler dieser Schrift ist wieder, dass sie weder Metaphysik, noch Psychologie, also eigentlich zu nichts brauchbar ist. Sie geht keinen Schritt aus den Phänomenen heraus, und will doch die Phänomene überhaupt erklären, sie ahndet nichts von einer ursprünglichen Kraft unsers Ichs und hat daher nie zureichende Erklärungsgrunde."

22 DuS, 1795-96, GS VII: 581-583.

23 Wilhelm Rössle (1952: 29): "... ich demonstrierte und demonstrierte, und nie brachten doch die Resultate eigentlich Ueberzeugung hervor."

24 Rössle (1952: 29): "... die Gegenstände selbst in ihrem ganzen Leben und ihrer Wahrheit anzuschauen, ..."

25 Rössle (1952: 30): "Wie ist nun da Wahrheit von Täuschung zu unterscheiden? Ich glaube durch kein anderes Mittel, als indem man den Gegenstand immerfort herumwendet und wieder von neuen Seiten betrachtet. Denn analyse der Begriffe kann, dünkt mich, da sie uns nie, auch nur mit dem kleinsten Schritte, aus dem Formalen heraus in das Materielle der Erkenntnis hinüberfuhrt, auch nicht einmal von kritischen Gebrauche heirbei sein. ... Sinnlichkeit ist, glaube ich, die einzige Bedingung, unter der wir neue Begriffe von aussen her erhalten können, jede Anschauung, die sich weder mittelbar noch unmittelbar auf Sinnlichkeit bezöge, würde ich für Sensation, nicht für Perzeption halten."

26 Rössle (1952: 48-49): "Meiner Empfindung nach ist zwischen Ihnen und Kant auch nicht der kleinste Berührungspunkt; überall gehen sie schlechterdings von einander ab. ... Bei Ihnen ist alles Erkennen unmittelbar, Offenbarung des Objekts, Perzeption des Subjekts, bei Kant Annehmen aus einer Art der Notwendigkeit. So nimmt er Dinge ausser uns überhaupt an, weil in unsern Vorstellungen, wenn wir sie entwickeln, doch etwas Materiales liegt, was sich auf etwas Wirkliches ausser uns beziehen muss, ...".

27 Rössle (1952: 60), letter to Friedrich Heinrich Jacobi, 22 August, 1791: "Vorzüglich beschäftigt mich jetzt wieder die Metaphysik. Ich habe mir vorgenommen, eine neue ernstliche Revision meiner eignen Ueberzeugungen vorzunehmen, und studiere das Kantische System von vorn an von neuem durch."

28 Albert Leitzmann (1900: 189): "Im Ganzen kann ich die Schrift nicht sehr wichtig nennen. Es ist mir keine einzige Idee aufgestossen, selbst den Grundsatz der Politik a priori nicht ausgenommen, welche nicht schon durch seine frühern Schriften gegeben wäre."

29 Leitzmann (1900: 213), letter to Schiller, 27 November, 1795.

30 Leitzmann (1900: 96): "Herders Parthenope ist ganz Herderisch, voll seiner Vorzüge, aber, wie es mir wenigstens scheint, auch seiner unarten. Das Stück hat im Ganzen einen schönen, ergreifenden Gang und einzelne unendlich liebliche Stellen, aber auch soviel Mystisches und ein so durchaus verbreitetes halbdunkel, dass mancher leicht daran irre werden kann." Cf. also Leitzmann (1900: 206-207).

31 Rössle (1952: 222): "Aber schrecklich ist es, dass er, auch nach dem Villers, immer noch nicht einsieht, dass Kantische Philosophie etwas anders als Lockische ist. Es wird mir immer mehr und mehr klar, dass nur unendlich wenige Menschen eigentlich fühlen, was Metaphysik ist, und dass wirklich aller Streit über Philosophie nur der zwischen diesen wenigen und der Menge ist -- ein Streit, in dem die ersteren die letzte blind und die letzte die ersteren verrückt nennt und der leicht interminabel sein mag. Denn ich, der ich immer sehr neutral bin, bin wirklich unentschieden, auf wessen Seite das Rechte ist."

32 Rössle (1952: 243), letter to Karl G. von Brinkmann, on 22 October, 1803: "Der deutschen Metaphysik, mit der Sie sich soviel beschäftigt haben, bin ich, wenn von Büchern die Rede ist, ganz abgestorben. Ich glaube aber auf metaphysische Ideen auf einem andern Weg gekommen zu sein. ... Fichtes absolutes Ich (ich rede aus blossen Erinnerungen) war mir sonst immer widrig und dunkel, weil es mir die wirklichen Ichs aufzuheben und ein durchaus chimärisches zu hypostasieren schein. Von dem Schellingschen Pantheismus habe ich kaum einen dunklen Begriff. Aber wenn sie mir zugeben, das in jeder Metaphysik ein fester und heller Punkt ist, von dem man

ausgeht und ein (nicht unsichrer, aber) dunkler, auf den man zugeht, so dünkt mich, nimmt Fichte zum ersten an, was eigentlich der letzte ist, das absolute, eigentliche Ich." Cf. also Rössle (1952: 244).

33 Cf. Leitzmann (1908), and Lefmann (1897).

34 Rössle (1952: 432): "In der Sprache glaube ich zwar, mich befestigt zu haben und selbst zu einer Einsicht gekommen zu sein, zu welcher die Philologie auf dem herkömmlichen Wege nicht führt. ... Aber das Lesen der Schriftsteller und der ästhetische und antiquarische Teil des Studiums leiden natürlich, da ich in meinen hauptsächlichen Untersuchungen eine andere Richtung genommen haben."

35 Kurt Müller-Vollmer (1976: 228): "Das Modell der menschlichen Geistestätigkeit, das der humboldtschen Kunst- und Sprachphilosophie zugrundeliegt, leitet sich aus der Wissenschaftslehre Fichtes her."

36 In conversation with the author in November, 1979.

CHAPTER TWO

37 Dualis, 1827, GS VI: 23: "Die Sprache ist aber durchaus kein blosses Verständigungsmittel, sondern der Abdruck des Geistes und der Weltansicht der Redenden, die Geselligkeit ist das unentbehrliche Hülfsmittel zu ihrer Entfaltung, aber bei weitem nicht der einzige Zweck, auf den sie hinarbeitet, ...".

38 Grundzüge, 1824-26, GS V: 377: "Ohne daher irgend auf die Mittheilung zwischen Menschen und Menschen zu sehn, ist das Sprechen eine nothwendige Bedingung des Denkens des Einzelnen in abgeschlossener Einsamkeit."

39 Grundzüge, 1824-26, GS V:374: "... die Sprache nicht bloss die Bezeichnung des, unabhängig von ihr geformten Gedanken, sondern selbst das bildende Organ des Gedanken ist."

40 DuS, 1795-96, GS VII: 581-583: I quote here from the translation by Nathan Rotenstreich (1974). The German text is as follows.

"1. Das Wesen des Denkens besteht im Reflectiren, d.h. im Unterscheiden des Denkenden von dem Gedachten.

2. Um zu reflectiren, muss der Geist in seiner

fortschreitenden Thätigkeit einen Augenblick still stehn, das eben Vorgestellte in eine Einheit fassen, und auf diese Weise, als Gegenstand, sich selbst entgegenstellen.

3. Die Einheiten, deren er auf diesem Wege mehrere bilden kann, vergleicht er wiederum unter einander, und trennt und verbindet sie nach seinem Bedürfniss.

4. Das Wesen des Denkens besteht also darin Abschnitte in seinem eignen Gange zu machen; dadurch aus gewissen Portionen seiner Thätigkeit Ganze zu bilden; und diese Bildungen einzeln sich selbst unter einander, alle zusammen aber, als Object, dem denkenden Subjecte entgegenzusetzen.

5. Kein Denken, auch das reinste nicht, kann anders, als mit Hülfe der allgemeinen Formen unsrer Sinnlichkeit geschehen; nur in ihnen können wir es auffassen und gleichsam festhalten.

6. Die sinnliche Bezeichnung der Einheiten nun, zu welchen gewisse Portionen des Denkens vereinigt werden, um als Theile andern Theilen eines grösseren Ganzen, als Objecte dem Subjecte gegenübergestellt zu werden, heisst im weitesten Verstande des Worts: Sprache."

41 DuS, 1795-96, GS VII: 582: "Der Sprache suchende Mensch sucht Zeichen, unter denen er, vermöge der Abschnitte, die er in seinem Denken macht, Ganze als Einheiten zusammenfassen kann."

42 Karl-Heinz Weimann (1965: 502), and cf. Aarsleff (1975: 397): "By virtue of his strong sense of the active role of words in thinking, Locke has much in common with von Humboldt."

43 Humboldt, Aeschylos Agamemnon metrisch übersetzt, 1816, GS VIII: 129: "Ein Wort ist so wenig ein Zeichen eines Begriffs, dass ja der Begriff ohne dasselbe nicht entstehen, geschweige denn fest gehalten werden kann; das unbestimmte Wirken der Denkkraft zieht sich in ein Wort zusammen, ... Nun ist es ein individuelles Wesen, von bestimmtem Charakter und bestimmter Gestalt, ...".

44 Humboldt, Ueber Religion, 1789, GS I: 60: "Ich verstehe aber hier unter der Vernunft das ganze intellektuelle Vermögen des Menschen, seine ganze Fähigkeit Ideen aufzufassen, seis durch Beobachtung der Sinne, oder durch das Anstrengen der Seele auf der Dinge innre Beschaffenheiten; und die aufgefassten Ideen zu verarbeiten durch Vergleichung, Verknüpfung und trennung."

45 Einleitung, 1836, GS VII: 54: "Er aber strebt nach

Vergleichung, Trennung and Verbindung und in seinen höheren Zwecken nach Bildung immer mehr umschliessender Einheit." Cf. also Vom gram. Baue, 1827-29, GS VI: 339-340: "Das zusammenhangende Denken, wie es der Selbstbetrachtung und der Rede zum Grunde liegt, besteht in einem Zusammennehmen des Einzelnen, einem Emporsteigen zu immer mehr unter sich befassender Einheit."

46 Cf. for example, the notion of an 'ursprüngliche Articulationsinn', at Einleitung, 1836, GS VII: 117.

47 vergl. Sprachstudium, 1820, GS IV: 26: "Der Mensch denkt nur vermittelst der Sprache; ..."; Entstehen, 1821, GS IV: 307: "Das Denken, welches vermittelst der Sprache geschieht, ..."; and Einleitung, 1836, GS VII: 162: "Denn da das Bedürfniss des Denkens die Sprache im Menschen weckt ...".

48 vergl. Sprachstudium, 1820, GS IV: 17: "Das durch die ganze Sprache herrschende Princip ist Articulation; der wichtigste Vorzug jeder feste und leichte Gliederung; diese aber setzt einfache, und in sich untrennbare Elemente voraus. Das Wesen der Sprache besteht darin, die Materie der Erscheinungswelt in die Form der Gedanken zu giessen; ...".

49 vergl. Sprachstudium, 1820, GS IV: 23: "Das Wort, welches den Begriff erst zu einem Individuum der Gedankenwelt macht, ...".

50 Humboldt, Versuch einer Analyse der mexikanischen Sprache, 1821, GS IV: 248: "Aus der Masse des unbestimmten, gleichsam formlosen Denkens reisst ein Wort eine gewisse Anzahl von Merkmalen heraus, verbindet sie, giebt ihnen ... Gestalt und Farbe und individualisirt sie dadurch."

51 Grundzüge, 1824-26, GS V: 374-375: "... die Sprache nicht bloss die Bezeichnung des, unabhängig von ihr geformten Gedanken, sondern selbst das bildende Organ des Gedanken ist. Die intellectuelle Thätigkeit, durchaus geistig, durchaus innerlich, und gewissermassen spurlos vorübergehend, wird durch den Ton in der Rede äusserlich und wahrnehmbar für die Sinne, und erhält durch die Schrift einen bleibenden Körper ... Die intellectuelle Thätigkeit und die sprache sind daher Eins und unzertrennlich von einander; man kann nicht einmal schlechthin die erstere als das Erzeugende, die andre als das Erzeugte ansehen. ... Die intellectuelle Thätigkeit ist an die Nothwendigkeit geknüpft, eine

Verbindung mit dem Ton einzugehen, das Denken kann sonst nicht zur Deutlichkeit gelangen, die Vorstellung nicht zum Begriff werden."

52 Grundzüge, 1824-26, GS V: 428: "..., der Begriffe aber erst selbst seine Vollendung durch das Wort erhält, und beide nicht von einander getrennt werden können. Dies zu verkennen, und die Wörter als blosse Zeichen anzusehen, ist der Grundirrthum, der all Sprachwissenschaft und alle richtige Würdigung der Sprache zerstört."

53 Dualis, 1827, GS VI: 26: "Er wird erzeugt, indem er sich aus der bewegten Masse des Vorstellens losreisst, und, dem Subject gegenüber, zum Object bildet."

54 Cf. for example, Vom gram. Baue, 1827-29, GS VI: 356-359, 361; Einleitung, 1836, GS VII: 53-57, 66-67, 79-80.

55 For example, the passage at Einleitung, 1836, GS VII: 53, is used earlier in Verschiedenheiten, 1827-29, GS VI: 152, and in Grundzüge, 1824-26, GS V: 374, quoted above.

56 Descartes (1976: xlvii). These comments illuminate the problem being discussed here, and it may be helpful to quote them at length. "The most important problem of a Descartes translation is the rendering of the verbs cogitare and penseur and their derivatives. Since Locke, the traditional English renderings have been the verb think and the noun thought. We have decided to abandon this tradition, which seems to us to run the risk of seriously misrepresenting what Descartes says. In everyday seventeenth century French, pensée had a rather wider application than in modern French; it was then natural, as it would not now be, to call an emotion une pensée. Similarly, cogitare and its derivatives had long been used in a very wide sense in philosophical Latin; ... Now, as may be seen, ... think and thought in English have always had a predominently intellectual reference; thought is naturally taken to be a cognitive process; and it would be most unnatural to call an act of will, and still more a fit of anger or a toothache, a 'thought'. To use think and thought as the standard rendering for cogitare and penser and their derivatives gives Descartes' conception an intellectualistic cast that is not there in the original."

57 Cf. McRae (1976: 15): "When Locke asserts a necessary connection between (present) thought and cons-

ciousness, he uses the word thought in the same broad way as Descartes, so that it covers everything of which we are conscious within ourselves, including pleasures and pains, and the perceptions of sense."

58 Descartes (1976: xlvii): "Locke's polemic against the idea that the soul always 'thinks' ... is pretty clearly ignoratio elenchi resulting from a misleading translation."

59 See, for example, Hobbes, Leviathan (1651), part 1, chap. 3; and also De Corpore chap. 3 (in Hobbes 1962: 32-33). In Locke, see Essay concerning Human Understanding, Bk. II, XIV, 3-4; II, VIII, 9; II, XIV, 13-14, and II, XIX, 1. In Kant the characterization of 'thinking' as mental activity 'prior' to the structure imposed by the categories, is always an abstract view of thinking, much more so than for the empiricists. Nevertheless, cf. his discussions of the 'sensory manifold' and the flux of 'inner sense' at Critique of Pure Reason A 107 and A 381. Also see the discussion of inner sense in the Anthropology (Kant 1974a: 39): "Inner sense is not pure apperception, consciousness of what we are doing; for this belongs to the power of thinking. It is, rather, consciousness of what we undergo insofar as we are affected by the play of our own thoughts."

60 Kant (1974b: 70). On the perception and consciousness of animals cf. also Leibniz (1951: 418ff, =1981: 134-140).

61 Gilbert Ryle (n.d.: 17-20).

62 Cf. Descartes (1973: Vol. I, 52): "Idea is a word by which I understand the form of any thought, that form by the immediate awareness of which I am conscious of that said thought; ... And thus it is not only images depicted in the imagination that I call ideas; nay, to such images I here decidely refuse the title ideas, ...". Cf. Leibniz (1951: 281, 418; 1981: 134).

63 E.g., Locke, Essay I, III, 21: "..., that whatever idea, being not actually in view, is in the mind, is there only by being in the memory; and if it be not in the memory, it is not in the mind, ...".

64 Cf. especially Leibniz (1951: 281): "What I mean by an idea is not a certain act of thinking, but a power or faculty such that we have an idea of a thing even if we are not actually thinking about it ...", and cf. McRae (1976: 74).

65 Cf. Locke, Essay II, XXII, 4: The complex idea "... has its unity from an act of the mind, combining those several simple ideas together, and considering them as one complex one, consisting of those parts; and the mark of this union, or that which is looked on generally to complete it, is one name given to that combination." Also cf. III, V, 19; II, VI, 39; III, III, 20; and II, XVIII, 7.

66 Descartes was skeptical about the influence of language on thinking. In his reply to Hobbes (Descartes 1973: Vol. II, 66), concerning the third meditation, he says; "Moreover, in reasoning we unite not names but the things signified by the names; and I marvel that the opposite can occur to anyone. For who doubts whether a Frenchman and a German are able to reason in exactly the same way about the same things, though they yet conceive the words in an entirely diverse way?"

67 Cf. McRae (1976: 130): "Thought is dependent upon sensible signs, whether natural or conventional. Despite, however, the immense potentialities which Leibniz, more perhaps than anyone else, attributed to the use of characters for bringing the human mind to its highest perfection, he did not take the view that they were essential to thought. He did not ... consider thought to be by nature internal speech. The original function of language was for Leibniz merely that of an instrument for the communication of thought." Compare the Dialogue of 1677, in Leibniz (1969: 183).

CHAPTER THREE

68 Cf. for example, Stephen Ullmann (1962: 55ff); and Gordon 1982.

69 Norman Kretzmann (1968: 180).

70 Kretzmann (1968: 187-188): "I have been calling this the argument from the doctrine of representative ideas because it is representative ideas, those that Locke thinks have corresponding non-ideas as their originals, that constitute the cases in which Locke's main thesis applies in full detail. Once it becomes clear that it is only immediately that words signify nothing but the user's ideas, it is clear also that where the ideas immediately signified are themselves signs --that is, are representative ideas-- their originals may be

mediately signified by those words."

71 Vom gram. Baue, 1827-29, GS VI/2: 361: "Es tritt alsdann eine zweifache Bezeichnung in die Sprache ein: die der Begriffe durch Wörter, und die der Verknüpfungen durch Gestaltung der Wörter, durch eigne Wörter oder auf andre, nunmehr näher zu beleuchtende Weise.". Cf. also Einleitung, 1835, GS VII: 78, 120: "Die Ideenentwicklung erfordert ein zweifaches Verfahren, ein Vorstellen der einzelnen Begriffe und eine Verknüpfung derselben zum Gedanken."

72 Einleitung, 1836, GS VII: 72-73: "Unter Wörtern versteht man die Zeichen der einzelnen Begriffe."; "... Da die Wörter immer Begriffen gegenüberstehen, ..."; and Grundzüge, 1824-26, GS V: 427: "Das Wort, als Bezeichnung des Begriffs, ...".

73 Entstehen, 1821, GS IV: 305: "Die Sprache bezeichnet ursprünglich Gegenstände, ...".

74 Einleitung, 1836, GS VII: 78: "In dem ganzen Bereiche des in der Sprache zu Bezeichnenden unterscheiden sich zwei Gattungen wesentlich von einander: die einzelnen Gegenstände oder Begriffe und solche allgemeine Beziehungen, die sich mit vielen der ersteren theils zur Bezeichnung neuer Gegenstände oder Begriffe, theils zur Verknüpfung der Rede verbinden lassen."

75 Kretzmann (1968: 188).

76 Grundzüge, 1824-26, GS V: 436: "... die Bezeichnung erst das Entstehen des zu Bezeichnenden vor dem Geist vollendet. Selbst bei Naturgegenständen ist dies der Fall, da das Wort ja nicht sie überhaupt, sondern die in der Sprache gegründete Ansicht derselben bezeichnet." Cf. also Grundzüge, 1824-26, GS V: 424: "..., und da das Wort nicht unmittelbar von dem Gegenstande, sondern von dessen Auffassung abhängt, ...".

77 vergl. Sprachstudium, 1820, GS IV: 23-24: "Das Object, dessen Erscheinung im Gemüth immer ein durch die Sprache individualisirter, stets gleichmässig wiederkehrender Eindruck begleitet, wird auch in sich auf eine dadurch modificirte Art vorgestellt."

78 Einleitung, 1836, GS VII: 89: "Wie bei der Lautform als die beiden hauptsächlichsten zu beachtenden Punkte die Bezeichnung der Begriffe und die Gesetze der Redefügung erschienen, ebenso ist es in dem inneren,

intellectuellen theil der Sprache. Bei der Bezeichnung tritt auch heir, wie dort, der Unterschied ein, ob der Ausdruck ganz individueller Gegenstände gesucht wird oder Beziehungen dargestellt werden sollen, welche, auf eine ganze Zahl einzelner anwendbar, diese gleichförmig in einen allgemeinen Begriff versammeln, so dass eigentlich drei Fälle zu unterscheiden sind. Die Bezeichnung der Begriffe, unter welche die Beiden ersteren gehören, machte bei der Lautform die Wortbildung aus, welcher hier die Begriffsbildung entspricht."

79 Engels Vortr., 1785-86, GS VII: 373.

80 For example, in section 21 of Vergl. Sprachstudium, 1820, GS IV: 28-29, Humboldt speaks first of "die Ausdrücke für unsinnliche Gegenstände", and then, in a derivative sense, of 'sinnlicher und unsinnlicher Ausdrücke ...".

81 Grundzüge, 1824-26, GS V: 423: "... und es entstehen mithin bei jedem Worte die Fragen: was fasst das Wort, als seinen Gegenstand, zusammen? wie bezeichnet es dies Zusammengefasste? und welchen Nebenbegriff verbindet es, nach begleitendem Gefühle, mit dieser Bezeichnung?

82 Grundzüge, 1824-26, GS V: 416: "In der Wahl der Laute für die Begriffe lässt sich die Sprache natürlich durch die klareren und dunkleren Beziehungen leiten, welche das Gefühl und die Einbildungskraft, der Individualität der Nationen gemäss, under ihnen findet."

83 Grundzüge, 1824-26, GS V: 426: "Ursprünglich liegt diese Bezeichnung (die eigentlich nur in Beziehung auf den Hörenden eine solche, von Seiten des Sprechenden aber eine Auffassung ist) in jedem Wort, bei den den Naturlauten nachgebildeten in dem Tönen der Gegenstände, bei andren für körperliche Dinge in andren ihrer Eigenschaften, bei intellectuellen in den zu ihrer Andeutung gewählten Metaphern."

84 Cf. also Grundzüge, 1824-26, GS V: 421: "Die Ausdrücke für körperliche Gegenstände sind gewiss zum grössten Theile aus Eigenschaften entstanden, die an denselben vorzüglich auffielen, und sind nichts anders, als zu Adjectiven gewordene Substantiva, unsinnliche Begriffe werden metaphorisch nach körperlichen bezeichnet, ...".

85 Einleitung, 1836, GS VII: 76: "Das Zusammenhang

zwischen dem Laute und dessen Bedeutung vorhanden ist, scheint gewiss; die Beschaffenheit dieses Zusammenhanges aber lässt sich selten vollständig angeben, oft nur ahnden und noch viel öfter gar nicht errathen."

86 Einleitung, 1836, GS VII: 76-78. English translation here is taken from Humboldt, Linguistic Variability and Intellectual Development, trans. G.C. Buck and F.A. Raven (Humboldt 1971: 52-54).

87 Einleitung, 1836, GS VII: 76: "... wie stehen, stätig, starr den Eindruck des Festen, das Sanskritische li, schmelzen, auseinandergehen, den des Zerfliessenden, nicht, nagen, Neid den des Fein und scharf Abschneidenden. Auf diese Weise erhalten ähnliche Eindrücke hervorbringende Gegenstände Wörter mit vorherrschend gleichen Lauten, wie wehen, Wind, Wolke, wirren, Wunsch, in welchen allen die schwankende, unruhige, vor den Sinnen undeutlich durcheinandergehende Bewegung durch das aus dem, an sich schon dumpfen und hohlen u verhärtete w ausgedrückt wird."

88 Einleitung, 1836, GS VII: 77 (Buck and Raven 1971: 53).

89 A good treatment of onomatopoeia, sound-symbolism, and word-motivation more generally, is included in Ullmann (1962: chapter 4). He treats 'sound-symbolism' as a secondary form of onomatopoeia; thus his three part distinction of (1) primary onomatopoeia; (2) secondary onomatopoeia; (3) morphological and semantic motivations, corresponds quite closely in spirit to Humboldt's distinctions discussed here.

90 T.V. Gamkrelidze (1974: 107)

91 Einleitung, 1836, GS VII: 109: "In allen hier zusammengefassten Fällen liegt in der innerlichen Bezeichnung der Wörter ein Doppeltes, dessen ganz verschiedene Natur sorgfältig getrennt werden muss. Es gesellt sich nemlich zu dem Acte der Bezeichnung des Begriffes selbst noch eine eigne, ihn in eine bestimmte Kategorie des Denkens oder Redens versetzende Arbeit des Geistes, und der volle sinn des Wortes geht zugleich aus jenem Begriffsausdruck und dieser modificierenden Andeutung hervor. Diese beiden Elemente aber leigen in ganz verschiedenen Sphären."

92 Vom gram. Baue, 1827-29, GS VI/2: 337: "Die Wörter stellen grossentheils körperliche Gegenstände dar. Was

die Grammatik bezeichnet, ist nichts Körperliches, nichts Sichtbares, kommt nirgends in der Aussenwelt vor, schwebt nur, wie eine unkörperliche form, an den Dingen, insofern eine Vorstellungskraft sie in sich aufnimmt, besteht durchaus in intellektuellen Verhältnissen."

93 Entstehen, 1821, GS IV: 285. Thus he wants to ask: "... wie in einer Sprache diejenige Bezeichnungsart grammatischer Verhältnisse entsteht, welche eine Form zu heissen verdient?"

94 Entstehen, 1821, GS IV: 295: "Was in einer Sprache ein grammatisches Verhältniss charakteristisch (so, dass es im gleichen Fall immer wiederkehrt) bezeichnet, ist für sie grammatische Form." Cf. further GS IV: 289. We investigate the determinate forms a language uses to "... jedes grammatische Verhältniss bezeichnet." Cf. also 291, and Vom gram. Baue, 1827-29, GS VI/2: 343.

95 See Vom gram. Baue, 1827-29, GS VI/2: 361; and also Entstehen, 1821, GS IV: 291: "Die Wörter, und ihre grammatischen Verhältnisse sind zwei in der Vorstellung durchaus verschiedne Dinge. Jene sind die eigentlichen Gegenstände in der Sprache, diese bloss die Verknüpfungen, aber die Rede ist nur durch beide zusammengenommen möglich."

96 Vom gram. Baue, 1827-29, GS VI/2: 360: "Zum Ausdruck verschiedner Gedanken muss sich der Sprechende derselben Wörter bedienen. Er muss diese Zeichen einzelner Begriffe alsdann von demjenigen entkleiden, was nur der bestimmten Verbindung angehört. Indem er auf diese Weise das bleibende Begriffzeichen von dem wechselnden Verbindungslaut scheidet, ...".

97 Bau der chines., 1826, GS V: 310: "Die Grammatik andrer Sprachen hat zwei abgesonderte Theile, einen etymologischen und einen syntaktischen, in der chinesischen Grammatik findet sich bloss dieser letztere. ... Mann muss unmittelbar das Wörterbuch zu Hülfe nehmen, und die Construction ergeibt sich bloss aus der Wortbedeutung, der Stellung und dem Sinne der Rede."

98 Vom gram. Baue, 1827-29, GS VII/2: 378: "Die grammatische Formung der Wörter (der sogenannte etymologische Theil der Grammatik) bereitet nur die Redeverbindung vor. Diese selbst bestimmen erst die Gesetze der Construction (der syntaktische theil der Grammatik)."

99 Vom gram. Baue, 1827-29, GS VI/2: 379.

[100] Vom gram. Baue, 1827-29, GS VI/2: 376: "Das grammatische Verhältniss wird nicht immer in seiner reinen Allgemeinheit aufgefasst. Wenn alsdann etwas Besondres in ihm zurückbleibt, so entsteht auch wohl eine Reihe von Formen an der Stelle einer einzelnen. Dies ist der Fall, wenn das Activum durch Einverleibung des Pronominalaccusative in das Verbum bezeichnet wird."

[101] Vom gram. Baue, 1827-29, GS VI/2: 371-372: "Sie können aber auch ganz eigentlich aus dem Gefühle des grammatischen Zwecks, dem sie dienen, entstanden seyn, und werden alsdann zu symbolischen ... Das Symbolische liegt gewöhnlich in einer solchen Umänderung, wie z.B. in der Reduplication als Charakteristik der Vergangenheit: es kann aber auch an der Natur der Buchstaben hängen, und alsdann entsteht, ebenso als bei den Wörtern, ein analogischen Zusammenhang zwischen dem Begriff und dem ihn bezeichnenden Laut."

CHAPTER FOUR

[102] Cf. Whorf (1956: esp. 57-64); and the review with bibliography of Lenneberg's work by Roger Brown (1976: 125-153).

[103] vergl. Sprachstudium, 1820, GS VII: 27: "Ihre Verschiedenheit ist nicht eine von Schällen und Zeichen, sondern eine Verschiedenheit der Weltansichten selbst. Hierin ist der Grund, und der letzte Zweck aller Sprachuntersuchung enthalten." Cf. also GS VII: 602.

[104] Nationalcharakter, 1822, GS IV: 420: "Ich habe in einer meiner früheren akademischen Vorlesungen die Aufmerksamkeit darauf zu richten versucht, dass die Verschiedenheit der Sprachen in mehr, als einer blossen Verschiedenheit der Zeichen besteht, dass die Wörter und Wortfügungen zugleich die Begriffe bilden und bestimmen, und dass, in ihrem Zusammenhange, und ihrem Einfluss auf Erkenntniss und Empfindung betrachtet, mehrere Sprachen in der That mehrere Weltansichten sind."

[105] Einleitung, 1836, GS VII: 86-87: "Bei der Lautform ist eine unendliche, nicht zu berechnende Mannigfaltigkeit begreiflich, ... Was aber, wie der intellectuelle Theil der Sprache, allein auf geistiger Selbstthätigkeit beruht, scheint auch bei der Gleichheit des Zwecks und der Mittel in allen Menschen gleich seyn zu müssen; und eine grössere Gleichförmigkeit bewahrt dieser Theil der

Sprache allerdings. Aber auch in ihm entspringt aus mehreren Ursachen eine bedeutende Verschiedenheit."

106 Einleitung, 1836, GS VII: 192: "Weit mehr aber, als bei den einzelnen Wörtern zeichnet sich die intellectuelle Verschiedenheit der Nationen in den Fügungen der Rede, ...".

107 Cf. Dualis, 1827, GS VI: 21, and Grundzüge, 1824-26, GS V: 454.

108 Einleitung, 1836, GS VII: 91: "Man bemerkt aber diesen Einfluss der nationellen Eigenthümlichkeit in der Sprache auf eine zwiefache Weise: an der Bildung der einzelnen Begriffe und an dem verhältnissmassig verschiedenen Reichthum der Sprache an Begriffen gewisser Gattung."

109 Humboldt, Ueber die in der Sanskritsprache durch die Suffixa twa und ya gebildeten Verbalformen, 1822, GS IV: 393: "So ist also das Gerundium nicht bloss eine Form gewisser Sprachen, sondern nach Begriffen der allgemeinen Grammatik gerechtfertigt, und als nothwendig dargestellt. Als Zwischenglied zwischen dem reinen Infinitiv und dem Verbalsubstantiv bedarf es sogar einer eignen Benennung."

110 The passage in German, from Ueber die in der Sanskritsprache durch die Suffixa twa and ya gebildeten Verbalformen, 1822, GS IV: 360, is as follows: "Wenn man die grammatischen Formen verschiedener Sprachen mit Rücksicht auf das vergleichende Sprachstudium untersucht, läuft man leicht Gefahr auf zwei Abwege zu gerathen, indem man entweder diese Formen gänzlich nach ähnlichen bekannter Sprachen beurtheilt, ...". Brown translates: "When one investigates the grammatical forms of various languages with respect to universal grammar, one runs slight danger of going astray, since one either judges these forms completely according to similar known languages, ...". The first part of this passage, however, surely should be read as: "When one investigates the grammatical forms of various languages with respect to the comparative study of language, one easily runs the danger of going astray in two ways, in that either ...".

111 Grundzüge, 1824-26, GS V: 450: "Das Gemeinsame in der Grammatik kann nur aus der Natur und dem Wesen der Sprache, den Gesetzen des Denkens und der Beschaffenheit der Sprachorgane, an sich und in ihrem Verfahren, her-

rühren, und nur die beiden ersten Stücke lassen Herleitungen aus blossen Begriffen zu."

112 Grundzüge, 1824-26, GS V: 453: "Die Gleichheit der Gesetze des Denkens bringt das Gemeinsame der Grammatik aller Sprachen hervor, vermöge dessen alle sich auf die allgemeine Grammatik und eine auf die andre beziehen lassen. Jede grammatische form lässt sich, in irgend einer Art sie wiederzugeben, in jeder Sprache nachweisen, ...".

113 Vom gram. Baue, 1827-29, GS VI: 342: "Die allgemeine Grammatik ist der Kanon, auf den jede einer besondren Sprache bezogen werden muss, in Rücksicht auf den überhaupt grammatische Sprachvergleichung möglich ist. Denn sie umfasst und entwickelt, was, vermöge der Einerleiheit der Gesetz des Denkens und der wesentlichen Natur der Sprache, in allen Mundarten Gemeinsames leigt."

114 Vom gram. Baue, 1827-29, GS VI: 374: "Der allgemeine grammatische Typus verliert seine abstracte Begriffsnatur, so wie er in das gestaltenreiche Leben der Sprache eintritt."

115 Vom gram. Baue, 1827-29, GS VI: 345-346: "Die Grundbestimmungen der Grammatik sind schon in den allgemeinen Gesetzen des Denkens enthalten. ... In diesem Theile fällt die allgemeine Grammatik mit der Logik gewissermassen zusammen, aber beide Lehren müssen, auch in dem Umfange, in dem sie sich wirklich berühren, sorgfältig jede in ihren eigenthümlichen Gränzen gehalten werden. ... Das logische Urtheil und der grammatische Satz stehen durch alle ihre Arten und Unterarten hindurch, in der Verbindung und Trennung der Begriffe genau auf derselben Linie. Aber die Logik behandelt diese idealen Verhältnisse bloss an und für sich, im Gebiete der Möglichkeit, des absoluten Seyns. Die Sprache setzt sie in einem bestimmten Moment, und stellt das Subject, als das Prädicat, thätig oder leidend, an sich reissend oder zurückstossend dar. Dadurch wird der todte Verhältnissbegriff, gleichsam das Verbindungszeichen der mathematischen Gleichung, zu lebendiger Bewegung." Cf. also Grundzüge, 1824-26, GS V: 452.

116 Vom gram. Baue, 1827-29, GS VI: 340-341: "Die grammatischen Verhältnisse müssen in allen Sprachen auf irgend eine Weise erkennbar seyn. ... Die Art aber, wie diesen Forderungen genügt wird, ist nicht in allen die nämliche." Cf. also GS VI: 374.

117 This three part division appears most clearly in Dualis, 1827, GS VI: 21, and in Grundzüge, 1824-26, GS V: 454.

118 Vom gram. Baue, 1827-29, GS VI: 343: "Unsre gegenwärtige Untersuchung hat es daher nicht bloss mit der Bezeichnung, der materiellen Darstellung der grammatischen Verhältnisse, sondern ganz vorzüglich auch mit der Verschiedenheit ihrer idealen Ansicht in Vergleichung mit der Einen unwandelbaren der allgemeinen Grammatik zu thun."

119 On the distinction of ausdrücklichen and stillschweigenden grammar, cf. Grundzüge, 1824-26, GS V: 462f.; Bau der chines., 1826, GS V:319; and Vom gram. Baue, 1827-29, GS VI: 364.

120 Bau der chines., 1826, GS V: 319: "In der Grammatik jeder Sprache giebt es einen ausdrücklich bezeichneten und einen stillschweigend hinzugedachten Theil."

121 Entstehen, 1821, GS IV: 287: "Die grammatischen Verhältnisse insbesondre hängen durchaus von der Absicht ab, die man damit verbindet. Sie kleben weniger den Worten an, als sie von dem Hörenden und Sprechenden hineingedacht werden."

122 Grundzüge, 1824-26, GS V: 469: "Wenn eine grammatische Form auch keine Bezeichnung in der Sprache besitzt, so ist sie, als leitendes Gesetz des Verständnisses doch in denen vorhanden, welche die Sprache reden."

123 Cf. Roger L. Brown (1967: 104); and B. den Ouden (1975: 42)

124 Grundzüge, 1824-26, GS V: 452-453: "So fliessen die vier ersten Casus der Declination von selbst und nothwendig aus der Kategorie der Relation, und diese Ableitung liesse noch einen fünften, den der Wechselwirkung zu; der Instrumentalis und Locativus dagegen entstehen erst durch die Dazwischenkunft der Begriffe des Werkzeugs und des Orts. Der gleiche Unterschied findet sich zwischen dem Conjunctivus, als nothwendigem Gegensatz des Indicativus, und dem Optativus, neben dem es noch manche andre modi des Pflegens, Müssens, u.s.f. geben könnte und giebt, zwischen dem Passivum, als nothwendigem Gegensatz des Activum, und der 9 und 11 Conjugationsform der Araber, die sich nur auf gewisse

Gegenstände, Farben, Körperfehler, bezieht, zwischen dem Pluralis, als nothwendigem Ausdruck der Mehrheit, und dem Dualis, welcher zufällig eine eigne Form für eine einzelne bestimmte Zahl einführt, u.s.f."

125 Grundzüge, 1824-26, GS V: 463: "In Sprachen ohne Casusbeugung, oder mit unvollkommener, sich nicht bestimmt unterscheidender, muss das in der Rede gemeinte grammatische Verhältniss hinzugedacht werden, da die Sprache es in ihren Lauten nicht anzeigt."

126 Cf. for example, Vom gram. Baue, 1827-29, GS VI: 340: "Die grammatischen Verhältnisse müssen in allen Sprachen auf irgend eine Weise erkennbar seyn."

127 See for example, Einleitung, 1836, GS VII: 87: "Einestheils wird sie (i.e., Verschiedenheit) durch die vielfachen Abstufungen hervorgebracht, in welchen, dem Grade nach, die Spracherzeugende Krafte, ... wirksam ist."

128 Einleitung, 1836, GS VII: 66. On deaf-mutes cf. also Verschiedenheiten, 1827-29, GS VI: 153; and Grundzüge, 1824-26, GS V: 375.

129 I have not considered 'Stimmung' here because Humboldt uses it only rarely, and in a way much like 'Anlage'. He usually talks of the 'Stimmung' of the intellect and its effect on language; e.g., Dualis, 1827, GS VI: 27; and Nationalcharakter, 1822, GS IV: 434.

130 Einleitung, 1836, GS VII: 58-59: "Man könnte gegen das hier Gesagte einwenden wollen, dass Kinder jedes Volkes, ehe sie sprechen, unter jedes fremde versetzt, ihr Sprachvermögen an dessen Sprache entwickeln. Diese unläugbare Thatsache, könnte man sagen, beweist deutlich, dass die Sprache bloss ein Wiedergeben des Gehörten ist und, ohne Rücksicht auf einheit oder Verschiedenheit des Wesens, allein vom geselligen Umgange abhängt. Man hat aber schwerlich in Fällen dieser Art mit hinlänglicher Genauigkeit bemerken können, mit welcher Schwerigkeit die Stammanlage hat überwunden werden müssen, ... Die Gewalt der Abstammung über diese liegt demungeachtet klar genug in ihren Vertheilung nach Nationen vor Augen."

131 Grundzüge, 1824-26, GS V: 385-86. Cf. also Humboldt, Essai sur les langues du nouveau continent, 1812, GS III: 324, and his mention of the differing Sprachanlagen of each nation in Ueber die Buchstaben-

schrift und ihren Zusammenhang mit dem Sprachbau, 1824, GS V: 107.

132 See for example, Humboldt, Ueber den französischen Nationalcharakter, 1799; and Ueber den Charakter der Griechen, die idealische und historische Ansicht desselben, 1807, both in GS VII; and the comments in Ross, (1970: 296ff).

133 Karl-Wilhelm Eigenbrodt (1969: esp. 11-24). Cf. similarly Conte (1976: 617-18).

134 Helmut Gipper (1965: 15): "Was Humboldt meint, ist nicht Forma im Sinne einer Forma formata, wie sie sich etwas im Ergon des grammatischen Formensystems zeigt, sondern form formans, alles Sprachliche durchdringende Formkraft, ...". See also on this H. Gipper and P. Schmitter (1975: 536).

135 Einleitung, 1836, GS VII: 49: "Es ergiebt sich schon aus dem bisher Gesagten von selbst, dass unter Form der Sprache hier durchaus nicht bloss die sogenannte grammatische Form verstanden wird. ... Der Begriff der Form der Sprachen dehnt sich weit über die Regeln der Redefügung und selbst über die der Wortbildung hin aus, ..."

136 Einleitung, 1836, GS VII: 49: "Der Form steht freilich ein Stoff gegenüber; um aber den Stoff der Sprachform zu finden, muss man über die Grenzen der Sprache hinausgehen. Innerhalb derselben lässt sich etwas nur beziehungsweise gegen etwas andres als Stoff betrachten, z.B. die Grundwörter in Beziehung auf die Declination. In andren Beziehungen aber wird, was hier Stoff ist, wieder als Form erkannt. ... Absolut betrachtet, kann es innerhalb der Sprache keinen ungeformten Stoff geben, da alles in ihr auf einen bestimmten Zweck, den Gedankenausdruck, gerichtet ist, ...".

137 Vom gram. Baue, 1827-29, GS VI: 383: "Nicht alle Lauteigenthümlichkeiten der Sprachen lassen sich aber unter das euphonische Princip bringen, ... Sie zerfallen in zwei Classen, nämlich in solche, zu welchen die Natur des Lauts selbst veranlasst, und solche, die in der nationellen Individualität liegen, ..."

138 Einleitung, 1836, GS VII: 160: "In dem Entwicklungsgange der Sprachen überhaupt wirken zwei sich gegenseitig beschränkende Ursachen zusammen, das ursprünglich die Richtung bestimmende Princip und der

Einfluss des schon hervorgebrachten Stoffes, ..."

139 Cf. e.g., Coseriu (1970: 56): "Der Begriff 'innere Form' bedeutet bekanntlich bei Humboldt die spezifische inhaltliche Gestaltung der Einzelsprache, die Gestaltung der einzelsprachlichen Bedeutungen, sowohl der grammatischen als auch der lexikalischen."

CHAPTER FIVE

140 Kant, Immanuel (1974b: 63-64). I here slightly revise the translation in a way suggested by Hartman and Schwarz themselves (64, nt 71). The German is as follows (Kant 1920: 64) "Die menschliche Erkenntnis ist von seiten des Verstandes diskursiv; d.h. sie geschieht durch Vorstellungen, die das, was mehreren Dingen gemein ist, zum Erkenntnisgrunde machen, mithin durch Merkmale, als solche. Wir erkennen also Dinge nur durch Merkmale; und das heisst eben Erkennen, welches von Kennen herkommt.

Ein Merkmal ist dasjenige an einem Dinge, was einen Teil der Erkenntnis desselben ausmacht; oder --welches dasselbe ist-- eine Partialvorstellung, sofern sie als Erkenntnisgrund der ganzen Vorstellung betrachtet wird. Alle unsere Begriffe sind demnach Merkmale und alles Denken ist nichts anderes, als ein Vorstellen durch Merkmale."

141 Herder (1966: 116). The German text is as follows (1960: 24): "Er beweist also Reflexion, wenn er nicht bloss alle Eigenschaften lebhaft oder klar erkennen, sondern eine oder mehrere als unterscheidende Eigenschaften bei sich anerkennen kann: der erste Aktus dieser Anerkenntnis gibt deutlichen Begriff; es ist das erste Urteil der Seele - und - wodurch geschah diese Anerkennung? Durch ein Merkmal, das er absondern musste und das, als Merkmal der Besinnung, deutlich in ihn fiel."

142 Nationalcharakter 1822, GS IV: 432: "Daraus entstehen zwei höchst merkwürdige Unterschiede unter den Sprachen; der eine aus dem Grade des Gefühls jener Unzulänglichkeit, und dem Streben sie aufzuheben, der andre aus der Verschiedenheit der vorherrschenden Ansichten in der Bezeichnungsart, da die Vielseitigkeit der Gegenstände, verbunden mit der Mannigfaltigkeit der Auffassungsorgane eine unbestimmbare Anzahl derselben

erlaubt." (I quote here in full although only the second 'Unterschied' among languages is directly relevant to the present discussion.)

143 Einleitung, 1836, GS VII: 90: "Denn die Sprache stellt niemals die Gegenstände, sondern immer die durch den Geist in der Spracherzeugung selbstthätig von ihnen gebildeten Begriffe dar;"

144 Grundzüge, 1824-26, GS V: 428: "Denn es schiebt der Idee eine Gestalt unter, und abstrahirt bei dem körperlichen Gegenstand von der totalität seiner Wirklichkeit, indem es ihn an Einem Merkmale fest hält, und ihn in diesem durch etwas, ihm fremdes, einen ton, bezeichnet."

145 vergl. Sprachstudium, 1820, GS IV: 23-24: "Das Object, dessen Erscheinung im Gemüth immer ein durch die Sprache individualisierter, stets gleichmässig wiederkehrender Eindruck begleitet, wird auch in sich auf eine dadurch modificirte Art vorgestellt."

146 Einleitung, 1836, GS VII: 170: "Daher entstehen in der Periode der Sprachbildung in einigen Sprachen die Menge der Ausdrück für denselben Gegenstand. Es sind ebenso viele Eigenschaften, unter welchen er gedacht worden ist und deren Ausdruck man an seine Stelle gesetzt hat."

147 Grundzüge, 1824-26, GS V: 420: ""Dadurch entstehen in den gleichbedeutenden Wörtern mehrerer Sprachen verschiedene Vorstellungen desselben Gegenstandes, und diese Beschaffenheit des Wortes trägt hauptsächlich dazu bei, dass jede Sprache eine eigne Weltansicht gewährt."

148 Müller-Vollmer (1967: 64): "Denn unser Verhältnis zu den Dingen ist, so glaubt Humboldt, immer unvollkommen und unbefriedigend. Sie entziehen sich letztlich dem Zugriff unseres Erkennens. Wir erfassen immer nur einen bestimmten Aspekt des Gegenstandes. Nie können wir alle seine Seiten übersehen, ...".

149 Einleitung, 1836, GS VII: 89: "Dies ist selbst bei äusseren, körperlichen, geradezu durch die Sinne wahrnehmbaren Gegenständen der Fall. Auch bei ihnen ist das Wort nicht das Aequivalent des den Sinnen vorschwebenden Gegenstandes, sondern der Auffassung desselben durch die Spracherzeugung im bestimmten Augenblick der Worterfindung. Es ist dies eine vorzügliche Quelle der Vielfachkeit von Ausdrücken für die nemlichen Gegenstände;"

150 Dualis, 1827, GS VI: 23: "Die Sprache trägt Spuren an sich, dass bei ihrer Bildung vorzugsweise aus der sinnlichen Weltanschauung geschöpft worden ist, oder aus dem Inneren der Gedanken, wo jene Weltanschauung schon durch die Arbeit des Geistes gegangen war."

CHAPTER SIX

151 Einfluss, 1821, GS VII: 640: "Man kann vielmehr als allgemein anerkannt annehmen, dass die verschiedenen Sprachen die Organe der eigenthümlichen Denk- und Empfindungsarten der Nationen ausmachen, dass ... "

152 Nationalcharakter, 1822, GS IV: 428: "In sich selbst aber äussert sich der aus dem Einfluss der Sprache hervorgehende Gewinn auf eine zweifache Weise, als erhöhete Sprachfähigkeit, und als eigenthümliche Weltansicht."

153 Einleitung, 1836, GS VII: 171: " ... so ist es gewiss, dass die Entwicklung der Sprache die nationellen Verschiedenheiten erst in das hellere Gebiet des Geistes überführt."

154 Ross (1970: 296ff); and Roger L. Brown (1967: 82): "In his later works Humboldt expresses various views on the relationship between national character and language, and leaves his reader with the impression of unresolved ambiguities."

155 Grundzüge, 1824-26, GS V: 397; and Einleitung, 1836, GS VII: 65).

156 Einleitung, 1836, GS VII: 43: "für die praktische Anwendung besonders wichtig ist es nur, bei keinem niedrigeren Erklärungsprincipe der Sprachen stehen zu bleiben, sondern wirklich bis zu diesem höchsten und letzten hinaufzusteigen und als den festen Punkt der ganzen geistigen Gestaltung den Satz anzusehen, dass der Bau der Sprachen im Menschengeschlechte darum und insofern verschieden ist, weil und als es die Geisteseigenthümlichkeit der Nationen selbst ist."

157 Humboldt, Ueber das Studium des Alterthums, 1793, GS I: 266: "Einzelne Beispiele in Absicht der Bildung der Wörter, der Beugungen und Verbindungen könnten hier die Uebereinstimmung der Sprache der Griechen mit ihrem Charakter zeigen."

158 Humboldt, Latium und Hellas, 1806, GS III: 167: "...; das Sprachstudium lehrt daher, ausser dem Gebrauch der Sprache selbst, noch die Analogie zwischen dem Menschen und der Welt im Allgemeinen und jeder Nation insbesondre, ..."

159 Humboldt, Latium und Hellas, 1806, GS III: 170: "Das Denken behandelt nie einen Gegenstand isolirt, und braucht ihn nie in dem Ganzen seiner Realität. Es schöpft nur Beziehungen, Verhältnisse, Ansichten ab, und verknüpft sie. ... und es lässt sich daher mit Grunde behaupten, dass auch bei durchaus sinnlichen Gegenständen die Wörter verschiedener Sprachen nicht vollkommene Synonyma sind, und dass wer hippus, equus und Pferd ausspricht, nicht durchaus und vollkommen dasselbe sagt."

160 Humboldt, Latium und Hellas, 1806, GS III: 164: "... aus dem allmähligen Einfluss einzelner Umstände gleichsam mechanisch herleiten zu wollen."

161 Humboldt, Latium und Hellas, 1806, GS III: 164: "..., dass diejenigen Dinge, auf deren Einfluss sie bestehen, grossentheils selbst nur Folgen des Charakters sind, den sie erklären sollen; und dass andre Nationen unter denselben Umständen eine andre Wendung des Charakters genommen haben."

162 For example, Humboldt, Essai sur les langues du nouveau continent, 1812, GS III: 329ff; and Ueber den Einfluss des verschiedenen Charakters der Sprachen auf Literatur und Geistesbildung, 1821, GS VII: 640-641.

163 Nationalcharakter, 1822, GS IV: 423: "Richtige Ansicht lebendiger Kräft muss allerdings die Hoffnung abschneiden, das Wirken derselben in seiner Individualität erschöpfend darszustellen. Man kann aber dem Umriss, dessen Linien wahrhaft zu beschreiben allerdings unmöglich bleibt, so nahe kommen, so viele Punkte bemerken, die seine Richtung bestimmen, dass sich dasjenige, was der genauen Schilderung widerstrebt, dennoch bis auf einen gewissen Grad empfinden und erahnden lässt."

164 Nationalcharakter, 1822, GS IV: 424-25: "..., wenn man die Nation mit der Sprache zusammendenkt, in der letzteren allemal ein ursprünglicher Charakter mit einem von der Nation empfangenen in Eins zusammengeschmolzen ist. Zwar darf man auch hier nicht, und am wenigsten geschichtlich, einen gleichsam festen Punkt annehmen, wo

eine Nation ihre Sprache im Entstehen empfängt, da das Entstehen der Nationen selbst nur ein Uebergehen in stätigen Reihen ist, und sich ebensowenig ein Anfangspunkt einer Nation, als einer Sprache gedenken lässt. Allein unsre Geschichtskunde rechtfertigt doch nirgends die Annahme, dass je eine Nation durchaus vor ihrer Sprache vorhanden gewesen, oder um es mit andren Worten auszudrücken, dass irgend eine Sprache allein durch die Nation, der sie angehört, gebildet worden wäre. Demnach liegt auch in jeder Sprache eine ursprüngliche Eigenthümlichkeit und Einwirkungsweise. Doch kann in den Sprach- en, deren Ursprung in das Dunkel der Zeiten zurückgeht, diese Verbindung eines doppelten Charakters gleichgültig erscheinen, da sich über den ursprünglichen nichts mehr ausmachen lässt."

165 Nationalcharakter, 1822, GS IV; also cf. Verschiedenheiten, 1827-29, GS VI: 244-245: "In den Sprachen des Lateinischen Europa, ... und im Persischen z.B. erkennt jeder auf den ersten Anblick gegen das Lateinische und das Sanskrit eine neue, vorher nicht da gewesene Sprachform und mithin das Entstehen wirklich neuer Sprachen."

166 Nationalcharakter, 1822, GS IV: 423-424: It remains true "... dass die Sprache durch die auf sie geschehende Einwirkung eine Individualität erhält, die insofern ganz eigentlich auch zu ihrem Charakter wird, als sie nun auch wiederum in demselben zurückwirkt, und als sie sich nur innerhalb der Gränzen desselben mit Willigkeit gebrauchen lässt."

167 Humboldt, Latium und Hellas, 1806, GS III: 165: "Die Kraft (und eine Kraft ist nie ohne irgend eine Richtung denkbar) ...".

168 Humboldt, Ueber Goethes Herrmann und Dorothea, 1798, GS II: 118: "Es giebt keine freie und kraftvolle Aeusserung unserer Fähigkeiten ohne eine sorgfältige Bewahrung unserer ursprünglichen Naturanlagen; keine Energie ohne Individualität."

169 Nationalcharakter, 1822, GS IV: 432-433: "Ungeachtet der unendlichen Verschiedenheit derselben, liegt in allen, indem sie von Einer Nation aufgefasst werden, etwas Gemeinsames der Erscheinung, das sich dem Worte, als Zeichen, mittheilt. Man kann dies wohl, in groben Umrissen, so charakterisiren, dass die Wörter einer Sprache mehr sinnliche Anschaulichkeit, einer andren mehr innre Geistigkeit, einer dritten mehr nüchterne Begriffesdarlegung u.s.f. besitzen, ... Keine jener

angeführten Eigenschaften steht so vereinzelt da, und wo sie sich auch in verschiedenen Nationen gemeinsam finden, sind sie in keiner dieselben."

170 Verschiedenheiten, 1827-29, GS VI: 187: "Wenn man die Wörter Volk, Nation, und Staat, als durch feste Gränzen von einander geschieden ansieht, so bezieht sich das erste auf den Wohnsitz und das Zusammenleben, das zweite auf die Abstammung, das letzte auf die bürgerliche Verfassung. ... Nation aber gilt vorzüglich als Bezeichnung derjenigen Völkereinheit, auf die alle verschiedenartigen Umstände einwirken, ohne dass man gerade darauf sieht, ob Abstammung oder Sprache innerhalb dieser Einheit dieselben sind, oder sich nicht noch über dieselbe hinauserstrecken. So redet man von der französischen Nation, ohne auf das in Sprache abgesonderte Völkchen der Nieder-Bretagne, von der Spanischen, ohne auf die Vasken, Valencianer und Catalanen zu sehen, von der Schweizerischen, ungeachtet Abstammung und Sprache ihnen mit den Deutschen gemeinschaftlich sind."

171 Verschiedenheiten, 1827-29, GS VI: 188: "In diesem Sinne ist eine Nation ein solcher Theil der Menschheit, auf welchen so in sich gleichartige und bestimmt von andren verschiedene Ursachen einwirken, dass sich ihm dadurch eine eigenthümliche Denk-, Empfindungs-, und Handlungsweise anbildet."

172 Verschiedenheiten, 1827-29, GS VI: 188: "Die wirkliche Verschiedenheit prägt sich allemal auch in Verschiedenheit der Sprache, wäre sie auch nur eine der Mundart, aus, ..."

173 Verschiedenheiten, 1827-29, GS VI: 189: "Die Sprache lebt und webt in der Nationalität und das Geheimnissvolle ihres Wesens zeigt sich gerade darin vorzüglich, dass sie aus der scheinbar verwirrten Masse von Individualitäten hervorgeht, unter welchen keine sich gerade einzeln auszuzeichnen braucht. Sie erhält ihre ganze Form aus diesem dunkeln Naturwirken bewusstlos zusammenstimmender Anlagen, ..."

174 Einleitung, 1836, GS VII: 165: "Mit dem grammatischen Baue, wie wir ihn bisher im Ganzen und Grossen betrachtet haben, und der äusserlichen Structur der Sprache überhaupt ist jedoch ihr Wesen bei weitem nicht erschöpft und ihr eigentlicher und wahrer Charakter beruht noch auf etwas viel Feinerem, tiefer Verborgenem und der Zergliederung weniger Zugänglichem".

175 Einleitung, 1836, GS VII: 166: "Man müss also, um die Verflechtung des Geistes in die Sprache genauer zu verfolgen, dennoch den grammatischen und lexicalischen Bau der letzteren gleichsam als den festen und äusseren von dem inneren Charakter unterscheiden, der wie eine Seele in ihr wohnt und die Wirkung hervorbringt, mit welcher uns jede Sprache, so wie wir nur anfangen, ihrer mächtig zu werden, eigenthümlich ergreift. Es ist damit auf keine Weise gemeint, dass diese Wirkung dem äusseren Baue fremd sey."

176 Einleitung, 1836, GS VII: 167: "Ich werde daher bei diesem Unterschiede zwischen dem Principe, aus welchem sich nach dem obigen die Structur der Sprache entwickelt, und dem eigentlichen Charakter dieser hier noch verweilen ...".

177 Einleitung, 1836, GS VII: 42: "Ohne aber über die Prioritat der einen oder andren entscheiden zu wollen, müssen wir als das reale Erklärungsprincip und als den wahren Bestimmungsgrund der Sprachverschiedenheit die geistige Kraft der Nationen ansehen, weil sie allein lebendig selbständig vor uns steht, die Sprache dagegen nur an ihr haftet."

178 Einleitung, 1836, GS VII: 43: "..., dass der Bau der Sprachen im Menschengeschlechte darum und insofern verschieden ist, weil und als es die Geisteseigentümlichkeit der Nationen selbst ist."

179 Einleitung, 1836, GS VII: 172: "Er ist eine natürliche Folge der fortgesetzten Einwirkung der geistigen Eigenthümlichkeit der Nation."

180 Einleitung, 1836, GS VII: 166: Die Denk- und Sinnesart eines Volkes, durch welche, wie ich eben sagte, seine Sprache Farbe und Charakter erhält, wirkt schon von den ersten Anfängen auf dieselbe ein."

181 Einleitung, 1836, GS VII: 170: "Der nationelle Charakter wird zwar durch Gemeinschaft des Wohnplatzes und des Wirkens unterhalten, verstärkt, ja bis zu einem gewissen Grad hervorgebracht; eigentlich aber beruht er auf der Gleichheit der Naturanlage, die Man gewöhnlich aus Gemeinschaft der Abstammung erklärt."

182 Einleitung, 1836, GS VII: 179-180. (I follow the Buck & Raven translation (1971) with slight revisions): "Wenn man nun die gesammte innere und äussere Thätigkeit des Menschen bis zu ihren einfachsten Endpunkten ver-

folgt, so findet man diese in der Art, wie er die Wirklichkeit als Object, das er aufnimmt, oder als Materie, die er gestaltet, mit sich verknüpft oder auch unabhängig von ihr sich eigene Wege bahnt. Wie tief und auf welche Weise der Mensch in die Wirklichkeit Wurzel schlägt, ist das ursprünglich charakteristische Merkmal seiner Individualität. Die Arten jener Verknüpfung können zahllos seyn, je nachdem sich die Wirklichkeit oder die Innerlichkeit, deren keine die andre ganz zu entbehren vermag, von einander zu trennen versuchen oder sich mit einander in verschiedenen Graden und Richtungen verbinden. ... Wenn aber auch, wie daran kein Zweifel seyn kann, der Charakter der Nation sich an allem ihr wahrhaft Eigenthümlichen offenbart, so leuchtet er vorzugsweise durch die Sprache durch.

... Das Gefühl des Unterschiedes zwischen dem Stoff, den die Seele aufnimmt und erzeugt, und der in dieser doppelten Thätigkeit treibenden und stimmenden Kraft, zwischen der Wirkung und dem wirkenden Seyn, die richtige und verhältnissmässige Würdigung beider und die gleichsam hellere Gegenwart des dem Grade nach obenan stehenden vor dem Bewusstseyn liegt nicht gleich stark in jeder nationellen Eigenthümlichkeit. ... Zwischen diesen beiden Extremen aber befindet sich eine zahllose Menge von Mittelstufen und sie selbst gründen sich offenbar auf vorherrschende Richtung nach dem Inneren des Gemüths und nach der äusseren Wirklichkeit."

183 <u>Einleitung</u> 1836, GS VII: 172: "Er ist eine natürliche Folge der fortgesetzten Einwirkung der geistigen Eigenthümlichkeit der Nation. Indem diese die allgemeinen Bedeutungen der Wörter immer auf dieselbe individuelle Weise aufnimmt und mit den gleichen Nebenideen und Empfindungen begleitet, nach denselben Richtungen hin Ideenverbindungen eingeht ..., ertheilte sie der Sprache eine eigenthümliche Farbe und Schattirung, welche diese fixirt und so in demselben Gleise zurückwirkt."

184 <u>Einleitung</u>, 1836,, GS VII: 181: "Ihr Sinn gieng vorzugsweise auf das, was die Dinge sind und wie sie erscheinen, nicht einseitig auf dasjenige hin, wofür sie im Gebrauche der Wirklichkeit gelten. Ihre Richtung war daher ursprünglich eine innere und intellectuelle."

CHAPTER SEVEN

185 This chapter is a revised version of an article

published in Historiographia Linguistica (Manchester 1982), and I gratefully acknowledge the permission of the publisher to use the material here.

186 Cf. especially P.A. Verburg (1949); K.-H. Weimann (1965); and E. Coseriu (1972).

187 Cf. E. Coseriu (1972: 111-117) for a brief summary of early language typology. Also useful are J.H. Greenberg (1974: 35-39), and R.H. Robins (1973)

188 Friedrich Schlegel (1975: 153: "Entweder werden die Nebenbestimmungen der Bedeutung durch innre Veränderung des Würzellauts angezeigt, durch Flexion; oder aber jedesmal durch ein eignes hinzugefügtes Wort, was schon an und für sich Mehrheit, Vergangenheit, ein zukünftiges Sollen oder andre Verhältnisbegriffe der Art bedeutet; und diese beiden einfachsten Fälle bezeichnen auch die beiden Hauptgattungen aller Sprache."

189 Greenberg (1974: 38) is guilty of the latter mistake.

190 Entstehen,, 1821, GS IV: 296: "Die Anfügung und Einschaltung bedeutungsloser Wortelement, und die Umänderung von Vocalen und Consonanten wäre, wenn eine Sprache durch wirkliche Verabredung entstände, das natürlichste und passendste Mittel. Es ist die wahre Beugung (Flexion) im Gegensatz der Anfügung, ..."

191 Vom gram. Baue, 1827-29, GS VI: 387-388: "Ich rede mit grossem Bedacht hier immer nur von Methoden, und verwechsle diesen Ausdruck nicht ohne besondre Gründe mit dem der Sprachen. Denn es liesse sich leicht zeigen, dass es wohl keine Sprache giebt, die nicht in ihrer Grammatik alle diese Methoden oder doch die meisten derselben zugleich anwendete."

192 Dualis, 1827, GS VI: 21: "Die Sprachen sind nemlich grammatische verschieden:

a) zuerst in der Auffassung der grammatischen Formen nach ihrem Begriff,

b) dann in der Art der technischen Mittel ihrer Bezeichnung,

c) endlich in den wirklichen, zur Bezeichnung dienenden Lauten."

Cf. also Grundzüge, 1824-26, GS V: 454.

193 The criterion is an uncontroversial one in the tradition. Schlegel and Humboldt speak of the Zusammenschmelzen of the inflectional changes with the Haupt-

wort. For example, cf. F. Schlegel (1975: 155), and Humboldt, Entstehen, 1821, GS IV: 300, 301, 308). Sapir discusses the meaning of 'fusion' extensively, and the term is acknowledged, although treated in a somewhat more restricted fashion, in Matthews (1972: 67-72).

194 Roberta Graber Ross (1970: 75): "The problem of the origin of grammatical endings in languages was of great interest during this period. Bopp and Humboldt contended that they were formed by the merging of two words which were originally separate (agglutination)."

195 Einleitung, 1836, GS VII: 116: "Die ursprünglich selbstständige Bedeutsamkeit der Suffixe ist daher kein nothwendiges Hinderniss der Reinheit ächter Flexion." Cf. also Einleitung, 1836, GS VII: 124.

196 Entstehen, 1821, GS IV: 304: "Denn die an sich durchaus bedeutungslose Beugung enthält nichts, als den reinen Begriff des Verhältnisses. In dem grammatischen Wort leigt ausserdem der Nebenbegriff, der auf das Verhältniss, um es zu bestimmen, bezogen wird, ..."

197 Entstehen, 1821, GS IV: 300: "Alles hier Zugegebne aber hebt den Unterschied zwischen wahren grammatischen Formen, wie amavit, époieisas, und zwischen solchen Wort- oder Silbenstellungen, als die meisten roheren Sprachen zur Bezeichnung der grammatischen Verhältnisse brauchen, nicht auf. Er leigt darin, dass jene Ausdrücke wirklich wie in Eine Form zusammengegossen, in diesen die Element nur an einander gereiht erscheinen."

198 Greenberg notes (1974: 37) that with Friedrich Schlegel's distinction of 'organic' from 'mechanical' languages, "... the valuational attitude so characteristic of most versions of the theory is to be found right at the beginning." For a discussion of the 'organic' metaphor in Humboldt and his predecessors, cf. R.L. Brown (1967: 40ff).

199 Grundzüge, 1824-26, GS V: 422: "Denn die Vorzüge der Sprachen werden nicht durch den partiellen Reichthum von Bildern und Begriffen bestimmt, den sie der Seele zuführen, sondern durch ihre Einwirkung auf das Denken und Empfinden überhaupt." Cf. also 434: "Insofern man unter dem Reichthum einer Sprache ihr Vermögen dem Bedürfniss des Ausdrucks zu genügen versteht, kann man alle gleich reich nennen."

200 Einleitung, 1836, GS VII: 162: "Da sie (die Flexionsmethode) jedes Element der Rede in seiner zwie-

fachen Geltung, seiner objectiven Bedeutung und seiner subjectiven Beziehung auf den Gedanken und die Sprache nimmt und dies Doppelte in seinem verhältnissmässigen Gewichte durch darnach zugerichtete Lautformen bezeichnet, so steigert sie das ursprünglichste Wesen der Sprache, die Articulation und die Symbolisirung, zu ihren höchsten Graden.".

201 Entstehen, 1821, GS IV: 308: "Das Erste und Wesentlichste ist, dass der Geist von der Sprache verlangt, dass sie Sache und Form, Gegenstand und Verhältniss rein abscheide, und nicht beide mit einander vermenge. ... Gerade aber diese Absonderung wird erst rein vorgenommen bei der Bildung der ächt grammatischen Form durch Beugung, oder durch grammatische Wörter, ..."

202 Entstehen, 1821, GS IV: 309: "Denn da sie den Ausdruck des Verhältnisses rein, und sonst nichts stoffartiges enthält, worauf der Verstand abschweifen könnte, dieser aber den ursprünglichen Wortbegriff darin verändert erblickt, so muss er die Form selbst ergreifen. Bei der unächten Form kann er dies nicht, da er den Verhältnissbegriffe nicht bestimmt genug in ihr erblickt, und noch durch Nebenbegriffe zerstreut wird."

203 Entstehen, 1821, GS IV: 304: "Denn die an sich durchaus bedeutungslose Beugung enthält nichts, als den reinen Begriff des Verhältnisses."

204 For Humboldt's views on the inflectional status of the auxiliary verb method, cf. Vom gram. Baue, 1827-29, GS VI: 369-370.

205 Vom gram. Baue, 1827-29, GS VI: 362: "Negativ geschieht die Darstellung der Gedankenheit in der Sprache durch die Entfernung jedes Sachbegriffs aus der grammatischen Bezeichnung. Der hier herausgehobene Unterschied wird durch die Vergleichung der Sprachen sichtbar, welche die Tempora des Verbum durch Zeitadverbien, die Praepositionen durch Theile des menschlichen Körpers, Rücken, Stirn u.s.f., und derer, die jene durch Endungen, diese durch bedeutungslose Wörter bezeichnen."

206 Grundzüge, 1824-26, GS V: 424: "Das erste hier vorwaltende Gesetz ist nun das einer richtigen Eintheilung des Gedankenstoffs durch die Sprache, oder anders ausgedrückt, dass der Gegenstand des Worts von festen Gränzen umschrieben sey, alles enthalte, was zur Vollendung seines Begriffs gehört, und nichts, was ihm nicht wesentlich ist, sondern nur zufällig anhängt."

207 Bau der chines., 1826, GS V: 323: "Der Gedanke erhält einmal bloss durch die Sprache Deutlichkeit und Bestimmtheit, und diese Wirkung ist nur vollständig, wenn alles auf ihn Einwirkende auch in der Sprache einen analogen Ausdruck antrifft. Jede Sprache, die darin zu ergänzen ubriglasst, befindet sich in dieser Rücksicht im Nachtheil."

208 Vom gram. Baue, 1827-29, GS VI: 364: "Sie fallen von selbst in zwei Hauptclassen, wenn das grammatische Verhältniss nicht hinlänglich, und wenn es nicht in reiner Formalität angedeutet ist."

CHAPTER EIGHT

209 Brown (1967: 114), for example, confuses this point by describing the linguistic relativity thesis in three propositions, the latter two of which are only concerned with the variation of languages.

210 Hamann, Herder and Humboldt are indeed often lumped together as the 'founding fathers' of the linguistic relativity thesis. Cf. R.L. Miller (1968: 14-34); Julia Penn (1972: 15-22).

211 Christmann (1967: 15): "Humboldt --ebenso wie Herder und Hamann-- entwickelte somit eine Konzeption weiter, die schon in der Aufklärung vorgebildet war. Das heisst, es handelt sich um einen jener Gedanken, die aus der Auflkärung erwachsen sind und dennoch bereits auf die Romantik weisen."

212 For a thorough discussion of this movement, in relation to the LRT, cf. R.L. Miller (1968); and for a shorter survey Harald Basilius (1952).

213 Nationalcharakter, 1822, GS IV: 420: "Ich habe in einer meiner früheren akademischen Vorlesungen die Aufmerksamkeit darauf zu richten versucht, dass die Verschiedenheit der Sprachen in mehr, als einer blossen Verschiedenheit der Zeichen besteht, dass die Wörter und Wortfügungen zugleich die Begriffe bilden und bestimmen, und dass, in ihrem Zusammenhange, und ihrem Einfluss auf Erkenntniss und Empfindung betrachtet, mehrere Sprachen in der That mehrere Weltansichten sind."

214 Grundzüge, 1824-26, GS V: 433: "Jede Sprache, welche sie seyn möge, trägt in jedem Zeitpunkt ihres Daseyns den Ausdruck aller Begriffe, die sich jemals in

der Nation entwickeln können, in ihrem Schooss. Jede ist ferner in dem jedesmaligen Zeitpunkte ihres Lebens genau dem jedesmaligen Gedankenumfange der Nation gleich. Jede endlich in jedem ihrer Zustände bildet das Ganze einer Weltansicht, indem sie Ausdruck für alle Vorstellungen enthält, welche die Nation sich von der Welt macht, und für alle Empfindungen, welche die Welt in ihr hervorbringt. Diese Sätze beruhen auf der Identität des Denkens und Sprechens. Was der Mensch denken kann, das vermag er auch zu sagen."

215 Grundzüge, 1824-26, GS V: 411: "... und in dem Wörtervorrath einer Sprache liegt also der gesammte Gedankenstoff einer Nation."

216 vergl. Sprachstudium, 1821, GS IV: 21: "Das Denken ist aber nicht bloss abhängig von der Sprache überhaupt, sondern, bis auf einen gewissen Grad, auch von jeder einzelnen bestimmten."

217 Vom gram. Baue, 1827-29, GS VI: 344: "... ein Volk spricht, wie es denkt, denkt so, weil es so spricht, und dass es so denkt und spricht, ist wesentlich in seinen körperlichen und geistigen Anlagen gegründet, und wieder in diese übergegangen."

218 Helmut Gipper (1972: 16ff), and (1976: 219).

219 vergl. Sprachstudium, 1821, GS IV: 29: "Die Ausdrücke sinnlicher Gegenstände sind wohl insofern gleichbedeutend, als bei allen derselbe Gegenstand gedacht wird, aber da sie die bestimmte Art ihn vorzustellen ausdrücken, so geht ihre Bedeutung darin gleichfalls auseinander. Denn die Einwirkung der individuellen Ansicht des Gegenstandes auf die Bildung des Wortes bestimmt, solange sie lebendig bleibt, auch diejenige, wie das Wort den Gegenstand zurückruft."

220 Cf. the notion of language taken 'in its broadest extent', and the definitions of the world-view doctrine as not a claim about phonetic 'sign' variation, but rather about the variation of 'meaning' designated by those signs. E.g., Nationalcharakter GS IV: 420, and Entstehen, 1821, GS IV: 286.

221 Entstehen, 1821, GS IV: 309: "In der Rückwirkung der Sprache auf den Geist macht die ächt grammatische Form, auch wo die Aufmerksamkeit nicht absichtlich auf sie gerichtet ist, den Eindruck einer Form, und bringt formale Bildung hervor."

222 Grundzüge, 1824-26, GS V: 388: "Wir sind im Vorigen darauf aufmerksam geworden, dass der in Sprache aufgenommene Gedanke für die Seele zum Object wird, und eine ihr insofern als etwas Fremdes zukommende Wirkung auf sie ausübt. Aber wir haben das Object vorzüglich als aus dem Subjekt entstanden, die Wirkung als aus demjenigen, worauf sie zurückwirkt, hervorgegangen betrachtet."

223 Entstehen, 1821, GS IV: 290-291: "Sind nun die Fälle, wo die Bezeichnung eines grammatischen Verhältnisses dem Begriff der wahren grammatischen Form nicht genau entspricht, häufig, machen sie die Eigenthümlichkeit und den Charakter der Sprache aus, so ist eine solche, wenn man auch im Stande wäre, Alles in ihr auszudrücken, noch weit von der Angemessenheit zur Ideenentwicklung entfernt."

224 Bau der chines., 1826, GS V: 322: "..., was nun eigentlich in der Seele dieser Zurückwirkung der Sprache durch vollständige Formenbezeichnung auf die Gedankengehalt entspricht, und was mithin, da wo, wie im Chinesischen, eine solche Wirksamkeit fehlt oder schwach ist, deshalb in dem Geiste der Sprechenden vermisst werden muss?"

225 Bau der chines., 1826, GS V: 322: "Diese so unbedeutend erscheinenden Formen erlauben, in dem sie Mittel darbieten, die Sätze zu erweitern und zu verschlingen, dem Geist einen freieren Schwung. Der Gedanke, der im dem Köpfe eine ununterbrochene Einheit bildet, findet in einer, alle Wörter organisch verknüpfenden Sprache dieselbe Statigkeit wieder."

CONCLUSION

226 Humboldt, Ueber Goethes Hermann und Dorothea, 1798, GS II: 132. "Aber es enthält eine Unbestimmtheit, die nur dadurch vermieden werden kann, dass man das Wesen der Kunst nicht (wie man bisher nur zu oft gethan hat) in der Beschaffenheit ihres Gegenstandes, sondern in der Stimmung der Phantasie aufsucht."

227 Humboldt, Ueber Goethes Hermann und Dorothea, 1798, GS II: 137. "Mehr aber als das Gemüth zu stimmen ist nicht die Absicht des Dichters, ..."

228 Cf. Ueber Goethes Hermann und Dorothea, 1798, GS

II: 127-28, 132; Essais aesthétique, 1799, (Müller-Vollmer 1967: 122); and Einleitung, 1836, GS VII: 169-70.

229 For a review of this background, cf. Knoll & Siebert (1969: 28-32).

230 Cf. Humboldt, Bericht der Sektion des Kultus und Unterrichts, 1809, GS X: 209-14.

231 Humboldt, Bericht der Sektion des Kultus und Unterrichts, 1809, GS X: 210: "Bei dem Unterricht geht (1) der Gesichtspunkt nicht, wie bisher gewöhnlich, davon aus, dass das Kind nur lesen, schreiben, rechnen u.s.f. lernen, sondern dass alle Hauptfähigkeiten seines Körpers und seiner Seele in möglichsten Zusammenstimmung entwickelt und geübt werden, wodurch denn jene Fertigkeiten von selbst entstehen."

232 Cf. e.g., Humboldt, Ueber die innere und äussere Organisation der höheren wissenschaftlichen Anstalten in Berlin, 1810, GS X: 255.

REFERENCES

1. Editions of Wilhelm von Humboldt's works

Humboldt, Wilhelm von. 1903ff. Gesammelte Schriften. 17 vols., ed. by Albert Leitzmann et al. for the Königlich Preussische Adademie der Wissenschaften Berlin: B.Behr. (Repr., Berlin: W. de Gruyter, 1967-68.)

Humboldt, Wilhelm von. 1960ff. Werke in fünf Bänden. Edited by Andreas Flitner and Klaus Giel. Stuttgart: Cotta.

Humboldt, Wilhelm von. 1971. Linguistic Variability and Intellectual Development. Translation of Einleitung by George C. Buck and Frithjof A. Raven. Coral Gables: Univ. of Miami Press.

2. Correspondence cited

Leitzmann, Albert, ed. 1900. Briefwechsel zwischen Schiller und Wilhelm von Humboldt. Stuttgart: Cotta.

Leitzmann, Albert, ed. 1908. Briefwechsel zwischen Wilhelm von Humboldt und August Wilhelm Schlegel. Forward by Berthold Delbrück. Halle a. S.: Niemeyer.

Lefmann, Salomon, ed. 1897. Franz Bopp, sein Leben und sein Wissenschaft: Nachtrag: Briefwechsel zwischen Humboldt und Bopp. Berlin: C. Reimer.

Rössle, Wilhelm, ed. 1952. Wilhelm von Humboldt: Briefe. München: Hanser.

3. Other works cited

Aarsleff, Hans. 1974. "The Tradition of Condillac: The problem of the origin of language in the eighteenth century and the debate in the Berlin Academy before Herder". Studies in the History of Linguistics Ed. by Dell Hymes, 277-306. Bloomington: Indiana Univ. Press.

________. 1975. "The Eighteenth Century, including Leibniz". Current Trends in Linguistics vol.13, 1. 382-479.

________. 1982. From Locke to Saussure: Essays on the study of language and intellectual history. Minneapolis: Univ. of Minnesota Press.

Basilius, Harald. 1952. "Neo-Humboldtian Ethnolinguistics". Word 8.95-105.

Baumann, Hans-Heinrich. 1971. "Die generative Grammatik und Wilhelm von Humboldt". Poetica 4.1-12.

Benfey, Theodor. 1869. Geschichte der Sprachwissenschaft und orientalischen Philologie in Deutschland. München: Cotta.

Bopp, Franz. 1856. Vergleichende Grammatik. 2nd ed. Berlin: F. Dümmler.

Borsche, Tilman. 1981. Sprachansichten: Der Begriff der menschlichen Rede in der Sprachphilosophie. Stuttgart: Klett-Cotta.

Brown, Roger L. 1967. Wilhelm von Humboldt's Conception of Linguistic Relativity. Hague: Mouton.

Brown, Roger. 1976. "Reference: In memorial tribute to Eric Lenneberg". Cognition 4.125-153.

Cassirer, Ernst. 1951. The Philosophy of the Enlightenment. Princeton: Princeton Univ. Press.

Cassirer, Ernst. 1953. The Philosophy of Symbolic Forms. vol. I: "Language". Transl. by Ralph Mannheim. New Haven: Yale Univ. Press.

Chomsky, Noam. 1966. Cartesian Linguistics: A Chapter in the history of rationalist thought. New York: Harper and Row.

Conte, Maria-Elizabeth. 1976. "Semantische und pragmatische Ansätze in der Sprachtheorie Wilhelm von Humboldts". History of Linguistic Thought and Contemporary Linguistics Ed. by Herman Parret, 616-632.

Coseriu, Eugenio. 1970. "Semantik, innere Sprachform und Tiefenstruktur". Folia Linguistica 4.53-63.

________. 1972. "Ueber die Sprachtypologie Wilhelm von Humboldts". Beiträge zur vergleichenden Literaturgeschichte. ed. by Johannes Hösle, 107-135. Tübingen: Niemeyer.

Descartes, René. 1973. Philosophical Works. transl. by E.S. Haldane and G.R.T. Ross. 2 vols. London: Cambridge Univ. Press.

________. 1976. Philosophical Writings. Transl. by Elizabeth Anscombe and Peter T. Geach. Sunbury on Thames: Nelson.

Diderichson, Paul. 1974. "The Foundations of Comparative Linguistics". Studies in the History of Linguistics Ed. by Dell Hymes, 93-156. Bloomington: Indiana Univ. Press.

Eigenbrodt, Karl-Wilhelm. 1969. Der Terminus 'innere Sprachform' bei Wilhelm von Humboldt: Versuch einer genetischen Erklärung. Doctoral Diss, Univ. Mainz.

Esper, Erwin Allen. 1968. Mentalism and Objectivism in Linguistics: The Sources of Leonard Bloomfield's Psychology of Language. New York: Elsevier.

Fontaine-De Visscher, Luce. 1970. "La pensée du langage comme forme: la 'form intérieure du langage' chez W. von Humboldt". Revue philosophique de Louvain 68.449-72.

Gamkrelidze, Tomas V. 1974. "The Problem of 'l'arbitraire du Signe'". Language 50.102-110.

Gipper, Helmut. 1963. Bausteine zur Sprachinhaltsforschung. Düsseldorf: Pädagogischer Verlag Schwann.

________. 1965. "Wilhelm von Humboldt als Begründer moderner Sprachforschung". Wirkendes Wort 15. 1-19.

________. 1972. Gibt es eine sprachliches Relativitätsprinzip? Frankfurt: S. Fischer.

________. and Peter Schmitter, 1975. "Wilhelm von Humboldt". Current Trends in Linguistics Vol.XIII. 532-546.

________. 1976. "Is There a Linguistic Relativity Principle?" Universalism versus Relativism in Language and Thought Ed. by R. Pinxten, 217-228. Hague: Mouton.

Gordon, W. Terrence. 1982. A History of Semantics. Amsterdam: J. Benjamins.

Greenberg, Joseph. 1974. Language Typology: A Historical and Analytic Overview. Hague: Mouton.

Hacking, Ian. 1975. Why does Language matter to Philosophy? Cambridge: Cambridge Univ. Press.

Heeschen, Volker. 1972. Die Sprachphilosophie Wilhelm von Humboldts. Doctoral Diss., Ruhr-Universität Bochum.

Herder, Johann Gottfried. 1960. Sprachphilosophie. Ed. by Erich Heintel. Hamburg: Meiner

________. 1966 (1770). Essay on the Origin of Language. Transl. by J.H. Moran and A. Gode, in On the Origin of Language, 87-166. New York: Unger.

Hobbes, Thomas. (n.d.) (1651). Leviathan. Ed. by Michael Oakeshott, Oxford: Blackwells.

________. 1962. Body, Man and Citizen. Ed. by Richard S. Peters. New York: Collier.

Hymes, Dell, Ed. 1974. Studies in the History of Linguistics. Bloomington: Indiana Univ. Press.

Kant, Immanuel. 1920. Sämmtliche Werke. Bd. 4: Logik, Anthropologie, Die Religion innerhalb der Grenzen der blossen Vernunft. Leipzig: Meiner.

________. 1965 (1781). Critique of Pure Reason. transl. by Norman Kemp Smith. New York: St. Martins Press.

________. 1974a (1797). Anthropology from a pragmatic Point of View. Transl. by Mary J. Gregor. Hague: Nijhoff.

__________. 1974b (1800). Logic. Transl. by Robert Hartmann and Wolfgang Schwarz. New York: Bobbs-Merrill.

Knoll, Joachim H. & Siebert, Horst. 1969 Wilhelm von Humboldt: Politik und Bildung. Heidelberg: Quelle & Meyer.

Kretzmann, Norman. 1968. "The Main Thesis of Locke's Semantic Theory". Philosophical Review 77.175-196.

Lammers, Wilhelm. 1936. Wilhelm von Humboldts Weg zur Sprachforschung: 1785-1801. Berlin: Junker & Dünnhaupt.

Leibniz, Gottfried Wilhelm. 1951. Leibniz Selections. Ed. by Philip Wiener. New York: Scribner's.

__________. 1969. Philosophical Papers and Letters. Ed. by Leroy Loemker. Dordrecht: D. Reidel

__________. 1981 (1765). New Essays on Human Understanding. Transl. and Ed. by Peter Remnant and Jonathan Bennett. Cambridge: Cambridge Univ. Press.

Lenneberg, Eric. 1953. "Cognition in Ethnolinguistics". Language 29.

Leroy, Maurice. 1967. The Main Trends in Modern Linguistics. Transl. by G. Price. Oxford: Blackwells.

Liebrucks, Bruno. 1965. Sprache und Bewusstsein. Bd. II: Sprache. Frankfurt am Main: Akademische Verlagsgesellschaft.

Locke, John. 1959 (1690). Essay on Human Understanding. Ed. by Alexander Campbell Frazier. 2 vols. New York: Dover.

Lyons, John. 1974. Semantics. Vol. I. Cambridge: Cambridge Univ. Press.

Manchester, Martin L. 1982. "Philosophical Motives in Wilhelm von Humboldt's Defense of the Inflectional Superiority Thesis". Historiographia Linguistica IX.107-120.

__________. 1983. Review of Borsche 1981. Historiographia Linguistica X.325-28.

Matthews, Peter. 1972. Inflectional Morphology. Cambridge: Cambridge Univ. Press.

McRae, Robert. 1972. "Descartes' Definition of Thought". Cartesian Studies Ed. by R.J. Butler, 55-70. Oxford: Blackwells.

________. 1976. Leibniz: Perception, apperception and thought. Toronto: Univ. of Toronto Press

Menze, Clemens. 1964. "Ueber den Zusammenhang von Sprache und Bildung in der Sprachphilosophie W. von Humboldts". Pädagogische Rundschau 18.768-86

________. 1976. "Die Individualität als Ausgangs- und Endpunkt des Humboldtschen Denkens". Universalismus und Wissenschaft im Werk und Wirken der Brüder Humboldt Ed. by Klaus Hammacher, 145-164. Frankfurt am Main: Klostermann.

Miller, Robert L. 1968. The Linguistic Relativity Principle and Humboldtian Ethnolinguistics. Hague: Mouton.

Mueller, Hugo. 1966. "On Re-Reading von Humboldt". Monograph Series on Languages and Linguistics 19.97-107.

Müller-Vollmer, Kurt. 1967. Poesie und Einbildungskraft: Zur Dichtungstheorie Wilhelm von Humboldts. Stuttgart: Metzler.

________. 1976. "Von der Poetik zur Linguistik: Wilhelm von Humboldt und der romantische Sprachbegriff". Universalismus und Wissenschaft im Werk und Wirken der Brüder Humboldt Ed. by Klaus Hammacher, 224-40. Frankfurt am Main: Klostermann.

Oesterreicher, Wulf. 1981. "Wem gehört Humboldt? Zum Einfluss der französischen Aufklärung auf die Sprachphilosophie der deutschen Romantik". Logos Semantikos: Studia Linguistica in honorem Eugenio Coseriu Vol.I, Ed. by Horst Geckeler, 117-135. Berlin: W. de Gruyter.

Ogden, C.K. and Richards, I.A. 1923. The Meaning of Meaning. London: Routledge and Kegan Paul.

Penn, Julia. 1972. Linguistic Relativity versus Innate Ideas. (Unrevised Ph.D. diss., Univ. of Texas, 1966.) Hague: Mouton.

Robins, Robert Henry. 1967. A Short History of Linguistics. Bloomington: Indiana Univ. Press.

________. 1973. "The History of Language Classification" Current Trends in Linguistics Vol.11.3-41.

Ross, Roberta Graber. 1970. Wilhelm von Humboldt's Philosophy of Language: the genesis of its basic Concepts. Ph.D. diss. Stanford University.

Rotenstreich, Nathan. 1974. "Humboldt's Prolegomena to Philosophy of Language". Cultural Hermeneutics 2: 3.211-227.

Ryle, Gilbert. (n.d.). "John Locke on the Human Understanding". Locke and Berkeley: A collection of critical essays Ed. by C.B. Martin and D.M. Armstrong, 14-39. London: Macmillan.

Sapir, Edward. 1921. Language. New York: Harcourt, Brace and Co.

Scharf, H.W. 1977. Chomskys Humboldt Interpretation: Ein Beitrag zur Diskontinuität der Sprachtheorie in der Geschichte der neueren Linguistik Doctoral diss., Univ. Düsseldorf.

Schlegel, August Wilhelm. 1971 (1818). Observations sur la langue et la littérature provencales. Tübingen: Fotodruck Präzis.

Schlegel, Friedrich. 1975.(1808). "Ueber die Sprache und Weisheit der Indier". Kritische Ausgabe seiner Werke. Bd. VIII, 104-432. Paderborn-München-Wien: F. Schoeningh. (New ed. of the original publication, with an introd. by Sebastiano Timpanaro, Amsterdam: J. Benjamins, 1977.)

Seidler, Herbert. 1967. "Die Bedeutung von W. von Humboldts Sprachdenken für die Wissenschaft von der Sprachkunst". Zeitschrift für deutsche Philologie 86.434-451.

Spranger, Eduard. 1908. "W. von Humboldt und Kant". Kantstudien 13.57-129.

Steinthal, Heymann. 1882. "Programm zu einer neuen Ausgabe der Sprachphilosophischen Werke Wilhelms von Humboldt". Zeitschrift für Völkerpsychologie und Sprachwissenschaft 13.201-232.

Stankiewicz, Edward. 1974. "The Dithyramb to the Verb in eighteenth and nineteenth century linguistics". Studies in the History of Linguistics Ed. by Dell

Hymes, 157-190. Bloomington: Indiana Univ. Press.

Ullmann, Stephen. 1962. Semantics. Oxford: Blackwells.

Verburg, Pieter A. 1949. "The Background to the Linguistic Conceptions of Bopp". Lingua 2.438-68.

________. 1974. "Vicissitudes of Paradigms". Studies in the History of Linguistics Ed. by Dell Hymes, 191-232. Bloomington: Indiana Univ. Press.

Weimann, Karl-Heinz. 1965. "Vorstufen der Sprachphilosophie Humboldts bei Bacon und Locke". Zeitschrift für deutsche Philologie 84.498-508.

Whorf, Benjamin L. 1956. Language, Thought and Reality. Ed. by John B. Carroll. Cambridge, Mass.: M.I.T. Press.

INDEX NOMINUM

INDEX RERUM

In the STUDIES IN THE HISTORY OF THE LANGUAGE SCIENCES (SiHoLS) series the following volumes have been published thus far, and will be published during 1985:

1. KOERNER, E.F. Konrad: *The Importance of Techmer's "Internationale Zeitschrift für Allgemeine Sprachwissenschaft" in the Development of General Linguistics.* Amsterdam, 1973.
2. TAYLOR, Daniel J.: *Declinatio: A Study of the Linguistic Theory of Marcus Terentius Varro.* Amsterdam, 1974. 2nd pr. 1986.
3. BENWARE, Wilbur A.: *The Study of Indo-European Vocalism; from the beginnings to Whitney and Scherer: A critical-historical account.* Amsterdam, 1974. t.o.p. 2nd pr. 1986.
4. BACHER, Wilhelm: *Die Anfänge der hebräischen Grammatik* (1895), together with *Die hebräische Sprachwissenschaft vom 10. bis zum 16. Jahrhundert* (1892). Amsterdam, 1974.
5. HUNT, R.W. (1908-1979): *The History of Grammar in the Middle Ages. Collected Papers.* Edited with an introduction, a select bibliography, and indices by G.L. Bursill-Hall. Amsterdam, 1980.
6. MILLER, Roy Andrew: *Studies in the Grammatical Tradition in Tibet.* Amsterdam, 1976.
7. PEDERSEN, Holger (1867-1953): *A Glance at the History of Linguistics, with particular regard to the historical study of phonology.* Amsterdam, 1983.
8. STENGEL, Edmund (1845-1935), (ed.): *Chronologisches Verzeichnis französischer Grammatiken vom Ende des 14. bis zum Ausgange des 18. Jahrhunderts, nebst Angabe der bisher ermittelten Fundorte derselben.* Amsterdam, 1976.
9. NIEDEREHE, Hans-Josef & Harald HAARMANN (with the assistance of Liliane Rouday), (eds.): *IN MEMORIAM FRIEDRICH DIEZ: Akten des Kolloquiums zur Wissenschaftsgeschichte der Romanistik/Actes du Colloque sur l'Histoire des Etudes Romanes/Proceedings of the Colloquium for the History of Romance Studies, Trier, 2.-4. Okt. 1975).* Amsterdam, 1976.
10. KILBURY, James: *The Development of Morphophonemic Theory.* Amsterdam, 1976.
11. KOERNER, E.F. Konrad: *Western Histories of Linguistic Thought. An annotated chronological bibliography, 1822-1976.* Amsterdam, 1978.
12. PAULINUS a S. BARTHOLOMAEO (1749-1806): *Dissertation on the Sanskrit Language.* Transl., edited and introduced by Ludo Rocher. Amsterdam, 1977.
13. DRAKE, Glendon F.: *The Role of Prescriptivism in American Linguistics 1820-1970.* Amsterdam, 1977.
14. SIGERUS DE CORTRACO: *Summa modorum significandi; Sophismata.* New edition, on the basis of G. Wallerand's *editio prima,* with additions, critical notes, an index of terms, and an introd. by Jan Pinborg. Amsterdam, 1977.
15. PSEUDO-ALBERTUS MAGNUS: *Quaestiones Alberti de Modis significandi.* A critical edition, translation and commentary of the British Museum Inc. C.21.C.52 and the Cambridge Inc.5.J.3.7, by L.G. Kelly. Amsterdam, 1977.
16. PANCONCELLI-CALZIA, Giulio (1878-1966): *Geschichtszahlen der Phonetik* (1941), together with *Quellenatlas der Phonetik* (1940). New ed., with an introd. article and a bio-bibliographical account of Panconcelli-Calzia by Jens-Peter Köster. Amsterdam, 1986. n.y.p.
17. SALMON, Vivian: *The Study of Language in 17th-Century England.* Amsterdam, 1979.
18. HAYASHI, Tetsuro: *The Theory of English Lexicography 1530-1791.* Amsterdam, 1978.

19. KOERNER, E.F. Konrad: *Toward a Historiography of Linguistics. Selected Essays.* Foreword by R.H. Robins. Amsterdam, 1978.
20. KOERNER, E.F. Konrad (ed.): *PROGRESS IN LINGUISTIC HISTORIOGRAPHY: Papers from the International Conference on the History of the Language Sciences, Ottawa, 28-31 August 1978.* Amsterdam, 1980.
21. DAVIS, Boyd H. & Raymond K. O'CAIN (eds.): *FIRST PERSON SINGULAR. Papers from the Conference on an Oral Archive for the History of American Linguistics. (Charlotte, N.C., 9-10 March 1979).* Amsterdam, 1980.
22. McDERMOTT, A. Charlene Senape: *Godfrey of Fontaine's Abridgement of Boethius the Dane's MODI SIGNIFICANDI SIVE QUAESTIONES SUPER PRISCIANUM MAIOREM.* A text edition with English transl. and introd. Amsterdam, 1980.
23. APOLLONIUS DYSCOLUS: *The Syntax of Apollonius Dyscolus.* Translated, and with commentary by Fred W. Householder. Amsterdam, 1981.
24. CARTER, M.. (ed.): *ARAB LINGUISTICS, an introductory classical text with translation and notes.* Amsterdam, 1981.
25. HYMES, Dell H.: *Essays in the History of Linguistic Anthropology.* Amsterdam, 1983.
26. KOERNER, Konrad, Hans-J. NIEDEREHE & R.H. ROBINS (eds.): *STUDIES IN MEDIEVAL LINGUISTIC THOUGHT,* dedicated to Geoffrey L. Bursill-Hall on the occassion of his 60th birthday on 15 May 1980. Amsterdam, 1980.
27. BREVA-CLARAMONTE, Manuel: *Sanctius' Theory of Language: A contribution to the history of Renaissance linguistics.* Amsterdam, 1983.
28. VERSTEEGH, Kees, Konrad KOERNER & Hans-J. NIEDEREHE (eds.): *THE HISTORY OF LINGUISTICS IN THE NEAR EAST.* Amsterdam, 1983.
29. ARENS, Hans: *Aristotle's Theory of Language and its Tradition.* Amsterdam, 1984.
30. GORDON, W. Terrence: *A History of Semantics.* Amsterdam, 1982.
31. CHRISTY, Craig: *Uniformitarianism in Linguistics.* Amsterdam 1983.
32. MANCHESTER, M.L.: *The Philosophical Foundations of Humboldt's Linguistic Doctrines.* Amsterdam 1985. n.y.p.
33. RAMAT, Paolo, Hans-Josef NIEDEREHE & E.F. Konrad KOERNER (eds.): *THE HISTORY OF LINGUISTICS IN ITALY.* Amsterdam, 1985. n.y.p.
34. QUILIS, Antonio & Hans J. NIEDEREHE (eds.): *THE HISTORY OF LINGUISTICS IN SPAIN.* Amsterdam, 1985. n.y.p.
35. SALMON, Vivian (ed.): *A READER ON THE LANGUAGE OF SHAKESPEARE.* Amsterdam, 1986. n.y.p.
36. SAPIR, Edward: *Appraisals of his Life and Work.* Edited by Konrad Koerner. Amsterdam, 1984.
37. Ó MATHÚNA, Seán P.: *William Bathe, S.J., 1564-1614: a pioneer in linguistics.* Amsterdam, 1986. n.y.p.
38. AARSLEF, Hans, Louis G. KELLY & Hans-Josef NIEDEREHE: *PAPERS IN THE HISTORY OF LINGUISTICS. Proceedings of ICHoLS III, Princeton 1984.* Amsterdam, 1986.